Launching the Grand Coalition:
The 2005 Bundestag Election and the Future of German Politics

GW00504681

Launching the Grand Coalition

The 2005 Bundestag Election and the Future of German Politics

Edited by
Eric Langenbacher

Berghahn Books
NEW YORK • OXFORD

Published in 2006 by

Berghahn Books

www.berghahnbooks.com

Library of Congress Cataloging-in-Publication Data

Launching the grand coalition : the 2005 Bundestag election and the
  future of German politics / edited by Eric Langenbacher.
    p. cm.
  Includes bibliographical references and index.
  ISBN 1-84545-283-6 (pbk. : alk. paper)
  1. Germany. Bundestag--Elections, 2005. 2. Coalitions--Germany.
  3. Germany--Politics and government--1990-   . I. Langenbacher,
  Eric.
  JN3971.A95L38 2006
  324.943'0882--dc22

2006029299

British Library Cataloguing in Publication Data

A catalogue record for this book is available
from the British Library.

Printed in the United States on acid-free paper.

Contents

There are many people and institutions behind a project such as this. First, I would like to thank *German Politics and Society* for providing the impetus and support for the special issue that forms the basis of this volume. The journal's editor, Jeffrey Anderson and the BMW Center for German and European Studies at Georgetown University deserve particular mention. The team at Berghahn Books, especially Vivian and Marion Berghahn, was likewise supportive, efficient, and, as always, very professional. I would also like to thank the contributors for their outstanding analyses, insights and punctuality with deadlines. Above all, I would like to express my undying appreciation to my wife, Kayoko, and my boys, Adam and Max, for everything.

Introduction

The Drama of 2005 and the Future of German Politics

Eric Langenbacher

I recall a conversation from a while back with a colleague. He was disdainful of German politics, stating that they are ponderous, lackluster, even boring. He prefers to follow Italian politics because of the intrigue, emotion, and, most of all, the drama. Although forced to agree at the time that the contrast between the two countries could not be greater, I was also immediately reminded of the old (apocryphal) Chinese curse, "may you live in interesting times."

My, how times have changed. German political life in 2005 witnessed some of the most dramatic events since at least the period of unification over fifteen years ago, and perhaps since the inception of the Federal Republic. It is this highly important and dramatic election to which *Launching the Grand Coalition: The 2005 Bundestag Election and the Future of German Politics* is dedicated.[1] The contributors analyze the results, but also locate current developments in the history and traditions of the Federal Republic. Just as important, they project trends and policies into the future. What will Chancellor Angela Merkel and her grand coalition achieve? What will become of the German party system? What long-term structural changes are affecting German politics and policy-making?

Drama on the Left

As with the interpretation of any drama, one must first begin with a plot summary—an overview of the major, attention-grabbing developments. The narrative begins with a string of electoral defeats at the regional level that culminated in the Social Democrats (SPD) losing the state election in North Rhine Westphalia in late May 2005. This in itself was remarkable, seeing that the old Ruhrgebiet was a heartland of SPD support, ruled by the Social Democrats (at least as senior coalition partners) for nearly forty consecutive years. One of the reasons for this defeat was Chancellor Gerhard Schröder's severe loss of support within his own party. Almost always fractious and divided between centrist moderates and trade union-oriented leftists, the party could not maintain solidarity and support in the face of the Red-Green government's reformist agenda and program (Agenda 2010, Hartz Reforms, etc.)—and one might add, in the face of the daunting and structural economic and social problems that the country has faced for at least a decade. Radicals led inside and outside of the government by Oskar Lafontaine and others were never enamored of the telegenic, "American" centrism that Schröder represented, but at least he could win elections for the team. The regional defeats in the Länder eroded even this tenuous reason for radical support. Schröder understood acutely the magnitude of the party's defeat in North Rhine Westphalia and elsewhere (and not just because of the legislative gridlock that this created in the opposition-controlled second house, the Bundesrat) and the dangers of the loss of internal support. He soon launched unprecedented political and constitutional machinations to salvage his power.

His first step was to bring down his own government by consciously staging and then losing a vote of confidence on 1 July 2005. Schröder engineered this as a last ditch attempt to maintain power, by forcing his party to declare support for him and by catching the opposition off-guard with the unexpected election that would have to follow. Of course, his official justification was that he lacked a mandate to govern and to implement his reforms and was calling the election early to obtain one. He added that Germany could not afford to lose another year or even two (until the next regularly scheduled Bundestag election) because of weak governance and gridlock. The constructive vote of non-confidence and other parliamentary norms were not supposed to allow for such a Weimaresque tactic. Yet, the Constitutional Court (Bundesverfassungsgericht) ruled on August 25 that it was constitutional and that a new election, already under way, was indeed necessary. Postwar Germany rarely had witnessed such expert maneuvering, nor such an adept political operative. Most surprising of all was that it almost worked, in light of the eventual result–with the SPD retaining 34.2 percent support–versus just 35.2 percent for the Christian Democrats CDU/CSU.[2] Despite this unexpectedly strong showing and some valiant attempts to try to remain chancellor, Schröder was gone quickly from the political stage (as were many other senior political figures). Finally, in the worst "American" fashion he very soon took up a high-level position on the board of a German-Russian pipeline consortium(Gazprom), a decision that generated enormous criticism because he had advocated this deal while in public office (and which was retrospective evidence for his overly close relationship with Putin and Russia).

Drama on the Right

There was also more than enough drama on the other side. The rise of Angela Merkel, the first female party leader and chancellor in German history (as well as the first Easterner since unification and the youngest chancellor ever), has been long in coming. Her steadfast, largely behind-the-scenes maneuvering, explored in-depth below by Myra Marx-Ferree and Clay Clemens, began already in earnest when she took over as General Secretary of the CDU in 1998. As in an ancient Greek tragedy, these traits were on full display when she denounced her original political sponsor Helmut Kohl and Wolfgang Schäuble in 1999 in the midst of the CDU party financing scandal, becoming party leader in 2000. Having lost the Right's chancellor candidate spot in 2002 to Bavaria's Edmund Stoiber (in retrospect an adept move, given the likelihood that the SPD-Green government would be re-elected and the importance of exhausting and overcoming her internal critics) she quietly assured herself of this position by 2005. Since her ascendance within the party and now to the chancellorship, she has faced vociferous opposition from traditional party bigwigs and especially from the entrenched regional bosses like Stoiber, Roland Koch of Hessen and Christian Wulff in Lower Saxony. Nevertheless, she has outmaneuvered them all, gaining the highest office in the land–and these behind-the-scenes political skills, though often ignored, are some of her greatest assets.

Yet, it should not be forgotten that one big component of Merkel's drama in 2005 was the unprecedented loss of voters' support by election day. Polling only 35 percent of the vote (less than Stoiber in 2002 and the one of the worst results for the conservatives since World War II), she blew a 20-point lead, according to public opinion polls taken in the early summer. The reasons behind "her" loss of support included: the exceptional political gifts of Schröder—both personally as exemplified by his resounding "victory" in the televised debate on September 4 and in terms of the slick, even populist campaign that his SPD ran; tepid support from her party, especially the regional bosses; her own lackluster campaigning style; some missteps on the campaign trail (especially controversial remarks from her shadow finance minister, Paul Kirchhof); a hurried campaign platform; and, last but not least, the extremely challenging economic and social issues that the country currently faces, where solutions are in short supply and support for radical reforms amongst the electorate is even lower. The eventual poor CDU result and the most fragmented Bundestag ever—with five parties achieving significant representation and the two people's parties receiving less than 70 percent of the vote between them—made traditional coalition options untenable. Despite weeks of dramatic speculation over unusual coalition options, the widely disparaged grand coalition between CDU/CSU and SPD emerged as the only viable option. She was sworn into office on 22 November 2005.

Minidramas

There were other dramatic sub-plots affecting the smaller parties that provided even more excitement. The free market and generally libertarian Free Democrats (FDP) scored their best result since the unity election of 1990 and seem to have returned to their levels of support in the 1970s and 1980s. Almost all of this support came from Western Germany (unlike the election of 1990) and the party did not even make nominal efforts to reach out to the East. Nevertheless, this strong result shows that support for the kinds of neoliberal reforms that Germany needs is not unsubstantial, at least amongst Westerners. The Greens also did relatively well, having avoided a

4

significant loss of support despite sharing governing responsibility for seven years and despite the persistent internal dissension between "realos" and "fundis." It is rather interesting that the SPD tore itself apart over the course of Schröder's chancellorship but the ever-feisty Greens (how many times did former Foreign Minister Joschka Fischer have eggs or paint thrown at him during party congresses?) did not.

More important was the formation and then strong result of a new party, formed by the former East German communist Party of Democratic Socialism (PDS) and dissident left-wing factions of the SPD. Led by the charismatic Gregor Gysi and Oskar Lafontaine (long the bane of the Schröder-Müntefering SPD), the new Left Party gained 8.7 percent of the vote nationwide, but over 25 percent (more than the CDU) in the East. Most importantly, this new party has been able to move beyond the old PDS' ghettoization in the East, making major in-roads in the West—in fact, gaining 4.9 percent of the vote there (although see Jeffrey Kopstein and Daniel Ziblatt's chapter for a different interpretation). The consequences of this new party and its occupation of the left side of the ideological spectrum are open and potentially massive. On the one hand, this might signify the resurgence of a radical and ideological left wing in German politics, un-checked by the moderating tendencies of the dominant pragmatic faction of the SPD. Splintering on this side of the spectrum may make the Left incapable of governing as a bloc for quite some time. On the other hand, radicals may leave the SPD to the pragmatists, making it easier for the rump party to govern and run postmodern election campaigns around valence issues, competence and leadership. Of course, there is often the need in any democracy for a protest movement and, one could say this is better coming from the Left (especially in Germany with its ever present past) than the Right.

On the other side of the spectrum, early in the year there was widespread fear that radical rightists would do much better than in the past and actually surmount the 5 percent electoral threshold to gain representation in the Bundestag. Many observers feared the worst because persistent economic problems, especially in the East, have created a significant support base for these parties, manifested in recent state electoral successes—most notably the National Democratic Party (NPD) receiving 9 percent in the Saxon Landtag election of 2004. There were also unprecedented efforts to achieve unity amongst extreme Right parties. But, once again, divisiveness, lack of professionalism, poor leadership, the existence of another protest party—the Left Party had engaged in antiforeigner, anti-immigrant scaremongering—and, one might add, the German electorate's continued reluctance to support such radical parties, resulted in a combined percentage well short of the threshold. But, as Lars Rensmann writes in his chapter, many of the underlying problems that empower these parties and the trends towards greater organization continue, making these parties a continued threat in the future (perhaps as a consequence of the grand coalition and the pervasive economic and social malaise in the East).

Real or Superficial Changes?

Of course, often in political life there can be much surface drama, but behind the scenes or structurally, not much changes. Postwar Italy is an excellent example—where much instability on the surface (a new government basically every year) misled observers away from the real problems—a hyper-stable, rather ossified party system centered on the Christian Democrats and an entrenched, corrupt ruling elite. What is the case in Germany? Was last year's drama merely superficial, or are there real, structural issues surfacing?

Two relative simple calculations over time can help to shed some light. First, electoral volatility (based on seats won by parties in the Bundestag) has increased, as Table One indicates:

Table 1: Electoral Volatility (based on seats) in the Bundestag

Election (compared to previous)	Volatility, %
2005	10.54
2002	7.97
1998	7.96
1994	9.37
1990	8.35
1987	5.61
1983	8.76
1980 (1976)	3.37

Source: www.bundeswahlleiter.de. Volatility is calculated: $Vt = 1/2 \ (\Sigma \mid P(t\text{-}1) - Pt \mid)$. Where Vt is volatility at any given year compared to the last election; Pt is the party's seat share (% rounded to two decimal places) in the current time; $Pt\text{-}1$ is seat share in the last election.

The 2005 result represents a 32 percent increase compared to 2002, yet a rather large 213% increase from the (exceptionally low) figure of 1980. Yet, according to Peter Mair, the five decade average volatility on Europe was about 8.9 percent, the 100 year average between 1885 and 1985 was 8.6 percent.[3] Some estimates show slightly higher volatility for the 1990s in Europe (perhaps about 12 percent).[4] By these standards, electoral volatility in Germany after unification has been at or below long-term cross-national averages and, hence, does not indicate precipitous changes in the fortunes of the parties.

Secondly, I look at seat allocation in the Bundestag and calculate the effective number of parties (based again on seats allocated).

Table 2: Seat Allocation in the Bundestag since 1980

	PDS*/Other**		Greens		SPD		FDP		CDU-CSU	
2005	54	8.79%	51	8.31%	222	36.16%	61	9.93%	226	36.81%
2002	2	0.33%	55	9.12%	251	41.60%	47	7.79%	248	41.13%
1998	36	5.38%	47	7.03%	298	44.54%	43	6.43%	245	36.62%
1994	30	4.46%	49	7.29%	252	37.50%	47	6.99%	294	43.75%
1990	17	2.57%	8	1.21%	239	36.10%	79	11.93%	319	48.19%
1987	2		42	8.09%	193	37.19%	48	9.25%	234	45.09%
1983	1		27	5.19%	202	38.85%	35	6.73%	255	49.04%
1980					228	43.93%	54	10.40%	237	45.66%

Source: www.bundeswahlleiter.de.

* in 2005 the PDS combined with rogue elements from the SPD to form the new Left Party

** in 1983 and 1987 Alternative Liste (AL) received these seats

Table 3: Effective Number of Parties (based on seats) in the Bundestag since 1980

Election Year	Effective Number of Parties
2005	3.44
2002	2.80
1998	2.90
1994	2.89
1990	2.65
1987	2.80
1983	2.51
1980	2.42

Source: www.bundeswahlleiter.de. Effective number of parties is: $(N)=1/\Sigma(p2)$, where p is the proportion of votes or seats in a given year.

Here, some more noticeable changes have set in, namely a greater than 0.6 increase in the number of effective parties between 2002 and 2005, which corresponds to a 23 percent increase–yet a larger 42 percent increase compared to 1980. Interestingly, the number of effective parties hovered within a narrow band of only 0.4 for twenty-two years and seven Bundestag elections–barely changing despite the entry of the Greens in 1983 and the potential convulsions of the first all-German unity election in 1990. The rather marked increase in 2005 compared to previous Bundestags is an important change. Even this development is nowhere near as dramatic as some of the changes in other countries after so-called electoral earthquakes–such as Italy in 1994 or Canada in 1993. Nevertheless, the qualitative nature and dynamics of the German party system have shifted: from a two or two-and-one-half party system firmly into the moderate multiparty category system, where the effective number of parties ranges between three and five or six.[5] Whether this trend toward more effective parties will continue in future elections, even leading to a Weimaresque "extreme multiparty system" is something important to ponder, perhaps for the first time since World War Two.

Detailed analyses of the results reveal or reinforce other important trends. For example, the turnout rate continues to decrease from 79.1 percent in 2002 to 77.7 percent in 2005, solidifying a long-term decline (over 90 percent in 1972 and 1976 and even 82.2 percent in 1998).[6] Similar to trends in other advanced democratic countries, young people increasingly are abstaining compared to older citizens: only 69 percent of the under thirty-five age group voted versus 84.6 percent in the sixty to sixty-nine segment of the electorate.[7] There is also a significant turnout gap between the much more apathetic East and the West. Although enviable compared to elections for the U.S. Congress or the European Parliament and despite various reasons behind individual voters' decisions to stay away from the polls (for some this is a form of high-minded protest, for others indifference and for others disgust), lower participation rates are cause for concern. Not only is representation and resulting public policy biased towards those that actually do vote, but the overall legitimacy of the system may be eroded thanks to creeping dissatisfaction (*Politikverdrossenheit*).

East-West differences continue to be highly salient. Indeed, it appears that very different party systems and competitive dynamics

8

are solidifying in both regions. It is not just that the PDS/Left Party actually gained a (slightly) larger share of the vote in the East than the CDU, but three parties are broadly similar in their levels of support. Moreover, both the Greens and the FDP have almost no presence or support in the region. Given the aging nature of the PDS/Left Party's electorate, this may change. Yet, on-going economic and social problems in the region may attract younger, disaffected voters in the future (although this segment is also voting for right radical parties disproportionately—see Jeffrey Kopstein and Daniel Ziblatt and Lars Rensmann in this volume for more detailed discussions).

In addition to the emergent dual party systems structured along East-West lines, there also increasingly seem to be dual systems on generational lines. Fully 77.3 percent of voters older than sixty preferred the two *Volksparteien*; versus just 63.2 percent for the twenty-five to thirty-four age group. Younger and middle-aged voters especially in the West voted disproportionately for smaller parties—the Greens and, for the youngest cohort, the FDP. In the East, the forty-five to sixty age group gave disproportional support to the Left party (29.3 percent). Gender differences were less pronounced—women preferred the SPD and CDU at the same rate; men chose the CDU by a margin of 2 percent. However, there was another tendency for men to choose smaller parties more frequently than women. Finally, one other electoral behavior that continues to solidify is vote-splitting (one partisan preference for the first, constituency vote; another for the second, party list vote—the latter being the more important for overall Bundestag seat allocation). The smaller parties (FDP, Greens, Left) benefited immensely from this practice. Not surprisingly, ideological proximity matters with most CDU first preferences going to the Liberals in the second vote; most Socialist voters choosing the Greens. There were no discernible gender differences, but, again a rather marked East-West difference with Westerners splitting much more often than Easterners.[8]

The authors in this collection provide even more detailed data on public opinion, voting trends within sub-groups of the German electorate (East-West, Catholics, unionized workers, right radicals), the changing ideological spectrum in the Federal Republic (David Conradt, Ludger Helms, Hermann Schmitt and Andreas Wüst), as well as more structural data on cleavage structures and social changes

(Jeffrey Kopstein and Daniel Ziblatt). Other contributors look at long-term changes and project trends into the future. Dorothee Heisenberg , for example, looks at recent characteristics of German EU policy-making and offers her prognosis of Chancellor Angela Merkel's likely attitudes and policies. Lars Rensmann analyzes extreme Right parties and their continuing inability to make an electoral breakthrough at the national level. Several more qualitative analyses embed and historicize current developments in postwar German traditions. Ludger Helms compares and contrasts the first grand coalition (1966-1969) to the current one, paying particular attention to the larger political context and the informal mechanisms and personal relationships that are necessary to make this kind of government work. Jackson Janes discusses transatlantic relations and the bilateral relationship between Germany and the United States, focusing especially on the relationships between presidents and chancellors. Myra Marx-Ferree looks at Merkel's relationship with German feminism and argues that the achievements of several generations of women and feminist leaders paved the way for her success (whether Merkel admits it or not). Finally, Clay Clemens explores the life and career of Angela Merkel, focusing especially on her leadership style (strengths and weaknesses), political and social alliances, and her tenure as leader of the CDU in opposition.

Looking Forward

Was this drama over the last year superficial or an indication of real shifts? The authors of *Launching the Grand Coalition* come to differing conclusions about the magnitude (or not) of these changes. There are surely many open questions regarding the short- and medium-term performance of the new government, as well as long-term, structural issues. Merkel's grand coalition was seemingly off to a positive start especially in terms of foreign policy. Many policy-makers (although many fewer German voters) have welcomed a rapprochement with the United States and the Bush Administration in particular–although the extent and depth of this change is still in question, especially after the differing reactions to the crisis between Israel and Hezbollah in the Summer of 2006–and EU policy where Merkel has reasserted forcefully the old German role of deal-maker and consensus-builder. There also seems to be major movement in terms of reforming the overly-constraining federal system, education, childcare, and health care spending. In fact, in the early spring of 2006, Merkel had the highest personal approval ratings ever for a postwar chancellor–over 80 percent.[9] In September 2006, she even displaced Condoleezza Rice as the most powerful woman in the world according to Forbes magazine.[10]

However, by the late summer of 2006 after the feel-good patriotic glow of the soccer World Cup had faded, things changed dramatically. Despite the best economic performance in years, a perceived lack of revolutionary reforms, dissension within the coalition and her party, and the hugely unpopular increase in the Value Added Tax to 19 percent, Merkel and her government became increasingly unpopular. By August, only 37 percent (55 percent in January) support her as the head of government. The Union parties stood at only 31 percent approval (down from 41 percent in February), one of their lowest ratings ever. Fully 65 percent of the German public thought that she did not have the backing of her party on most issues.[11] The honeymoon had come to an end.

Will she be able to continue or regain her early momentum? Will her reformist efforts be too piecemeal and fail to address the deep, structural problems that the country faces? Will the persistent, even growing East-West cleavage be overcome? Will her grand coalition last a full term? And what comes after that? A strong and reformist CDU-FDP majority? Or weak and fragmented "Weimar" coalitions? These are questions that only time and further research will be able to address. Of course, the greatest questions of them all will be whether the theatrics continue, whether Germany has been "Italianized" and whether this potential drama will be Germany's salvation or curse.

Notes

1. The contributions in this volume were previously published in "Special Issue: The 2005 Bundestag Election," *German Politics and Society*, vol 24 (1) Spring 2006. Clay Clemens' chapter appeared in *German Poltiics and Society*, vol 24 (3) Fall 2006.
2. All national vote totals correspond to "second" party list results. All electoral data are from http://www. bundeswahlleiter.de/bundestagswahl2005
3. Peter Mair, *Party System Change: Approaches and Interpretations* (Oxford, 1997), 80, 67. See also Stefano Bartolini and Peter Mair, *Identity, competition, and electoral availability: the stabilisation of European electorates 1885-1985* (Cambridge, 1990).
4. Michael Gallagher, Michael Laver, Peter Mair, *Representative Government in Modern Europe* (Boston, 2001), 263. These figures are meant to contextualize the German case. Volatility can be calculated based on parties' vote or seat share, and the two calculations are usually correlated, especially in the highly proportional German system.
5. My party system categories are: one party, two party (N<3), moderate multiparty (3<N>5), and extreme multiparty (N>5). This modified formulation is based on Jean Blondel, *An Introduction to Comparative Government* (New York, 1969), 166; Giovanni Sartori, *Parties and Party Systems: A Framework for Analysis* (Cambridge, 1976), 125; Arend Lijphart, *Patterns of Democracy: Government Forms and Performance in Thirty-Six Countries* (New Haven, 1999), ch. 5. For all calculations I have counted the CDU/CSU as one party, diverging from Lijphart who counts them as one-and-a-half (1999, 71).
6. See http://www.destatis.de/presse/deutsch/pk/2003/rep_wahlstatistik.pdf accessed through www.bundeswahlleiter.de.
7. All data are from http://www.bundeswahlleiter.de/bundestagswahl2005/ presse_en/pd430211.html; http://www.bundeswahlleiter.de/bundestagswahl2005/ presse_en/pd410211.html
8. Ibid.
9. Andrew Purtis, "Land of Smiles," *Time Europe*, 1 April 2006.
10. http://www.forbes.com/execpicks/forbes/2006/0918/052.html
11. David Crosslands, "Tough Times for Angela Merkel," *Spiegel*-online, 21 August 2006, http://service.spiegel.de/cache/international/0,1518,432765,00.html; Eric Kirschbaum, "Merkel Under Attack from her Own Party," 6 August 2006, http://news.yahoo.com/s/nm/20060806/wl_nm/germany_dc_1

Chapter 1

The Tipping Point

The 2005 Election and the Deconsolidation
of the German Party System?

David P. Conradt

For the past quarter century the only constant in German election research has been the focus on change. Relying on a rich store of survey and aggregate data, analysts have documented a steady growth in voter volatility measured through a variety of indicators: the proportion of the electorate changing parties, splitting their ballots, deciding late in the campaign or not voting at all. But while volatility has been amply confirmed, analysts have been far less certain about how much change must take place on the demand side (voter) before major structural change takes place on the supply side (party system). Some observers argue that such a change is long overdue. In a recent essay Tobias Dürr, citing the social and economic upheavals (*Umbrüche*) of the past twenty-five years, considers it a "minor miracle" that the size and number of parties have remained relatively stable since "the old party system no longer fits our society."[1] Warnfried Dettling contends that the 2005 vote "could be the beginning of the end of the party system we have known for sixty years."[2] Others see remarkable resiliency. Thomas Saalfeld, writing before the 2005 vote, argues that "the fundamentals of the Federal Republic's party system and 'grand coalition structures' have remained remarkably stable ... Two party, ideologically compact and centrist minimal-winning coalitions, based on politically moderate center-left and center-right parties, persist."[3] In 2005 for only the second time in the Republic's history and for the first time as a matter of electoral necessity, not elite choice, no "minimal-winning coalition" was formed.

What is the bottom line on this volatility? Will it produce fundamental changes in the size and number of parties? Will the traditional exchange between the large parties be supplemented or replaced by voter flight from both large parties and the subsequent growth in the smaller and/or newer parties? Will German voters reject the sharp budget cuts and tax increases that the grand coalition intends to pass and flock to the three opposition parties waiting in the wings? These questions involve the supply side (voters), and the demand side (the party-system), of the political-electoral equation.

We begin with a brief overview of the development of the post-war party system. We then address the social and political meltdown of the two major parties during the past thirty years. The major differences between the current grand coalition and its 1966-1969 predecessors are analyzed briefly. We conclude with an examination of the prospects for the grand coalition and the party system.

Consolidation and Deconsolidation, 1949-2005

Figure One presents the two party share of the vote since 1949. This simple line clearly shows that the Federal Republic's party system from 1949 to 1976 consolidated around two large parties, in spite of a centrifugal institutional structure, i.e., proportional representation and federalism. These two parties increased their combined proportion of the vote from 60 percent to over 90 percent, a figure quite comparable to that achieved by the two largest parties in the classic two-party systems of the United States and Great Britain. Moreover, the number of parties represented in parliament declined from nine in 1949 to only three by 1961, where it remained for twenty-two years.

Postwar prosperity, the plebiscitary character of Konrad Adenauer's appeal, especially in the 1953 and 1957 elections and the subsequent embrace of the center by the SPD were factors that far outweighed the centrifugal tendencies of the proportional law. By the 1960s the bulk of the electorate was firmly anchored in the major demographic cleavages of class and religion and region, or via a growing psychological identification with the CDU/CSU, SPD, their images and their leaders. Both parties and their constant governing partner, the Free Democrats, embraced a consensus through distribution paradigm that meant only marginally different economic policy positions between them.[4] The great milestones of the welfare state introduced during

14

this period–housing subsidies (*Eigenheimzulage*), child allowances (*Kindergeld*), the dynamic pension system, health care insurance–were all supported by both major parties. Indeed, most of these programs date from the initial period (1949-1966) of CDU/CSU dominance. The constitutional structure of the Federal Republic, especially the federal system and the electoral law, played little or no role in the changes that took place in this consolidation phase. Maurice Duverger's fabled "law" was clearly contradicted by what took place between 1949 and 1976.[5]

Figure 1: Two Party (CDU/CSU-SPD) Share of Vote, 1949-2005

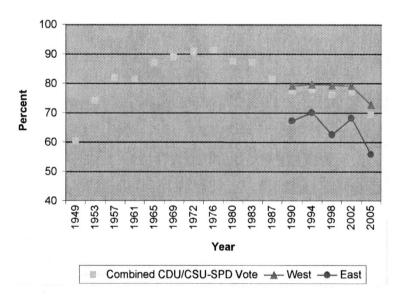

In the late 1970s and early 1980s, however, attachment and support for the three "system" parties (CDU/CSU, SPD, and Free Democratic Party (FDP)) started a slow decline. Noticeable cracks in this stable party-state (*Parteienstaat*) structure became visible as the economic motor began to sputter and a growing generational cleavage that began in the 1960s could no longer be contained by the major parties.[6] New political issues such as the environment and citizen participation also surfaced in public opinion. The young, educated offspring of Germany's economic winners embraced most enthusiastically this new set of "postmaterialist" issues. The first institutional manifestation of these new concerns was the appearance in 1983 of the Green party, the first new party to surmount the five percent barrier and end the twenty-two year-old reign of the established parties. To be sure the electoral system's five percent barrier held the Greens back in 1980 just as the federal opportunity structure gave the party national visibility when it entered the Bremen senate in 1979 and the state parliament in Baden-Württemberg a year later with little more than 5 percent of the vote. The Greens' emergence was fueled in part by the successes of postwar economic and social reconstruction.

The initial Green success had its major impact not via the size of their vote or presence in parliament, but rather through the shock waves it sent through the SPD. In the 1983 and 1987 campaigns the Social Democrats were focused less on returning to power than on keeping the Greens as far removed from power as possible. The 1983 SPD debacle was memorable for its blatantly postmaterialist quest for the phantom majority "beyond the Union" (*jenseits der Union*). This campaign by the "new Left", for the "new Left" yielded a paltry 37 percent of the vote, but far more importantly in the minds of its creators, it failed to keep the Greens out of the Bundestag. In 1987 the SPD again allowed itself to pursue the conflicting goals of returning to power and denying the Greens reelection to parliament.

Figure 2: Split Ticket Voting, 1957-2005

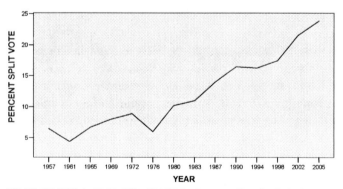

PERCENT SECOND BALLOT VOTERS SUPPORTING DIFFERENT PARTY ON FIRST BALLOT

Source: 1957-1990, 2002-2005 Federal Statistical Office; 1994-1998, Forschungsgruppe Wahlen Post-Election Survey

The emergence of the Greens and the continued survival of the FDP were facilitated by another centrifugal feature of the electoral system, the two ballot vote. This provision almost invites the voter to divide his or her support between two parties. Almost all splitting occurs at the expense of the CDU/CSU and SPD as their supporters seek to help their respective "small" partner, the FDP or the Greens, over the five percent hurdle. Thus Figure Two, which shows the proportion of voters splitting their ballots, is another indication of deconsolidation. Splitting, not surprisingly, was relatively seldom in the period of consolidation, but increased after 1976 and reached the record level of about 25 percent in 2005.

Deconsolidation and electoral volatility accelerated following the 1990 unification and the addition of over twelve million new voters. In no other European country has such an expansion occurred so suddenly. In no other western democracy was it necessary to integrate an entire socialist society and economy. Unification increased the number of parliamentary parties to five as the remnants of the former ruling communist party of the former East Germany, now renamed the Party of Democratic Socialism (PDS) secured representation under special one-time provisions of the electoral law applied to the eastern states. As Table One shows eastern voters are more likely to change parties than their western counterparts. The 1990-1994 eastern volatility score of 32 percent (range 0 to 100) is indeed one of the highest ever recorded in any modern European election. The Italian meltdown election of 1994 produced a score of 37 percent and between 1900 and 1989 only four elections yielded scores over 35 percent (Germany in 1919, France in 1945, and Greece in 1951 and 1959).[7] Less locked in via class or religion to a particular party, easterners are also more likely to be influenced by the candidates of the major parties.[8] According to one analysis, since 1990 the importance of the candidate factor has more than doubled with candidate voting especially high in the eastern states.[9] After fifteen years the exogenous shock of unification continues to impact the party system as seen in the 2005 emergence of the Left Party, a unique alliance of the "old" eastern PDS and dissatisfied, largely SPD western voters.

17

Table 1: Electoral Volatility*: West-East Germany 1990-2005

Years	West	East
1990-1994	11.2	31.8
1994-1998	12.8	23.2
1998-2002	13	18.6
2002-2005	14.2	24.6

* Pederson Index (Sum of differences between electoral support for party *i* in election *t-1* and election *t.*)

In the two elections of the 21st century the trend toward deconsolidation has accelerated. Neither the Christian Democrats nor the Social Democrats have been able to gain the support of 40 percent of the electorate and neither election produced a clear winner. By 2005 the two major parties, adjusting for turnout, were supported by only 54 percent of the eligible electorate. In the eastern states after five national elections, the two major parties have been unable to establish an electoral base comparable to their (declining) position in the western states. In 2005 only about 41 percent of the eligible eastern electorate supported the CDU/CSU or the SPD.

The Meltdown of the Core

The demographic core of the once great people's parties (*Volksparteien*) has been eroding for decades. This erosion has involved the core itself becoming smaller because of socio-economic and cultural change and the declining support within the remaining core electorate for their party. In the case of the CDU/CSU, we are referring to church-going Catholics. For the SPD the corresponding group is blue collar trade union members. While the proportion of the population affiliated with the Catholic church has declined over the past half century from about 47 percent to 40 percent, a much larger drop has occurred among Catholics with a "strong " (as measured by church attendance) attachment to the church. In 1953, six of every ten Catholics reported attending services every Sunday or almost every Sunday. By 2005 only two out of ten Catholics regularly attended services.[10] As Figure Three shows, within group support for the CDU/CSU has also declined from 82 percent in 1953 to 72 percent in 2005. Thus the combined (size x vote) contribution of strong

Catholics to the CDU electorate has dropped from over 50 percent in the 1950s to only 12 percent at the 2005 vote. While the decline in party loyalty among strong Catholics is less than the decline in the size of this group both contribute to the erosion of the core.

Figure 3: Catholics with Strong Attachment to Church and Support for CDU/CSU, 1953-2005

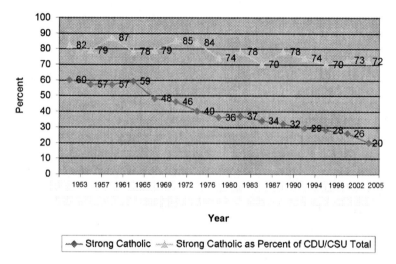

Source: 1953-1972: Institut für Demoskopie.
Survey Nos. 0061, 1010, 1055, 2005, 2085; 1976-2002: Forschungsgruppe Wahlen (2005, 36); 2005: Forschungsgruppe Wahlen Post-election survey. "Strong" Catholic = regular church attendance (weekly or almost weekly).

Historically, unionized blue collar workers have constituted the SPD core. Since the 1950s support for the SPD among this group has been roughly comparable to that given by strong Catholics to the CDU/CSU. SPD support among unionized blue collar workers for the period from 1952-1959, for example, ranged between 65 and 76 percent.[11] As Figure Four indicates, the SPD continues to lose market share among this group dropping from 73 percent in 1953 to 54 percent in 2005. In 1953 unionized blue collar workers accounted for almost 40 percent of the SPD vote, today about 10 percent of SPD voters comes from this socio-demographic group. This decline is also a function of the diminished size of the blue collar work force. In 1950 over half of all (West) Germans were in blue collar occupations. Today less than a third is in a blue collar occupation.

19

Figure 4: Support for SPD Among Unionized Blue Collar Workers, 1953-2005

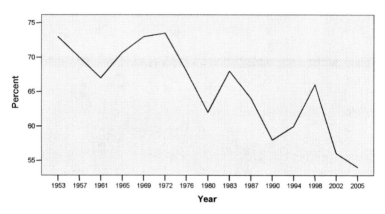

Source: See Figure Three.

The erosion of demographic bonds has been accompanied by a declining psychological identification with the political parties. Between 1972 and 2005 the proportion of western voters with "very strong" or "strong" ties to a political party has dropped from 55 percent to 34 percent.[12] By 2005 those with a "weak" attachment or none at all now constitute about 60 percent of the western electorate. In the eastern states, the relationship to the parties is weaker. Roughly one in four eastern voters report a very strong or strong attachment to a party and over 70 percent have no attachment or a weak attachment to the parties. From their ranks come disproportionately the millions of undecided voters, the ticket splitters, the "candidate personality" voters and the media-driven "campaign event" voters. Thus, in the first two elections of the 21st century, voting analysts point to candidate remarks and physical appearance at television debates (choice of clothing, hair style), their performance at natural disasters, and their reaction to breaking world news as decisive influences on the election.[13] In 2005 about one in eight voters were late deciders.[14] It is estimated that between Saturday night and the Sunday election, about 1.5 million voters who intended to vote for Angela Merkel's CDU switched to the Free Democrats.[15] Large and late swings in the voters' mood are another consequence of the eroding core. In 2005 between mid-July and the September 18 election date, Merkel and the CDU/CSU managed to lose a 20-point lead over Red-Green. Never before in the history of the Federal Republic has an opposition or incumbent candidate lost such a large lead.[16]

Grand Coalitions: Choice or Necessity?

Unlike the first grand coalition, the current alignment was *electorally* and not *elite-driven.*[17] The crisis of 1966 was largely about the conflicting ambitions and goals within the leadership of the major parties. Key leaders in the CDU/CSU, above all Rainer Barzel and Franz Josef Strauß, used a relatively mild recession and fiscal "crisis" to challenger Ludwig Erhard's chronically shaky leadership of the party. Fearing they could go down with the sinking Union, the Free Democrats left the coalition fully expecting they would return under a Chancellor Barzel. But the FDP badly underestimated the intensity of Strauß's desire to return to Bonn following his banishment over the Spiegel Affair in 1962.

Meanwhile the Social Democrats and especially their de facto leader, Herbert Wehner, had been patiently working toward a grand coalition as a key stepping stone to their goal of replacing the Christian Democrats as the dominant party. Wehner had some key allies in the Christian Democratic camp above all the CDU's labor wing led by Hans Katzer and the then Federal President Heinrich Lübke. In the end of course, the "K question" (*K Frage*) produced a deadlock between Barzel and Strauß and the Union turned to an outsider Kurt-Georg Kiesinger to head the new coalition with the FDP. Under Kiesinger's broker-style leadership the SPD saw the coalition as an opportunity to demonstrate to Germany's middle class that it could govern successfully. Above all, Karl Schiller's economic policies convinced many middle-class voters that the Socialists could indeed "handle money."[18] The winners of the first grand coalition were the Social Democrats. Consistent with Wehner's strategy, the SPD at the 1969 election made substantial inroads into the middle of the electorate at the expense of the Christian Democrats. The grand coalition made the Social Democrats acceptable to both Catholic and middle-class voters. The CDU after two decades in power could no longer project itself as the party that gave Germans economic security and prosperity. Even Erhard was largely forgotten by 1969. Only 40 percent in one 1969 voter survey remembered that he was the Union's chancellor candidate in 1965![19] In 2005 the voters left the leadership of the major parties with no choice, but to form a grand coalition. The only alternative, new elections, was unacceptable to all parties. In 1966 both major parties, especially the Social Democrats, expected to profit substantially from a grand coalition. There was no such plan for either party in 2005. Indeed Gerhard Schröder's decision in May 2005 to seek new elections via the use of the vote of confidence procedure marked the third time that Article 67 was used for this purpose. But the Brandt (1972) and Kohl (1982) governments employed this from a position of strength. Schröder, following eleven straight losses in state elections and growing discontent bordering on revolt within his own party, resorted to the procedure out of weakness.

In 1966 the Free Democrats were the sole opposition party. For dissatisfied voters this liberal, middle-class, pro-business party with a very limited clientele was the sole institutionalized alternative to the governing parties. Little wonder that after 1966 major opposition movements on the Left and Right developed outside of parliament: on the left the fabled APO (*ausserparlamentarische Opposition*) and on the right the National Democratic Party (NPD). Voters desiring something other than the Free Democrats had no choice. The APO emerged in the wake of the grand coalition to challenge both the legitimacy of the "established parties" and the constitutional order itself. Both the APO and the NPD enjoyed substantial success. Some APO participants eventually gravitated into what would become the Greens and the NPD scored some remarkable results in state elections. In 1966 the NPD received 8 percent of the vote in Hesse. In 1967 they easily surmounted the 5 percent barrier in Lower Saxony, Rhineland-Palatinate (7 percent), and Bremen (9 percent). The electoral high point for the party came at the 1968 state election in Baden-Württemberg when it secured almost 10 percent of the vote thus sparking wide-spread speculation that the party would enter the Bundestag the following year.

The current institutionalized opposition offers few opportunities for anti-system movements. The Left Party is an alternative for discontented voters at both political poles. The lack of success of right-wing populist parties in 2005 was indeed widely attributed to the anti-foreigner image of the Left especially in the eastern regions. It draws exceptionally strong support from the unemployed and it is also an electoral alternative for discontented Social Democrats. The three opposition parties should be able to offer an institutionalized political home for a wide variety of potential protest movements.

Conclusion: A New Party System?

"Despite the melting of the old order, a new party system has yet to emerge."[20] This statement about the Italian party system, based on voting patterns from 1987-1996, also applies to the current German situation. The Italian system was convulsed by the end of the Cold War (erosion of communist and Catholic subcultures), major scandals, a sharp economic downturn in the Mezzogiorno, and a major change in the electoral law. The German system has been hit with unification, soaring public debt, demographic decline, and changes in the classical or "Fordist" economic model. E. Spencer Wellhofer also considers a high proportion of voters "available for mobilization" as a further indicator of impending party system change in Italy. This is certainly the case in Germany as well. The "available" proportion of the German electorate—non-voters, supporters of splinter parties and the opposition party or parties—has grown from 17 percent in 1976 to 46 percent in 2005. In the eastern states, of course, it is even higher. Only 41 percent of eligible voters in 2005 supported the CDU or SPD.

Thus far, however, the German "center," unlike its Italian counterpart, has not collapsed. The 2005 election was more of a dealigning vote in which the existing party structure was severely shaken, but without any signs of a replacement. Can the current coalition save the old party system, or will it spark further deconsolidation and give the Federal Republic a multi-party system based on four or five parties of roughly equal strength? Is this the end of reform gridlock (*Reformstau*), or the continuation of the "catastrophic equilibrium," the disconnect between social-economic reality and political rhetoric, that Kenneth Dyson and others argue has characterized German politics since unification?[21]

Both governing parties must accept the reality of scarcity and frugality. The Federal Republic's distributive capacity is at its limits. The Christian Democrats could become the winners of this version of the grand coalition if they can be identified with job growth, debt reduction and a sustainable reform of the welfare state. The grand coalition may offer the SPD the opportunity to continue to free itself from its traditional, social-protectionist image.[22] If it does not, it could become a permanent minority party which could eventually be absorbed by Lafontainist populism.[23] The Greens could then become the modern party of the progressive center-left.

If the SPD and CDU/CSU remain in the current 34-38 percent range, they will need two smaller parties, instead of one, to form a future government. The initial, admittedly half-hearted, efforts to form such a three party alignment (so-called "traffic light" or "Jamaica" coalitions) after the 2005 election were unsuccessful. Surely, game and coalition theorists will be in high demand at both SPD and CDU headquarters after future elections.

The future of the two governing parties will also be affected by the development of the opposition. Currently, the party no one wants to play with is the Left which in 2005 ran a pure protest campaign. The Left leadership and most of its voters, according to one study, however, have other plans and would like to position the party as a possible coalition partner for the SPD and perhaps the Greens following the next federal election. "Red-Red-Green" governments are not unknown. In fact, Norway is governed currently by such a coalition.[24]

Moreover the improved supply-side condition of the opposition appears to be stable, i.e., none of the three opposition parties are likely to depart from the parliament in the near term. Already, all three have registered post-election membership gains and they all appear to have a core electorate that assures them of the required five percent. For the Left Party/PDS not surprisingly, the demographic core is among unemployed manual voters in the eastern states. In this group the Left Party received an astonishing 42 percent of the vote, a clear plurality and four times greater than its national average. Chronic unemployment coupled with the Hartz IV policies created a powerful impetus to support the Left which promised to repeal Hartz IV and institute a massive public works program. Fully 25 percent of all jobless voters supported the Left

Party/PDS in 2005. Among those with jobs, the party received less than 8 percent of the vote. The FDP now has a core electorate of young, middle-class voters. In 2005 it received 12 percent of the vote among 18-29 West Germans.[25] The party would gain more from the ranks of the CDU/CSU by emphasizing its market-liberal credentials at the expense of its traditional support for special interests (e.g., officials, artisans and dentists).[26]

All three opposition parties also have the ability and the opportunity to draw voters from the governing parties. The FDP is well-positioned to pursue a liberal reform program *pur* without any short-run need to consider a coalition partner. The way is clear for a form of German Thatcherism emphasizing the deregulation of markets, lower taxes, welfare state reform, and accelerated privatization. This would be attractive to voters in the neoliberal (i.e., Friedrich Merz) wing of the Union. The Greens are now free from their ties to the SPD and their need to support policies they fundamentally opposed such as subsidies for coal mining and ship-building, as well as the traditional health and pension systems. They can focus on issues that speak to their fundamentally new middle-class, post-materialist clientele: education reform, consumer protection, civil liberties, minority rights (women, children, foreign residents, gays), market-based, individualized pension and health care programs. They should also be able to target those segments of the SPD electorate that seek an alternative to traditional social democratic policies. The Left Party of Lafontaine and Gysi has already benefited from the defection of thousands of traditional SPD voters. Absent any significant economic upturn and with continued cuts in welfare programs, especially for the unemployed, this will continue. The Left Party is ideally positioned to mobilize these "modernization losers" as well as non-voters. Another ominous development for the SPD is reports of increasingly closer relations between several trade union organizations such as IG Metall and Ver.di and the Left Party.[27] Already in 2005 the Left Party received the support of 12 percent of trade union voters.

At what point will significant segments of the electorate cease to consider the CDU/CSU-SPD "major" or "*groß*" parties? In the eastern regions they are close to that level among the unemployed, young voters, and blue collar workers. The cycle of state elections which began in March 2006 will serve as early indicators of government and opposition support. At state elections will the two coalition parties attempt to focus their campaigns on local and state issues to avoid campaigns and election results that will raise tensions in Berlin? An attempt to denationalize state elections would mean the reversal of a twenty-five year-old trend toward the nationalization of state politics. Yet such a "don't rock the boat" approach will almost certainly benefit all or some of the three opposition parties thereby increasing the pressure on the two national governing parties. How will policy successes and failure be spun by the coalition partners?

Most economists predict real GDP growth of about 1.8 percent in 2006. That would be the best year since 2000, but far short of what is needed to reduce unemployment. This modest growth in 2006 will be fueled in part by increased consumer spending prior to the scheduled 3 percent increase in the Value Added Tax in 2007. If that tax increase produces a consumer spending strike and a significant drop in growth, the grand coalition will experience its first major domestic crisis. However, there is only one state election in 2007 in the small city-state of Bremen. With major state elections on the horizon, 2008 appears to be the critical year for the coalition. If there is no discernible improvement in the economy by 2008 both parties will suffer at the polls and the opposition parties should profit. In its early decades, support for the institutions, processes and values of the Federal Republic was performance-driven. Now in its sixth decade, it appears that the same can be said of the Republic's fractured party system.

Notes

1. Tobias Dürr, "Bewegung und Beharrung: Deutschlands künftiges Parteiensystem," *Aus Politik und Zeitgeschichte*, no. 32-33 (2005): 31, 36. He writes: "The 2005 election could be the beginning of the end of the party system we have known for 60 years." See also Warnfried Dettling, "Regierungswechsel? Gezeitenwechsel!, *Berliner Republik*, no. 4 (2005).
2. Dettling, see note 1.
3. Thomas Saalfeld, "Political Parties," in *Governance in Contemporary Germany*, eds. Simon Green, William E. Paterson (Cambridge and New York, 2005), 76.

4. Herbert Kitschelt, "Political-Economic Context and Partisan Strategies in the German Federal Elections, 1990-2002," *West European Politics* 26, no. 4 (2003):125-152.

5. With the Federal Republic less than twenty-five years old, Rudolf Wildenmann, on the basis of only six national elections, made a fundamental point about the party system that is still true today: "In contrast to many theoretical assumptions, the 5 percent clause built in the present proportional representation has only a slight effect on defractionalization ... the major cause of defractionalization is voting behavior." Rudolf Wildenmann, "Germany 1930/1970. The Empirical Findings," in *Sozialwissenschaftliches Jahrbuch für Politik,* ed. Rudolf Wildenmann, vol. 2, (Munich, 1971), pp. 13-60.

6. David P. Conradt and Russell J. Dalton, "The West German Electorate and the Party System: Continuity and Change in the 1980s." *Review of Politics* 50, no. 1 (1988): 3-29; See also Karl H. Cerny, ed., *Germany at the Polls .The Bundestag Elections of the 1980s* (Durham, 1990).

7. E. Spencer Wellhofer, "Party Realignment and Voter Transition in Italy, 1987-1996," *Comparative Political Studies,* 34, no. 2 (2001): 163.

8. Russell J. Dalton and Wilhelm Bürklin, "The Two German Electorates," in *Germans Divided. The 1994 Bundestag Elections and the Evolution of the German Party System.,* ed. Russell J.Dalton (Oxford and Washington, 1996), 183-207; See also Russell J. Dalton and Wilhelm Bürklin "The German Party System and the Future," in *The New Germany Votes. Unification and the Creation of the New German Party System,* ed. Russell J. Dalton (Providence and Oxford, 1993), 233-256.

9. Dieter Ohr, "Wahlen und Wahlverhalten im Wandel: Der individualisierte Wähler in der Mediendemokratie," in *Die Bundestagswahl 2002,* eds. Manfred Güllner, et al., (Wiesbaden, 2005), 27.

10. Forschungsgruppe Wahlen, "Zweite Runde für Rot-Grün: Die Bundestagswahl vom 22. September 2002," in *Wahlen und Wähler Analysen aus Anlass der Bundestagswahl 2002,* eds. Jürgen Falter, et al. (Wiesbaden, 2005), 15-49.

11 Institut für Demoskopie (Allensbach) cumulated data file, (Survey nos. 0050, 0061, 0073, 0083, 0095, 1010, 1020, 1031).

12. Russell J. Dalton, "Voter Choice and Electoral Politics," in *Developments in German Politics 3,* Stephen Padgett, William E. Paterson and Gordon Smith (Houndmills, 2003), 72. Data for 2005 are from the Forschungsgruppe Wahlen pre-election surveys.

13. After an exhaustive, multi-variate analysis of 2002 survey data , Klein and Rosar conclude: "By the end of the campaign, the knowledge of a voter's chancellor preference was more important than party identification or the perceived problem-solving competence of the party ... This relates to the Iraq crisis, the Elbe flood and the TV-duel. All enabled Schröder to expand his lead over Stoiber and compensate for his party and government's perceived policy failures. The voters considered the CDU more competent to deal with the economy and jobs, and the party with the best program." Markus Klein, Ulrich Rosar, "Die Wähler ziehen Bilanz: Determinanten der Wahlteilnahme und der Wahltschedtung," in Güllner, see note 9, 187, 198. Anticipating the analysis for 2005, we suggest that the "Kirchhof caper," the TV debate and Merkel's "campaign of honor," will be the equivalents of the flood and Iraq war in 2002.

14. The proportion of late deciders grew from 7 percent in 2002 to 12 percent in 2005, among the FDP's electorate, 18 percent decided late. Forschungsgruppe Wahlen, Bundestagswahl, 2005, p. 38

15. Forschungsgruppe Wahlen, post-election surveys.

16. This disappeared in stages. The first hemorrhage occurred in July when the CDU/CSU presented its election program which included a proposed increase in the Value Added Tax and cuts in various tax breaks for overtime, night-shift and holiday work. This increase would be used to further reduce payroll taxes and labor costs, specifically a drop in the unemployment insurance tax from 6.5 percent to 4.5 percent. But the connection between raising consumption taxes to reduce labor costs and thus stimulate economic growth was not understood by most voters. This was followed by the addition of Professor Kirchhof to the Kompetenz Team. Kirchhof quickly became the major target of the Social Democrats. Finally, Merkel's TV debate with Schröder in early September brought further decline in the polls. Forschnungsgruppe Wahlen, "Bundestagswahl. Eine Analyse der Wahl vom 18. September 2005," (Mannheim, 2005), 39-40. See also Frank Brettschneider, "Bundestagswahl und Medienberichterstattung," Aus *Politik und Zeitgeschichte*, no. 51-52 (2005): 19-26 for an account of the Kirchhof factor.

17. Matthias Jung and Andrea Wolf, "Der Wählerwille erzwingt die große Koalition," *Aus Politik und Zeitgeschichte*, no. 51-52 (2005): 3-12.

18. David P. Conradt, *The West German Party System: An Ecological Analysis of Social Structure and Voting Behavior, 1961-1969* (Beverly Hills and London, 1972).

19. Conradt, see note 18, 9.

20. Wellhofer, see note 7, 150-151.

21. Kenneth Dyson, "Economic Policy Management: Catastrophic Equilibrium, Tipping Points and Crisis Interventions," *Governance in Contemporary Germany*, see note 3, 115-137.

22. Herbert Kitschelt, "Political-Economic Context and Partisan Strategies in the German Federal Elections, 1990-2002," West *European Politics* 26, no. 4 (2003): 134.

23. In a recent analysis, the German political scientist Frank Decker argues that the SPD was the "structural loser" of the 2005 election since it lost the most voters to the Left Party and is unlikely to get them back. The CDU/CSU's losses to the Free Democrats, on the other hand, were within the bourgeois camp and were based on the FDP voters' assumption that Merkel together with the FDP would win a clear majority. Many of these voters can be expected to return to the Union if needed. Frank Decker, "Die Zäsur", *Berliner Republik*, no. 6 (2005).

24. "Operation Norwegen", *Der Spiegel*, 19 December 2005.

25. Forschungsgruppe, Bundestagswahl 2005, 65.

26. Kitschelt, see note 22, 151-152.

27. Markus Deggerich, "Schub für den Westen," *Der Spiegel*, 16 January 2005.

Chapter 2

The Extraordinary Bundestag Election of 2005

The Interplay of Long-term Trends and Short-term Factors[1]

Hermann Schmitt & Andreas M. Wüst

Introduction

The German federal election of September 2005 was an extraordinary election in many senses. Its premature calling came as a surprise, and, even more so, its result–not least with reference to the forecasts of German pollsters who largely failed to predict the outcome. While this is not our primary concern here, at the end we return to this issue. This chapter addresses the structural context of the election, illuminating the evolution of public opinion during the campaign, and discusses the result and likely consequences.[2] Before we begin, however, we address some conceptual and theoretical issues that guide us in defining the variables that we investigate.[3] At the time of writing,[4] it is too early to engage in analyses of individual-level data of the German Election Study 2005[5] in a hypothesis-testing manner. This must wait until the different data sets become available and analyses can be conducted. Hence, we are left with extant individual-level evidence. Based upon this, we relate (more or less) long-term trends on relevant variables to one another and draw conclusions from it for the future of German electoral politics.

Theoretical Considerations

Institutions matter at least somewhat, according to a series of empirical studies on the effect of institutional arrangements on political behavior.[6] Within the German political system, variations in the institutional context of federal politics are, of course, limited. The constitution has hardly changed, nor the procedures of federal policy-making or the competences of its actors. In fact, one might wonder why the institutional context should play a role here at all. Yet, there is one critical aspect: the power relation between the federal parliament (Bundestag) and the federal government that depends on it, on the one hand, and the house of representatives of state governments (Bundesrat), on the other. Every state parliament election (*Landtagswahl*) can change this power relation with the ultimate effect that a concordant majority in the two houses can change into a discordant majority, or vice versa. Concordant majorities usually allow the federal parliament to get its legislative projects through. Discordant majorities tend to cause problems because the Bundesrat has to approve two-thirds of all federal laws (among them all that involve co-funding of the states).

The consequences of discordant majorities on federal politics are immense. Most obviously, they affect policy output, i.e., legislation. In addition, discordant majorities in the two houses also have a moderating effect on the depth of ideological conflicts (see Figure One). When the federal government and its constituent parties need the consent of the main party of the opposition to legislate, they cannot afford to accommodate deep ideological cleavages. They know that, at the end of the day, they will need to compromise and

Figure 1: The Arguments

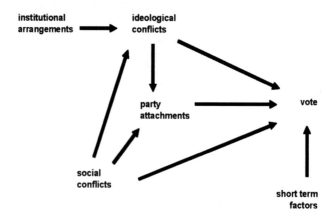

finally agree on less than the originally preferred policy. Under these circumstances, consensus-seeking strategies and the ability to cooperate are more useful and, hence, prevalent than persistent competition and conflict.[7] This is why party competition in the German federal system is less ideological than it sometimes appears to be. All of this is relevant for an analysis of the German federal election of 2005 because ideological conflict is one important source of partisanship,[8] which, in turn, is an important determinant of vote choices–certainly of stable vote choices.[9] Indeed, ideological conflict is all the more relevant in times when traditional social cleavages have lost some of their stabilizing impact on political attitudes and behavior.[10]

When the stabilizing cues from ideological, partisan and social divisions are weakening, short-term factors gain importance[11] and the timing of vote choices gradually approaches the date of the election.[12] Short-term factors originate in the issues that shape the campaign and in the candidates standing for election.[13] There are all sorts of candidates standing for election, but what increasingly counts in a German parliamentary election are the contenders for the position of head of government.[14] Much the same holds for issues. Among many sorts of issues, the ones that count most in the voting decision are often not very divisive between party camps–so-called "valence issues." The mechanism that translates their perceived importance is the competence that a voter attributes to a candidate or a party to resolve the issue.[15]

These claims have been corroborated in a number of empirical analyses and they do not need to be reinvestigated here at the micro level. In contrast, we analyze longitudinal empirical evidence on each of the factors in order to see whether trends covary over time. Because of vastly differing time frames, this can be done only in a somewhat impressionistic "eye-balling" manner. Imperfect as this methodology may appear, we nevertheless claim to support the arguments that due to the institutional properties of the federal system of government and the decline of ideological and social cleavages, German vote choices are increasingly dependent upon the issues that prevail during the election campaign and the image of "chancellor candidates"–that is, short-term factors. Numerous vote choices are made only during the campaign. This development poses mounting problems on the capability of the polling industry to accurately predict the result ahead of election day.

Ungovernability, Ideological Centrism, and the Decline of Core-Electorates

The German political system is characterized by two rival principles of government: federalism and party government. The first suggests a consensual, the second a competitive mode of policy-making.[16] Which of the two principles or modes of government prevails depends upon the majorities in the Bundesrat. There are two basic alternatives. The federal government can rely on a majority of state governments (and their votes) of the same political colors, in which case competitive party government is the prevailing characteristic. When the government cannot rely on this support, consensual policy-making, package deals, and more generally, the politics of the smallest common denominator are the prevailing characteristics.

Figure 2: Deadlock

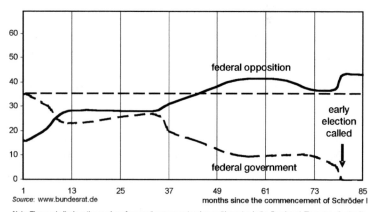

Source: www.bundesrat.de

months since the commencement of Schröder I

Note: The graph displays the number of „secure" government and opposition votes in the *Bundesrat*. The votes of „mixed" land colaitions, e.g. the SPD-FDP-coalition in Rhineland-Palatinate, are not displayed. In controversial decisions, these *Länder* usually abstain. After re-unification the federal states (*Bundesländer*) together have 69 votes, 35 being the absolute majority.

The evolution of majorities in the Bundesrat during the two terms of chancellor Gerhard Schröder (Schröder I and II) points to a growing trend towards consensual government in the Federal Republic of Germany (Figure Two). Displayed are "secure" Bundesrat votes for the federal government and the federal opposition (Social Democratic Party, SPD and SPD-Green state governments' votes included on the federal government side, and Christian Democratic Union/Christian Social Union, CDU/CSU or CDU-Free Democratic Party, FDP state governments' votes added to the federal opposition side).

Only during the first year of its first term could the federal SPD-Green coalition government rely on a relative majority of Bundesrat votes. Never did it control the absolute majority required to pass or block federal legislation. However, during the whole period of the second Schröder government, the federal opposition could count on such an absolute majority and hence obstruct federal legislation at will. The decision to call an early election was taken after the results of the 2005 Landtag election in North Rhine-Wesphalia became known—that is, at exactly the time when the share of Bundesrat votes of the federal government had declined to zero.

Discordant majorities in the two houses are a relatively recent phenomenon in the Federal Republic. They only emerged during the first period of SPD-led governments, between 1972 and 1983, and reappeared again ten years later, during the third and the fourth government of Helmut Kohl. Their potential effect on ideological polarization therefore should only become manifest during the 1980s and 1990s. Thanks to the *Politbarometer* surveys produced by the Forschungsgruppe Wahlen, this is also the period for which we have perceptional data on where the German parties stand in ideological terms. Ten representative samples of the voting age population were asked to place each of the relevant parties on an eleven-point Left-Right scale. The mean scores of these individual placements are depicted in the following figure (Figure Three). If we start from the right-hand side, in the absence of a relevant far Right party, the CSU comes first, followed less than a scale point apart towards the center by the CDU. The small FDP occupies the middle ground, but with a clear alignment: from 1983 onwards with the Right. The SPD places itself center-Left, the Greens are more or less left of the SPD. And the Party of Democratic Socialism, (PDS/Left Party) finds itself left of the Greens. In 2005, the two major parties—the SPD on the Left and the CDU on the Right—were 2.5 scale points apart, whereas in 1980, the

Figure 3: Ideological Bandwith

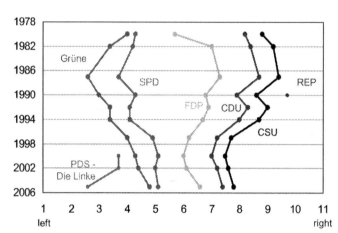

Source: Politbarometer of the Forschungsgruppe Wahlen

respective figure was 3.9. The Greens and CSU are now 3.1 scale points apart, compared to 4.8 scale points in 1980 (and 6.6 points in 1987, when the perceived ideological distance between these parties was the largest). Although the parties of the Right–CDU/CSU and FDP–have reoriented themselves somewhat more to the Right after they lost power in 1998, the bandwidth of German party competition has never been narrower than at present.

One of the consequences of a shrinking ideological spectrum is the opening up of niches in the electoral market–"open flanks" in military jargon that can be occupied with little effort. One example is the formation of a new Left Party (*Die Linke*), which integrates in addition to the Eastern based PDS a sizeable leftwing break-away of the SPD.[17] From the perspective of the system, there is little reason why similar developments should not also be expected on the right side of the political spectrum.[18] Institutional constraints and ideological conflicts are important motivations for political behavior. But is not social conflict the core of it all? What about the cleavage structure? Are "core electorates," defined in social-structural terms, still relevant for our understanding of electoral outcomes? Before we turn to this, we briefly recapitulate the traditional cleavage structure of the German party system. This basic structure has been made up

Figure 4: Traditional Cleavage Structure

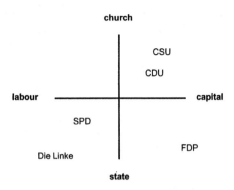

by two cross-cutting cleavages, state vs. church on the one hand, and labor vs. capital on the other (Figure Four).

Within this structure, the SPD used to stand for secular and labor interests while the CDU, and even more so the CSU, represented religious and business positions. The FDP has been the party of secular business, thereby balancing a rightist score on the business dimension with a leftist score on the religious dimension and henceforth occupying the middle ground. The new far-Left formation "the Left Party" fits very well in this traditional cleavage structure by being more "social democratic" than the original SPD. The same does not apply to the Greens, for whom a third dimension of "new politics" was needed to represent adequately their political claims and appeals.[19] Nevertheless, if placed solely within the traditional cleavage system, they would position themselves somewhere between SPD and the Left Party.

Decades of social change rendered this approach largely inadequate for our understanding of contemporary voting behavior. While practicing Catholics and unionized laborers continue to vote predominantly CDU/CSU and SPD respectively, the size of these social groups has declined dramatically to about 10 percent each (see Table One). This is not to say that social divisions are now a less powerful predictor of the vote than they were in the early years of the Federal Republic. While the old cleavage characteristics have lost most of their vote structuring power, new social inequalities have become associated with party preference and vote choice, among them age,

Table 1: Core Electorates (figures are percentages)

election year	SPD voters among unionized workers	unionized workers in the SPD electorate	CDU/CSU voters among practising catholics	practising catholics in the CDU/CSU electorate
1969		25		46
1972		19		42
1976	68	13	84	36
1980	62	14	74	31
1983	68	19	78	25
1987	64	18	70	29
1990	58	16	79	23
1994	60	13	74	15
1998	66	11	70	15
2002	55	11	73	12
2005	54	9	72	12

Source: Forschungsgruppe Wahlen. West Germany only.

education, and the regional context.[20] There is one difference, however, between the new inequalities and the old cleavages: the latter are organized, which adds stability to their political meaning.

Partisanship

Rooted in social oppositions partisanship, once established, lives a life of its own. It is reaffirmed through recurring election campaigns and voting decisions.[21] It flourishes when ideological conflicts between the electoral contenders are profound, and it weakens in the absence of such conflicts.[22] In addition to this "conflict theory" of partisanship, there are competing conceptions, most notably the theory that cognitively mobilized citizens would be less in need of partisan cues and thus more independent, not only functionally, but also politically.[23] This view, however, could not be confirmed in systematic diachronic tests for six West European countries that compared the likelihood of partisan ties among educated and politically interested people with that same likelihood in the general populace.[24]

What we should expect, then, is a decline of partisanship in Germany mainly as a result of the declining ideological bandwidth of party competition which, to an important degree, is caused by the increasing institutional deadlock between Bundestag and Bundesrat. Figure Five shows the evolution of the proportion of "independents" from 1976 on.[25]

Figure 5: German Party Identification, 1976-2005

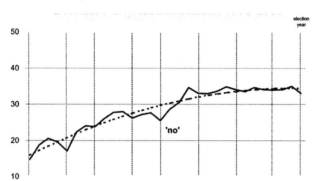

Source: Forschungsgruppe Wahlen; West Germany only. Note that the yearly figures are arithmetic mean scores of the porportions determined by the monthly Politbarometer surveys.

In 2005, one in three West Germans said "no" when asked whether they lean towards one of the political parties.[26] This proportion roughly has doubled over the past three decades, with the steepest increase in the years immediately following German unification in 1990. While the polynomial trend line suggests a slowly continuing increase of independents, the raw data indicate that a plateau of "nonpartisanship" was reached in 1993 and has been maintained since.

East German partisanship is not covered in this figure. Because of the changing universe of the samples (West Germany before 1990, united Germany thereafter) the trend line would become blurred. This is not to say that there is no empirical information available. Early in the unification process, it had been established that East Germans were no "virgins" in terms of affiliation with West German parties—many had every opportunity to align themselves "virtually" with a party of the Federal Republic.[27] In the year after unification, East Germans started out with 41 percent independents, which, however, as a result of dissatisfaction with the material consequences of unification, quickly rose to 52 percent in 1993. From then on, nonpartisanship in the East declined more or less continuously to reach again the 40 percent level from which it started in 1990.[28] The diminishing of ideological polarization, the diversification of social oppositions, and the dwindling of partisan ties all suggest that short-term factors have become extraordinarily important influences for Germans' voting decisions. These short-term factors are what we look at next.

Short-term Factors

Short-term factors can distort longer-term trends. They come in two types: issues and candidates. Both issue and candidate effects on the vote are election-specific, which is to say that both can change from election to election. Before we start analyzing this, we need to address again what the longer-term trends are. Some of the literature suggests that governmental support tends to follow a cyclical pattern. After some sort of post-electoral euphoria, governments usually lose support until after midterm and only then recover, rising to a level close to the previous score.[29] This pattern does not appear everywhere and does not emerge all the time.[30] Nevertheless, research into European Parliament election results repeatedly has provided evidence that confirms such an electoral cycle in consolidated electoral systems.[31]

Previous research into German electoral cycles has shown that the popularity of SPD-led governments does not follow cyclical developments as smoothly as CDU/CSU-led governments.[32] The two Schröder governments are no exception to the rule (see Figure Five). In particular, Schröder I does not fit the expected pattern: the government had a very bad start in its first year, enjoyed high ratings during midterm, deteriorated in the winter of 2001/2002, but recovered again during a spectacular election campaign.[33] Immediately after the 2002 election, satisfaction with Schröder II dropped even more dramatically than it did four years earlier and remained at a very low level over the first two years. A short period of increasing support was followed by another downturn (because of the loss of another state election in February 2004), which then marked the start of the 2005 election campaign.[34] All in all, these results demonstrate that satisfaction with government has been very volatile in

Germany lately. Long-term causes, we think, are the shrinking of ideological distances and the complementary decline of partisanship that has been referred to before.

Figure 6: Satisfaction With Government

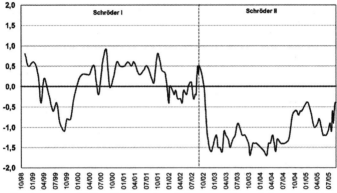

Source: Forschungsgruppe Wahlen – Politbarometer and other surveys. Respondents are asked how satisfied they are with government (displayed) and opposition (not shown). The graph indicates mean scores on an 11 point scale (+5/-5).

Issues

We distinguish two classes of issues: position and valence issues. Position issues are at the core of spatial models of vote choice. The simplest and most popular form of these models assumes that voters have policy preferences on a given issue. Parties position themselves on a policy dimension in order to maximize their vote share, while voters maximize their utility by choosing the party that is closest to their own position on this dimension.[35] It has been shown that this mechanism is indeed related to vote choices, if only modestly. However, even more important for vote choices are valence issues.[36] Valence issues do not involve a decision for or against, or for more or less of, a political measure. Everybody tends to agree on valence issues. What differs between voters is the importance that they assign to different valence issues, and the competence that they attribute to the competing parties to solve these issues/problems.

Issue competence is the mechanism that relates the perceived importance of valence issues to actual vote choices.[37] Unlike other national survey research traditions, the German series of election studies early on concentrated on this saliency/competence approach to issue voting.[38] It is in this tradition that a representative sample of the German voting age population was asked, shortly ahead of the 2005 election: (1) what the most important problems are; and (2) who is considered to be most competent to deal with these problems.

The results are clear. In the eyes of voters, the one issue overshadowing anything else is unemployment (85 percent mentioned it as the most important or second-most important issue). Shortage of money, i.e., inflation and salaries, comes next (14 percent), followed by general references to the state of the economy (13 percent). Welfare state concerns are clearly lagging behind these economic issues: 10 percent mention the pension system, 9 percent taxation, and 8 percent health. At the time of the 2005 election, the state of the economy in general

Figure 7: Political Agenda

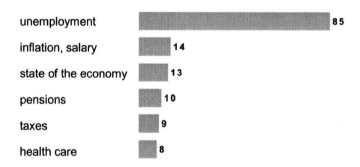

Source: Forschungsgruppe Wahlen – "flash survey" conducted during the week preceding the election.
Figures are percent "very important" of two possible responses to the agenda question.

and unemployment in particular were seen as the political problems of utmost importance (Figure Seven).

Competence attributions relate saliency perceptions to vote choices. High competence scores in economic matters should translate in a clear electoral advantage. The parties who did best in these fields were the CDU and CSU: roughly 40 percent of Germans referred to them as most competent in dealing with unemployment and the economy (Figure Eight). The SPD was mentioned only by some 20 percent, and about the same number held the opinion that none of the parties was competent. If it comes to welfare state policies, the clear competence advantage of the CDU/CSU for the economy is not reversed in favor of the SPD, as one could have expected on the basis of the traditional policy profile of this party, but rather turns into a

Figure 8: Competence

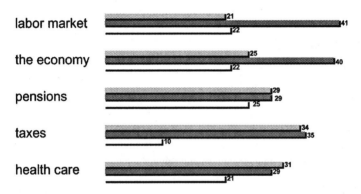

Source: Forschungsgruppe Wahlen, 'flash survey' conducted during the week preceding the election. Note that light grey bars represent percent 'SPD' responses, dark grey bars represent percent 'CDU/CSU' responses, and white bars represent percent responses 'none of the parties'.

tie between the two big parties. Altogether, issue effects on the vote favored CDU and CSU and a CDU/CSU-led government.[39]

Candidates

These findings do not pertain with respect to the candidates standing for office. The SPD chancellor Gerhard Schröder, not the CDU candidate Angela Merkel, was the more attractive candidate. If we compare the ratings of Schröder and the SPD over the eighteen months preceding the election, Schröder was always ahead of his party–he was clearly adding to the electoral attractiveness of the SPD (data not shown). The contrary emerges for Merkel and the CDU; she has been clearly less popular than the CDU, and only could close the gap and climb up to the level of her party's popularity during the campaign.

A more direct comparison of the two chancellor candidates is presented in Figure Nine. It shows which of the two candidates was the most preferred, and the evolution of these preferences during the campaign. Gerhard Schröder is clearly in the lead here as well. Only in the very early phase of the campaign, when the plan for an early election was just announced, did pro-Merkel preferences outnumber

Figure 9: Chancellor Preference

Source: Forschungsgruppe Wahlen – Politbarometer

those in favor of Schröder. From mid-July on, Schröder more or less continuously increased his support base. On election day, 53 percent of all Germans preferred him as the next chancellor, while only 39 percent desired Angela Merkel.

One should not underestimate the impact of these short-term factors on vote choices at times when the decision for which party to vote is taken closer and closer to election day. In 2005, one in three voters—more precisely 31 percent—decided during the election campaign, "a few days," or "a few weeks" ahead of the election. The corresponding figure in 2002 was 24 percent and 22 percent in 1998.[40]

In 2005, these short-term factors were favoring both of the two competing camps differently. On the candidate side, the SPD could profit from the popularity of its chancellor Gerhard Schröder. With respect to issues, the CDU/CSU was clearly ahead in terms of competence attributions for the most pressing political problems: unemployment and the economy. With a stronger candidate, and, one is tempted to add a better campaign, Christian Democrats and Christian Socials could have "really won" the election and formed a Christian-conservative/liberal government coalition as intended.

Results and Likely Consequences

This however was not the result of the election (Table Two). The two major parties came out about equally strong, with 34.2 and 35.2 percent of the valid vote respectively. The FDP did remarkably well (9.8 percent), as did the Left Party (8.9 percent)—the latter being a new formation combining the Eastern-based PDS and the left-wing SPD breakaway group Electoral Alternative Work and Social Justice (Wahlalternative-Arbeit und soziale Gerechtigkeit, WASG). The Greens could about hold their electoral support (8.1 percent). Upon this basis, neither a continuation of the Red-Green government of SPD and the Greens nor the formation of a Christian-Liberal government was numerically possible. A broadening of the Red-Green coalition with the inclusion of the Left Party was not seriously considered, least so perhaps by the SPD and the Left Party itself. A so-called "traffic light coalition" including SPD, FDP and Greens was ruled out on policy grounds by the FDP. Another option, a so-called "Jamaica coalition" of CDU/CSU, FDP and Greens was equally energetically ruled out by the Greens and the CSU. The formation of a minority government has no tradition in postwar Germany and was not even considered. The only option that remained to be pursued was the formation of a "grand coalition" of CDU/CSU and SPD.

What are the likely consequences of this grand coalition? One is that some of the causes of the policy deadlock produced by discordant majorities in Bundestag and Bundesrat might be addressed and eliminated. The grand coalition commands a solid majority in each of the two chambers and should therefore be able to pave the way for a reform of state and federal competences, with the aim of reducing the requirement of dual majorities as much as possible. Another likely consequence of this election is less positive. It might bring about a further reduction of ideological and policy alternatives in the

43

Table 2: The 2005 Election Result (figures are vote percentages and number of seats)

	1st vote	diff 2002	2nd vote	diff 2002	seats	diff 2002
participation	77,7	-1,4	77,7	-1,4		
SPD	38,4	-3,5	34,2	-4,3	222	-29
CDU	32,6	0,6	27,8	-1,7	180	-10
CSU	8,2	-0,8	7,4	-1,6	46	-12
Grüne	5,4	-0,3	8,1	-0,4	51	-4
FDP	4,7	-1,1	9,8	2,5	61	14
Linke	8,0	3,6	8,7	4,7	54	52
others	2,7	1,5	4,0	0,8	-	-

Source: Federal Statistical Office.

center of the German party system. The two major players, CDU/CSU and SPD, almost certainly will move closer together as a result of their cooperation in the grand coalition. This will open up new chances for political entrepreneurs. Empty spaces, for example on the far Right, might be filled by new or revitalized political formations such as the NPD.

As a result of these processes, the grand coalition will certainly contribute to a further reduction of the vote share of the two major parties. CDU/CSU and SPD have already lost a fifth of their 1972 proportion of the valid vote. The current developments will lead to further fractionalization of the German party system and, perhaps in the long run, to a gradual change in the direction of party competition from centripetal to centrifugal tendencies. Last but not least, this election result might be remembered as another step towards the volatile voter. A further decline of ideological polarization will contribute to continuing dealignment and the weakening of partisanship. This will strengthen existing tendencies towards vote switching and late vote decisions. German voters will become even less predictable than they were in 2005.

Notes

1. An earlier version of this chapter was presented at a conference on the German Federal Election of 2005 which was held in Athens, Greece, on 25 October, 2005. This conference was organized by the Greek Association of Political Science and supported by the Friedrich-Ebert-Stiftung Athen and the Goethe-Institut Athen.

2. See Dieter Roth and Andreas M. Wüst, "Abwahl ohne Machtwechsel," in *Bilanz der Bundestagswahl 2005: Voraus – Setzungen, Ergebnisse, Folgen*, eds. Eckhard Jesse and Roland Sturm (Wiesbaden, 2006), 43-70, for another account of contextual factors that contributed to the outcome of the 2005 election.

3. All survey information presented in this chapter has been gathered and made available by the Forschungsgruppe Wahlen in Mannheim. This is gratefully acknowledged.

4. This chapter was finished mid-November 2005, revised in April, 2006.

5. The German Election Study consists of more than one individual study. At least four deserve mention–three at the mass and one at the elitelevel: (1) a study on the role of political parties, directed by Oskar Niedermayer and Bettina Westle; (2) a study on the evolution of public opinion and campaigning, directed by Rüdiger Schmitt-Beck; (3) a study on the effects of a limited choice set, directed by Berhard Weßels and Hermann Schmitt; and (4) a study into attitudes and behavior of both direct and list candidates for the German Bundestag, directed by Thomas Gschwend, Hermann Schmitt, Andreas M. Wüst and Thomas Zittel. At the time of writing, these data were available only in preliminary form, and the the candidates' survey was only started.

6. See the list of publications at http://www.cses.org.

7. See Gerhard Lehmbruch, *Parteienwettbewerb im Bundesstaat* (Opladen, 1998); Arend Lijphart, *Patterns of Democracy* (New Haven and London,1999).

8. See Hermann Schmitt and Sören Holmberg, "Political Parties in Decline?," in *Citizens and the State*, eds. Hans-Dieter Klingemann and Dieter Fuchs (Oxford, 1995), 95-133; Hermann Schmitt, "Partisanship in Western Europe and the US: Causes and Consequences," Paper presented at the Annual Meeting of the American Political Science Association (Boston, 2002); Hermann Schmitt, "Politische Parteien, Links-Rechts-Orientierungen und die Wahlentscheidung in Frankreich und Deutschland," in *Wahlen und Wähler. Analysen aus Anlass der Bundestagswahl 2002*, eds. Jürgen W. Falter, Oscar W. Gabriel, and Bernhard Wessels (Wiesbaden: 2005), 551-571.

9. Angus Campbell, Philip E. Converse, Warren E. Miller, and Daniel E. Stokes, *The American Voter* (New York, 1960); Warren E. Miller and J. Merrill Shanks, *The New American Voter* (Cambridge and London, 1996); Hermann Schmitt, *Politische Repräsentation in Europa* (Frankfurt, 2001).

10. See Russell J. Dalton, Scott Flanagan, and Paul E. Beck, eds., *Electoral Change in Advanced Industrial Democracies: Realignment or Dealignment?* (Princeton, 1984); Mark N. Franklin, Thomas Mackie, and Henry Valen, eds., *Electoral Change.* (Cambridge, 1992); Hermann Schmitt, "Zur vergleichenden Analyse des Einflusses gesellschaftlicher Faktoren auf das Wahlverhalten: Forschungsfragen, Analysestrategien und einige Ergebnisse," in *Wahlen und Wähler. Analysen aus*

Anlaß der Bundestagswahl 1998, eds. Hans-Dieter Klingemann and Max Kaase (Opladen, 2001), 623-45.

11. Russell J. Dalton. "Political Cleavages, Issues, and Electoral Change," in *Comparing Democracies,* eds. Lawrence Leduc et al. (Thousand Oaks, 1996).

12. Pippa Norris, *Electoral Engineering* (Cambridge, 2004).

13. Campbell et al., see note 9.

14. *Kanzlerkandidaten;* See Markus Klein and Dieter Ohr, "Gerhard oder Helmut? 'Unpolitische' Kandidateneigenschaften und ihr Einfluss auf die Wahlentscheidung bei der Bundestagswahl 1998," *Politische Vierteljahresschrift* 41 (2000): 199-224; Hermann Schmitt and Dieter Ohr, "Are Political Leaders Becoming More Important in German Elections? Leader Effects on the Vote in Germany, 1961-1998," Paper prepared for delivery at the Annual Meeting of the American Political Science Association (Washington, 2000).

15. Donald E. Stokes, "Spatial Models of Party Competition," in *Elections and the Political Order,* eds. Angus Campbell, Philip E. Converse, Warren E. Miller and Donald E. Stokes (New York, 1966); Donald E. Stokes, "Valence Politics," in *Electoral Politics* ed. Dennis Kavanagh (Oxford, 1992); Hermann Schmitt, "Issue-Kompetenz oder Policy-Distanz?," in *Wahlen und Wähler,* eds. Max Kaase and Hans-Dieter Klingemann (Opladen, 1998), 145-72; Harold D. Clarke et al., *Political Choice in Britain* (Oxford, 2004).

16. Lehmbruch, see note 7.

17. The most well-known of earlier SPD followers being the former SPD chairman and now head (with Gregor Gysi) of the parliamentary group of the Left Party, Oskar Lafontaine.

18. In particular in a situation in which the CDU/CSU is becoming the leading force of a grand coalition which will pull the two parties even further towards the center and leave the far-right fully unguarded. What could speak against such an expectation is that the extreme right in Germany, in the aftermath of the Nazi regime, has been stigmatized. However, these Federal Republican reflexes to the fascist past might have weakened in united Germany where national pride has become more widespread again and acquired a positive connotation while Europe has become less of an auxiliary "fatherland" than it used to be.

19. Wilhelm Bürklin, *Grüne Politik.* (Opladen, 1984); Hermann Schmitt, *Das Parteiensystem der Bundesrepublik Deutschland. Eine Einführung aus politik-soziologischer Perspektive* (Hagen, 1987).

20. Schmitt, see note 10, tables two and three.

21. Philip E. Converse, "Of time and partisan stability," in *Comparative Political Studies* 2 (1969): 139-171.

22. Schmitt and Holmberg, "Political Parties in Decline?"; Schmitt, "Partisanship in Western Europe and the US: Causes and Consequences"; Schmitt, "Politische Parteien, Links-Rechts-Orientierungen und die Wahlentscheidung in Frankreich und Deutschland."

23. Russell J. Dalton, "Cognitive Mobilization and Partisan Dealignment in Advanved Industrial Democracies," *Journal of Politics* 46 (1984): 264-284; Russell J. Dalton and Martin P. Wattenberg, eds. *Parties without Partisans* (Oxford, 2000).

24. Frode Berglund, Sören Holmberg, Hermann Schmitt, and Jacques Thomassen, "Party Identification," in *The European Voter,* ed. Jacques Thomassen (Oxford, 2005), 106-124.

25. We look at "independents" because this is the most clear-cut information that the German version of party identification produces (see the question wording in the following footnote). Gradations of partisanship are much harder to compare between different systems.

26. The German question wording goes as follows: "Viele Leute in Deutschland neigen längere Zeit einer bestimmten Partei zu, obwohl sie auch ab und zu eine andere Partei wählen. Neigen Sie, ganz allgemein gesprochen, einer bestimmten Partei zu?" [yes, no]; "Wenn ja, welcher?" [party list]; "Und wie stark oder schwach neigen Sie alles zusammen genommen dieser Partei zu: sehr stark, ziemlich stark, mäßig, ziemlich schwach, sehr schwach?" Displayed here is the proportion of respondents saying "no" to the first question.

27. Hermann Schmitt, "So dicht war die Mauer nicht! Über Parteibindungen und *cleavages* im Osten Deutschlands," in *Die Entwicklung der Volksparteien im vereinten Deutschland,* ed. Gerhard Hirscher (München, 1992), 229-52.

28. *Politbarometer* results, data not shown.

29. Edward R. Tufte, "Determinants of the outcomes of midterm congressional elections," in *American Political Science Review* 67 (1975): 540-54; James A. Stimson, "Public Support for American Presidents: A Cyclical Model," *Public Opinion Quarterly* 40 (1976): 1-21; Reiner Dinkel, *Der Zusammenhang zwischen der ökonomischen und der politischen Entwicklung in einer Demokratie* (Berlin, 1977); Karlheinz Reif and Hermann Schmitt, "Nine Second-order National Elections. A Conceptual Framework for the Analysis of European Election Results," *European Journal of Political Research* 8 (1980): 3-44.

30. Cees van der Eijk, "Testing theories of electoral cycles: The case of the Netherlands," *European Journal of Political Research* 15 (1987): 253-270.

31. Michael Marsh, "The results of the 2004 European Parliament elections and the second-order model," in *Europawahl 2004,* eds. Oskar Niedermayer and Hermann Schmitt (Wiesbaden, 2005), 142-158; Hermann Schmitt, "The European Parliament elections of June 2004: Still second-order?," *West European Politics* 28 (2005): 650-679; Andreas M. Wüst and Dieter Roth, "Parteien, Programme und Wahlverhalten," in *Wahl-Kampf um Europa,,* ed. Jens Tenscher (Wiesbaden: 2005), 56-85.

32. Hermann Schmitt and Karlheinz Reif, "Der Hauptwahlzyklus und die Ergebnisse von Nebenwahlen," in *Politbarometer,* ed. Andreas M. Wüst (Opladen, 2003), 239-254.

33. These midterm heights are attributed to a CDU scandal over illegal donations for that party plus the 9/11 events which favored—as every international crisis does—the national government.

34. One could assume that these ups and downs of government satisfaction are accompanied by complementary evaluations of the parties of the federal opposition. There is no systematic evidence for this, however.

35. Anthony Downs, *An Economic Theory of Democracy* (New York, 1957).

36. Stokes, see note 15.

37. Schmitt, see note 9.

38. See the data file of the "European Voter", documented in Jacques Thomassen, ed., *The European Voter* (Oxford, 2005).

39. Note that both the agenda and the competence measures were taken at the end of a short but intensive election campaign. During the first two months, the SPD lagged far behind. Campaign advantages changed with the growing involvement

of the "communication champion" of the SPD, Gerhard Schröder, but also as a result of apparent leadership deficiencies and mistakes in the CDU/CSU campaign. An example for the latter is Angela Merkel's invitation of law professor Paul Kirchhof to join her campaign as shadow finance minister. Instead of promoting the Christian democratic tax concept, however, Kirchhof advertised his own "flat tax" model. Needless to say that the SPD in concert with the Greens, did their best to nurture this conceptual confusion.

40. The source of these figures is again the "flash surveys" of the Forschungsgruppe Wahlen during the week preceding election day. The percentage base includes all respondents with a "valid" vote intention, and excludes those who will not vote or do not know which party.

Chapter 3

The Grand Coalition
Precedents and Prospects

Ludger Helms

In his influential article on Germany's political institutions, Manfred G. Schmidt famously characterized the Federal Republic as a "grand coalition state."[1] By this, he referred to the strong power-sharing character of public policy-making in the postwar German political system, which is largely a result of the exceptionally numerous and powerful institutional checks and balances. As different political institutions, such as the Bundestag or the Bundesrat, are often controlled in practice by different political parties, the German political system has been marked not only by a high degree of "institutional pluralism," but also by a significant amount of "divided government." To avoid or overcome structural gridlock, the two major parties within the system, the Christian Democratic Union/Christian Social Union (CDU/CSU) and the Social Democratic Party (SPD), have tended to cooperate closely with each other—more often than not to an extent that would appear to justify talk of an informal grand coalition.[2]

If, by contrast, the focus is on the party composition of postwar governments, the Federal Republic could hardly be labeled a "grand coalition state." This is true in particular for the party complexion of German federal governments. While many of the Länder (states) have had more-or-less extended experiences with grand coalitions, or even all-party governments, the dominant pattern at the federal level has been a series of differently composed "small coalitions." Marking a major difference between Germany and the two other (mainly) German-speaking countries of Western Europe, Austria and Switzerland, which were governed by grand coalitions or even all-party coalitions for decades, the Federal Republic's historical record up until the eve of the 2005 Bundestag election included only a scant three-year experience of formal grand coalition government. This dated back to the late 1960s, when the Christian Democrats shared power with the Social Democrats under Chancellor Kurt Georg Kiesinger (CDU).

In historical assessments of the Federal Republic's political history the Kiesinger government has hardly been highlighted as a particularly notable, let alone fortunate experience. According to the title of a book-length study on the 'grand coalition', the Kiesinger government has been a "forgotten government."[3] The few aspects that escaped from oblivion carried mainly negative associations, such as the growing support for extremist parties in parliamentary elections and the increase in extra-parliamentary opposition. The formation of a new grand coalition at the federal level, under Chancellor Angela Merkel (CDU), in the aftermath of the 2005 Bundestag election provides an apt opportunity to revisit the experience of 1966-1969 and to look at the key features and prospects of the current CDU/CSU-SPD government from a comparative historical perspective.

Comparing governments that share a common key variable (the type of coalition and the party complexion) is not only the "fairest" way of making comparative judgments, especially when it comes to assessing such aspects as the chancellor's leadership performance. In our case, it also offers a unique opportunity to highlight the key differences in the political and social leadership environment now and then—an approach which has much to contribute to a deeper understanding of the overall conditions of democratic governance in early twenty-first-century Germany compared to those of the late 1960s. Thus, rather than trying to provide a neat historical account of the lengthy formation and the first steps of the Merkel government, this chapter concentrates on drawing some more specific comparisons between the two grand coalition experiments. Necessarily, many observations and judgments concerning the Merkel government are of a preliminary character.

Comparing the Merkel and the Kiesinger Governments: A Preliminary Assessment

The Government Formation Process

The first grand coalition at the federal level came to life on 1 December 1966, in the middle of the 5th German Bundestag. It emerged from the ashes of the last Erhard government that had been transformed into a helpless one-party minority government in October 1966 by the Free Democratic Party's (FDP) angry departure from the CDU-led cabinet. However, rather than marking a snap decision designed to overcome a sudden government crisis, the formation of a grand coalition had been on the cards for quite some time. In fact, different attempts to forge a coalition between the CDU/CSU and the SPD at federal level can be traced back until the last years of the Adenauer era.[4] Yet, the formation of the first grand coalition government at federal level was by no means a foregone conclusion. Considered out of context, the formation of a SPD-FDP coalition would seem to have marked the natural solution to the crisis of the Erhard government. After all, Ludwig Erhard's fate as the CDU/CSU's chancellor candidate was sealed only after the SPD and FDP joined forces in the Bundestag. On 8 November 1966 they won a vote on a motion urging Erhard to launch a vote of censure. While this did not come about, the CDU/CSU abandoned Erhard and agreed on Kurt Georg Kiesinger, then minister-president of Baden-Wurttemberg, as their new chancellor candidate only two days later. Rather than responding to this move by stepping up their efforts to bring about a SPD-FDP coalition, which would have enjoyed a slim parliamentary majority, the Social Democrats signaled their willingness to join a CDU/CSU-led government by not nominating a SPD chancellor candidate.[5]

There were obvious strategic considerations among the Christian Democrats and the Social Democrats that favored the formation of a grand coalition. For the CDU/CSU–which by that time had come to view itself as the Federal Republic's natural party of government–a coalition with the SPD marked the only chance to cling to power. For the Social Democrats, such alliance appeared as the safest (if not the only) way to seize power at the federal level after seventeen years in opposition and to demonstrate their fitness to govern. Those supporting the formation of a grand coalition could point to the tangible affinities between both parties at the programmatic level, which were very much the result of the SPD's constant movement toward the center since the late 1950s. There were, however, also "objective" reasons suggesting the formation of a grand coalition, namely a variety of serious challenges and issues ranging from constitutional policy through economic and social policy that had proven too hot to handle for any of the numerous CDU-led cabinets.

Unlike the Kiesinger government, the Merkel government was formed after a parliamentary election, that is, at the start of a new legislative term. Nevertheless, it hardly could claim to possess a significantly more impressive electoral mandate than its historical predecessor. While the scenario of a grand coalition government had long enjoyed a reasonable amount of support among the German public during the run-up to the 2005 Bundestag election,[6] the campaign activities of all established office-seeking parties were focused clearly on a bipolar confrontation between the CDU/CSU-FDP and the SPD-Alliance '90/Greens. In fact, the stunning gains of the FDP, which were partly responsible for the poor electoral performance of the Christian Democrats, to a large extent came from those sections of the electorate desperately seeking to prevent a grand coalition.[7] The final electoral result would have allowed the formation of several different majority governments under the leadership of either SPD or CDU/CSU. None proved politically viable, however: neither the so-called "Jamaica coalition" (CDU/CSU, FDP, Greens); nor a government of the "united left" (SPD, Greens, and the Left Party); nor a "traffic light coalition" (SPD, FDP, and Greens). Thus, already from the second week of the postelection period onwards, a grand coalition emerged as the only realistic option. Nevertheless, with more than sixty days elapsing between the election and the appointment of the chancellor, the 2005 government formation process was exceptionally drawn-out.

With hindsight, Gerhard Schröder's rather self-serving (and untenable) assertion that he had been confirmed as the Federal Republic's natural chancellor candidate—even though the Red-Green coalition had been clearly defeated and the SPD lost its status as the strongest party in the Bundestag—served the Social Democrats extremely well. While the CDU eventually gained the chancellorship, the price to pay for the SPD's willingness to join a grand coalition led by a CDU chancellor was rather high, certainly higher than it had been in 1966. The Kiesinger government was composed of ten CDU and nine SPD ministers, a distribution of power that many CDU/CSU supporters considered unduly generous given the 8-point lead that the Christian Democrats had secured over the SPD in the previous Bundestag election of 1965. Even taking into account that the difference between the CDU/CSU and the SPD in terms of electoral support was just 1 percentage point in 2005, it remains remarkable that SPD ministers outnumbered CDU ministers in the Merkel cabinet by eight to seven (though it was agreed to reserve a tie-breaking vote to the chancellor as the eighth cabinet member from the ranks of the CDU/CSU).

Another obvious difference between the two grand coalition cabinets concerned the representation of female politicians. Not only was the federal government formed in late 2005 the first in postwar German history to be chaired by a woman chancellor, but the number of women among ministers was several times higher than under Chancellor Kiesinger—five compared to one, even though the overall number of cabinet ministers in the first grand coalition was even higher than in 2005. It would, however, be misconceived to regard the formation of the Merkel government as the decisive breakthrough in terms of female representation in federal cabinets. Representation of women in the German executive steadily increased since the early 1990s, and, if there was a historical watershed, it clearly dated to the various Schröder cabinets between 1998 and 2005.[8]

Whereas the number of female ministers serving under Merkel was incomparably higher than in Kiesinger's cabinet, the representation of real political heavyweights within the Merkel cabinet remained conspicuously modest. Kiesinger included numerous political stars from both parties—characters such as Willy Brandt, Gerhard Schröder, Franz Josef Strauß, Herbert Wehner and Karl Schiller, who, even forty years later, are well remembered for their exceptional political stature. There were very few comparable figures in the Merkel team, with the notable exception of Wolfgang Schäuble, the Christian Democrat interior minister, who could claim to enjoy such status. Also, a comparison of the leadership personnel of the CDU/CSU and SPD parliamentary party groups in the Bundestag during the first and the second grand coalition contributes to the impression that the pool of available political talent in both major parties has grown smaller. This finding raises the awkward question as to whether the structural conditions of politics as a vocation in the age of "media democracy" may have discouraged political talent from joining the game.[9]

Sticking to the conventions that have marked any coalition-building process at the federal level since 1980, the parties forming the Merkel government decided to lay down the bargaining results in a written coalition contract that had to be ratified formally by special party conferences of the coalition partners. This marked another difference to the government formation process in 1966 that did not produce any specific written agreement.[10] An immediate consequence was the greater freedom that Kiesinger enjoyed, compared to Merkel, when putting together his parliamentary inauguration speech as chancellor. In fact, judging by the size of the 2005 coalition agreement–the document had nearly 200 pages, and was the most extensive of its kind in the Federal Republic's history–Merkel's room for maneuver in highlighting her political agenda as "chief executive" was more restricted than that of any other recent German chancellor. Acknowledging the specific parameters defining her chancellorship, most observers refrained from criticizing Merkel for what otherwise could have been taken as a lack a vigor, rather hailing her gentleness in giving direction to the government.[11]

Intra-Governmental Decision-Making

In terms of political decision-making in core executive competencies, the Kiesinger government has been widely associated among contemporary observers with notions of the ultimate failure of "chancellor democracy." In a paper published towards the end of the Kiesinger chancellorship Arnulf Baring asked bluntly, "is there Kiesinger?," and suggested "the disappearance of the chancellor in German constitutional practice."[12] Such harsh judgments were clearly influenced by the high standards of "chancellor rule" that had marked much of the Adenauer era and that continued to shape perceptions of political leadership well into the late 1960s. Even a more sober and balanced assessment cannot, however, escape the fact that the impact of the "chancellor factor" was more limited than in any previous government–notwithstanding Kiesinger's bold claims that precisely a grand coalition needed a strong chancellor, as well as his publicly voiced determination to tighten his grip on the government.[13] In the more recent literature on political leadership in Germany, Kiesinger's rather unspectacular performance as chancellor has generally been attributed to the specific constraints of the unusual coalition format of his government, rather than to any short-comings in his personal leadership skills. This argument is supported by Kiesinger's rather different leadership performance as minister-president of Baden-Wurttemberg.[14]

Whereas scholars agree that the years 1966 to 1969 witnessed a departure from the established model of "chancellor democracy," and its replacement by a more consensus-oriented type of governance, it has remained a moot question as to where exactly the government's center of decision-making was located. In light of more recent research, conventional assessments that the cabinet effectively was sidelined from the beginning are in need of revision. In fact, during the first half year or so, the cabinet functioned as the real decision-making center of the Kiesinger government. The large number of heavyweight ministers, the sophisticated system of cabinet committees, and not least the near balance of strength of both parties at the cabinet table all added up to a set of structural conditions that favored the emergence of a cabinet-centered decision-making system.[15] Needless to say, this did not preclude conflict and dissent–the relationship between Chancellor Kiesinger and Foreign Minister (and Vice Chancellor) Willy Brandt, in particular, was rather strained. Despite divergent views on many issues, the overall atmosphere in the cabinet remained rather collegial for most of the time with few formal votes being taken.[16]

Nevertheless, as early as mid-1967 the cabinet gradually ceased to be the real decision-making center of the Kiesinger administration. Regular meetings including the party chairmen, the general secretaries and the chairmen of the CDU/CSU and SPD parliamentary party groups were arranged. Other members of the cabinet and policy specialists from the parliamentary parties were invited to participate on an ad hoc basis. This so-called "Kressbronn Circle" (named after Kiesinger's summer retreat near Lake Constance where the first meetings were held) initially met once a week on Tuesdays with intervals becoming longer as the government's term progressed. There is no consensus as to whether the "Kressbronn Circle" may be properly characterized as a "subsidiary government." Described by some authors as the effective "collective owner of policy guideline competence,"[17] more recent works have pointed to the body's limited authority, especially when it came to producing final decisions.[18]

Such differences in judgment apart, it is beyond contention that the practice of informal governance within the core executive arenas reached an early peak between 1967 and 1969.

Unlike the Kiesinger government, the Merkel government did not even try to live without an informal decision-making body. The 2005 coalition contract specifically mentioned a "coalition committee," designed to gather at least once a month or more often if requested by one of the coalition partners. It included the chancellor, vice chancellor, party chairs, the parliamentary party group leaders, and, in order to give reasonable representation to the CSU, the deputy chair of the CDU/CSU parliamentary party group (who is always a CSU member).[19] The small size of the coalition committee—standing out especially in comparison with the sixteen member coalition committee of the Red-Green coalition—nurtured expectations among observers that it could develop into the definitive steering body of the Merkel government. As during the Kiesinger years, and in fact within any administration, there were other forms of informal cooperation. Among the more notable were attempts by the Social Democrats to establish an informal network within the core executive. The Ministry of Labor, headed by Vice Chancellor Franz Müntefering, emerged early on as the hub of the various "subgovernments" designed to coordinate the activities of SPD ministers within the Merkel government. There were weekly meetings of the SPD ministers, chaired by Müntefering, that were held immediately before cabinet meetings.[20] These were strongly reminiscent of the regularly held informal gatherings among SPD ministers during the Kiesinger years, yet there seemed to be no neat equivalent to the full-blown informal shadow government that formed part of the party's informal infrastructure during the late 1960s.[21]

Towards the end of the grand coalition's first one hundred days, it remained uncertain as to how much room, if any, there would be for even the softest possible form of "chancellor rule" within the Merkel government. Manifestations of policy leadership by the chancellor were confined to the area of foreign policy (from EU policy through transatlantic relations), where Merkel's various activities largely overshadowed the actions of Foreign Minister Frank-Walter Steinmeier. There were no comparable examples of "chancellor government" in domestic policy. In an early journalistic inquiry into the inner workings of the core executive, Merkel appeared as a highly analytical, pragmatic and determined leader,[22] a judgment that did not fit too well with her notable inclination to readily adopt Social Democratic positions on many key issues, or to shelve contested decisions altogether. While Merkel's somewhat cautious style prompted occasional comparisons with her former political sponsor, Chancellor Helmut Kohl,[23] an arguably more important parallel between Merkel and Kohl related to their much-proven quality of exploiting the advantage of being underestimated.

Executive-Legislative Relations

In parliamentary systems of government, the size of the government's parliamentary majority marks the single most important variable determining its room for maneuver in the parliamentary arena. Other things being equal, governments enjoying a sizeable majority in parliament are considerably better off than minority governments or governments depending on the support of small and shaky majorities. Thus grand coalitions are generally in an exceptionally privileged position when it comes to pushing their legislative agendas through parliament. However, a closer look reveals that there can be significant differences even between key features and the structural position of different grand coalitions in the parliamentary arena.

The Kiesinger government commanded a parliamentary majority of more than 90 percent of all deputies represented in the 5th Bundestag. By contrast, the Merkel government enjoyed a parliamentary basis of "just" 72.9 percent (448 out of 614 Bundestag seats). This was only a moderately more generous parliamentary basis than that of the second Adenauer government (1953-1957), which was made up of four parties–CDU/CSU, FDP, German Party (DP), All-German Bloc/Federation of the Displaced and Dispossessed (GB/BHE)– and together held 68.6 percent of the seats in the 2nd Bundestag. The comparatively modest parliamentary basis of the Merkel government was accompanied, and, in fact, was caused by the remarkably strong electoral performance of the minor parties and the large number of third parties that gained parliamentary representation. Whereas the Kiesinger government faced just a single opposition party in the Bundestag, the FDP, the parliamentary opposition in the 16th Bundestag was composed of no less than three different parties

(FDP, Greens, and the Left Party), each of which held between 8.3 and 9.9 percent of the total seats.

There is no convincing way of forecasting the performance of the parliamentary opposition by looking at basic indicators, such as the number of parties and their ideological and programmatic distance from each other. Regarding the 16th Bundestag, different scenarios may be conceived. It could be argued that the striking ideological fragmentation of the opposition will prove an advantage from the government's point of view, as it should be difficult, if not impossible, for the three parties to agree on any coordinated move, let alone a more complex common strategy. Alternatively, it could be maintained that the very heterogeneity of the parliamentary opposition in the 16th Bundestag, which represents competing views and interests from the far Left to the moderate Right, will help to prevent the emergence of a powerful extra-parliamentary opposition that so troubled the Kiesinger government.[24]

However political opposition to the Merkel government will evolve in the years to come, an even more important issue relates to the cohesion of the parliamentary majority of the government in the Bundestag. The history of parliamentary government in Western Europe and elsewhere provides ample empirical evidence that oversized parliamentary majorities tend to produce an unusually large amount of dissention from government backbenchers—partly because individual MPs do not always consider their support indispensable to save the government from parliamentary defeat. Research shows that at times governing with small majorities may be easier than holding together a sizeable majority. This is true for one-party governments and "minimum-winning coalitions," and is all the more applicable for grand coalitions that bind together actors that tend to share a rather limited number of views.[25]

A major test for any incoming German government stems from Article 63 of the Basic Law that requires any would-be chancellor to secure a reasonable amount of parliamentary support in a secret ballot before he or she can be appointed by the federal president. The standard procedure, which may be relaxed only if no candidate has been elected within a fortnight after the first ballot, stipulates an absolute majority. While it is difficult to demonstrate a clear correlation between the parliamentary support that a chancellor secures in the

Bundestag's "vesting vote" and his or her grip on the government and parliament, voting results nevertheless provide important insights into the dynamics of an emerging government. On 22 November 2005, Angela Merkel was elected by 397 of the 612 attending members of the Bundestag, which meant that less than 89 percent of the MPs from coalition parties supported her.[26] In terms of the voting cohesion of majority parliamentary party groups, this was the third worst result in the Federal Republic's history. Yet, the natural yardstick for comparison for the Merkel government remains the performance of the Kiesinger government. With just over 78 percent of MPs from the coalition parties voting for Kiesinger on 1 December 1966, reservations both about the chancellor candidate and the unusual party composition of the emerging government were considerably stronger than in 2005.[27] Nevertheless, from a broader historical perspective executive-legislative relations during the Kiesinger years were remarkably smooth and efficient. Much of the excellent working relationship between the cabinet and the Bundestag was due to the two caucus leaders of the coalition parties, Rainer Barzel (CDU/CSU) and Helmut Schmidt (SPD). Neither before nor after 1966-1969 has there been a similarly close working relationship between chairs of the governing parliamentary party groups. During the final year of the Kiesinger government the influence of the two chairmen increased to an extent that led many to consider them as the key actors keeping the grand coalition project running.[28] It remains to be seen if, and to what extent, the two new protagonists at the top of the CDU/CSU and SPD parliamentary leadership, Volker Kauder (CDU/CSU) and Peter Struck (SPD), who were elected in November 2005, will be able to follow in the steps of their unusually influential predecessors. In early interim assessments of the informal networks and working relationships within the grand coalition, Kauder and Struck already appeared as one of four important "inter-party couples." The three others were Chancellor Merkel and SPD party leader Matthias Platzeck, Olaf Scholz and Norbert Röttgen as prominent members of the leadership circles of the SPD and CDU/CSU parliamentary party groups, and the health policy specialists and cabinet ministers Ulla Schmidt (SPD) and Horst Seehofer (CSU).[29]

Under the exceptional conditions of grand coalition government, the majority parties in parliament cannot just content themselves with performing the various tasks of governing, such as giving government initiatives a smooth ride through the parliamentary arena. The parties can be expected to support a structurally weakened parliamentary opposition by scrutinizing the government both in public and behind closed doors. Indeed, a normative perspective on democratic quality in parliamentary systems of government considers public scrutiny and control of the government a no-less-important value than effective decision-making. This theoretical position comes very close to the dominant views on parliamentary government that characterized the late 1960s in the Federal Republic. In fact, the bulk of public reservations against the Kiesinger government were driven by concerns that a grand coalition might undermine the virtues of a reasonably powerful parliamentary opposition and effective parliamentary control of the government. Such fears were taken seriously and answered by the CDU/CSU and the SPD through an impressive number of initiatives designed to strengthen parliamentary scrutiny of the government "from within."[30]

The structure of public expectations and reservations that accompanied the formation of the Merkel government belongs to the most glaring differences that set the 1966-1969 experience and the current "grand coalition experiment" apart. While overall public support for a grand coalition was even slightly weaker, rather than stronger, in late 2005 than it was in late 1966/early 1967,[31] it had different reasons. Rather than being anxious about the possible negative effects of a "grand coalition leviathan" on the opposition, a majority of opinion leaders were against the formation of a CDU/CSU-SPD government for no other reason than because they suspected it would be too internally constrained to govern effectively.[32]

Legislative Agendas and Policy Ambitions

Some of the most important aspects of the Kiesinger government's legacy relate to its policy record, which was rather impressive. In fact, there has been no other government in the Federal Republic's history that passed so many major bills, including many constitutional amendments, in a period of less than three years. Key legislative achievements included the "emergency laws," a major finance reform and other structural reforms that altered the German federal system, as well as several major bills in the fields of social, education and labor market policy.[33]

Of the major projects drawing much attention during the run-up to and the eventual formation of the grand coalition, only a single one—the introduction of a plurality electoral system designed to give rise to a Westminster-style two-party system—was eventually dropped. Whereas for many in the CDU/CSU, an agreement on installing a British-style plurality system was considered the very raison d'être of a grand coalition, the SPD had a much less decided view on the issue from the beginning.[34] In the end, forces in both parties prevailed that regarded a radically altered electoral system and an institutionally "streamlined" party system to be seriously at odds with the strongly power-sharing and compromise-orientated nature of the postwar German model of democracy. However, there were also some more tactical considerations at work, especially among the Social Democrats, which related to the potentially negative effects of a first-past-the-post electoral system for the SPD and its future prospects to win governmental office. In particular, there was little doubt by 1968 that saving the FDP from political extinction by continuing the existing proportional representation electoral system would pay off for the Social Democrats in terms of future Social-Liberal cooperation in government.[35]

The inconclusive result of the 2005 Bundestag election temporarily threatened to revitalize demands for a party system with a simpler competition structure and a greater potential for producing clear-cut governing majorities. Still, electoral reform did not become part of the public agenda. Neither of the two major parties even dared to touch the issue, which would have been considered by many as little short of an assault on democracy itself. Apart from such cultural checks on electoral reform, enthusiasm and confidence in electoral engineering has tended to decline on a global scale since the Kiesinger government debated the issue. Given the specific parameters of party competition and electoral support in unified Germany, unintended (or at least unwelcome) effects of electoral reform would in fact appear to be even more likely to develop in the Federal Republic than in many other West European countries. Especially the strong regional imbalance that has come to mark the postunification German party system[36] could modify—and in fact largely undermine—the widely acknowledged virtues of plurality or majoritarian electoral systems. There would be no institutional guarantee that a plurality electoral system would preclude effectively the representation of the Left Party in the Bundestag.

While electoral system reform did not become an issue, a public debate emerged early in the government's term about the benefits and drawbacks of extending the legislative period from four years to five after 2009 (or later). There was a reasonable amount of support for this proposal among the majority parliamentary groups, though it soon became clear that there would be no easy compromise. Whereas many in the CDU/CSU tended to consider such plans positively, in terms of improving the chances of governments to concentrate on governing rather than campaigning, support among the Social Democrats was considerably more conditional. Echoing demands from the Greens and the Free Democrats, there was a strong faction within the SPD that considered a prolongation of the Bundestag's term acceptable only if accompanied by a set of direct democratic devices designed to compensate citizens for relaxing the established standards of electoral control.

Elsewhere, the Merkel government's agenda in the area of constitutional reform looked like an outright counterprogram to that of its historical predecessor—most obvious regarding reform of the federal system. The Kiesinger government effectively gave birth to what has become known as "interlocking federalism"—a system marked by a closely integrated multilevel system of public finances and a notably powerful second chamber (the Bundesrat) in federal legislative decision-making. While multilevel governance in Germany was not completely absent before the major constitutional amendments of the late 1960s,[37] it was the grand coalition under Chancellor Kiesinger that codified the hitherto largely informal practice of interlevel cooperation, thereby contributing to its persistence and its eventual "unreformability." Trying to revive previous (failed) efforts to "disentangle" the immensely complex German federal system, the Merkel government set out to introduce a larger degree of financial independence between the federation and the Länder, to prune the Bundesrat's far-reaching veto powers, and (in return for the latter) to extend the independent legislative decision-making capacities of the Länder.

However, even though the Merkel government could draw on the detailed work of an inter-party commission on federal system reform

(2003-2004), by early February 2006 none of these proposals was certain to be put into effect. Whereas the government's leverage in the Bundestag was formidable, the majority of the governing parties in the Bundesrat was uncomfortably slim. As of February 2006, there were seven out of sixteen state governments which included one of the smaller parties (FDP or the Left Party) as junior partners of either the CDU or the SPD. They operated on the basis of coalition agreements obliging them to abstain in the Bundesrat if there was no consensus between the coalition partners on a given issue. Those state governments exclusively composed of the parties forming the federal government enjoyed a working majority in the Bundesrat of just one vote, making an exceptionally high amount of cooperation and consensus indispensable.

The lengthy quarrels about making salary regulations for civil servants a matter of state rather than federal law[38] came as a reminder that the Federal Republic continues to practice a form of federalism that values equality higher than diversity and competition. Not surprisingly, conflicts between the federation and the Länder and, even more markedly, among the individual Länder, were particularly manifest in the area of finance reform. It was therefore postponed in order not to delay, or even derail, the whole federalism reform process.

Most of the Merkel government's legislative agenda focused on the overriding goal of budget consolidation, to be achieved by a mix of eliminating tax privileges and increasing public revenues. The signs sent out were somewhat ambiguous, though. While CDU/CSU and SPD agreed on an unprecedented Value Added Tax (VAT) increase of 3 percent—a remarkable compromise given the CDU/CSU's election pledge of a 2-point rise and the SPD's fierce opposition to any VAT increase—this reform was scheduled to take effect only in January 2007. The immediate effects of the change of government on the extremely strained federal budget were not particularly promising. Indeed, the Merkel government continued the problematic practice of several recent German governments to pass a federal budget that was in obvious conflict with the constitutional limits to public deficit spending set by Article 115 of the Basic Law (though it differed from its predecessors in that it did not even try to conceil this fact).[39] With a net borrowing sum exceeding EURO 38 billion, the public deficit at the federal level for 2006 set a new historical record.[40]

Many issues that had received a large amount of public attention during the election campaign such as approaches and instruments to fight Germany's soaring unemployment or the future of the German health system and pensions proved too complicated and conflictual for the coalition partners to agree on a swift compromise. There were little, if any, concrete commitments regarding these policy fields in the 2005 coalition contract. Issues like pensions, health and labor market reform seemed, therefore, all the more certain to become a litmus test for the Merkel government early in the 16th Bundestag. A two-day cabinet conclave at Genshagen on 9/10 January 2006 proved a welcome opportunity for the government to hail the unusual amount of harmony governing intra-coalition relations, but it left many of the key issues–including especially reform of the health system–completely untouched. The only tangible outcome of this special meeting was a major "growth program" worth EURO 25 billion, which was a patchwork of largely uncoordinated measures in such different fields as taxes, transport and research.[41] Foreign policy remained another area marked by few binding commitments in the coalition contract, which reflected the rather different concepts and visions of the CDU/CSU and SPD in some subfields such as European integration. Nevertheless, foreign policy appeared unlikely to become a major source of intra-governmental conflict, if only for the fortunate personnel constellations governing the relationship between the chancellery and the foreign ministry. In stark contrast to the cool and distrustful atmosphere that characterized the relationship between Chancellor Kiesinger and Foreign Minister Brandt, working relations between Chancellor Merkel and Foreign Minister Steinmeier were notably faithful and close.

Conclusion

Among the established liberal democracies, Germany has itself earned the reputation as a bastion of government stability. This holds true not only in terms of the exceptional length of some spectacular political careers of individual office-holders, such as Konrad Adenauer and Helmut Kohl, who together held the German chancellorship for more than thirty years. It also, and more importantly, has experienced a notable amount of stability in the party composition of governments. Whereas many postwar governments emerged in the midst of a legislative term, lacking a clear electoral mandate, voters have been remarkably reluctant to punish governing parties in elections. From a comparative perspective, Germany stands out as one of the few West European countries in which parties faced exceptionally modest electoral costs of governing. In fact, while in the vast majority of countries' governments tend to suffer severe electoral losses, almost half of all German federal governments of the period 1949 through 1999 were able to improve their strength in subsequent elections.[42]

In purely numerical terms, even the Kiesinger government managed to enlarge its electoral support base in the 1969 Bundestag election. The combined share of the vote for the CDU/CSU and the SPD increased from 86.9 percent in 1965 to 88.8 percent in 1969. That said, neither the Christian Democrats nor the Social Democrats ever seriously campaigned for a continuation of the grand coalition. There was a clear understanding among both parties that the grand coalition enterprise was to remain an exception with a strictly limited time frame.

Whereas many parameters of governing in the Federal Republic have changed since the late 1960s, the conviction of all relevant political players that the most desirable option for Germany is to have a "normal-sized" majority government and a reasonably powerful "alternative government" largely has persisted. Hence, the basic challenges facing the CDU/CSU and the SPD in the 16th Bundestag are not fundamentally different from that marking the close of the 1960s. Of all the possible coalition scenarios that may emerge after the next federal election, a prolongation of a grand coalition government would appear to be among the least likely options. This widespread awareness inevitably will have a major impact on the strategic behavior of the relevant players. Both the CDU/CSU and the SPD will struggle to gain electoral advantage at the direct expense of their respective coalition partner long before the close of the current legislative term. For this reason, time might turn out to be an even more precious commodity for the Merkel government than for most of its historical predecessors and contemporary foreign counterparts.

Notes

1. Manfred G. Schmidt, "Germany: The Grand Coalition State," in *Political Institutions in Europe*, ed. Josep M. Colomer (London/New York, 1996), 62-98.
2. For a closer empirical look at the nature and extent of the cooperation between the CDU/CSU and the SPD in the policy-making arena at the federal level see Uwe Wagschal, "Der Parteienstaat der Bundesrepublik Deutschland: Parteipolitische Zusammensetzung seiner Schlüsselinstitutionen," *Zeitschrift für Parlamentsfragen* 32 (2001): 861-886.
3. Reinhard Schmoeckel and Bruno Kaiser, *Die vergessene Regierung. Die große Koalition 1966 bis 1969 und ihre langfristigen Wirkungen* (Bonn, 1991).
4. Rudolf Morsey, "Die Vorbereitung der Großen Koalition von 1966: Unionspolitiker im Zusammenspiel mit Herbert Wehner seit 1962," in *Von der Arbeiterbewegung zum modernen Sozialstaat. Festschrift für Gerhard A. Ritter zum 65. Geburtstag*, eds. Jürgen Kocka, Hans-Jürgen Puhle and Klaus Tenfelde (München, 1994), 462-478.
5. Klaus Schönhoven, *Wendejahre. Die Sozialdemokratie in der Zeit der Großen Koalition: 1966-1969* (Bonn, 2004), 57-59.
6. In fact, the grand coalition headed the list of preferred coalition scenarios until the last week of the campaign, after which there was a swing in favor of a CDU/CSU-FDP coalition. See Forschungsgruppe Wahlen e.V., *Bundestagswahl: Eine Analyse der Wahl vom 18. September 2005* (Mannheim, 2005), 43.
7. Ibid., 39.
8. Ludger Helms, *Regierungsorganisation und politische Führung in Deutschland* (Wiesbaden, 2005), 102-103.
9. It cannot be seriously denied that the rise of the commercial media has led to a new intensity in scrutinizing politicians, both in the public and private spheres, which has reduced the room for maneuver of political leaders and increased the personal costs of being in politics. See Jean Seaton, "Public, Private and the Media," *The Political Quarterly* 74 (2003): 174-183; see also James Stanyer and Dominic Wring, eds., *Public Images, Private Lives: The Mediation of Politicians around the Globe*, a special issue of *Parliamentary Affairs* 57, no. 1 (2004).
10. Schönhoven (see note 5), 66.
11. *Frankfurter Allgemeine Zeitung*, 1 December 2005.
12. Arnulf Baring, "Über deutsche Kanzler," *Der Monat* 21, no. 252 (1969): 21-22.
13. Schönhoven (see note 5), 180.
14. Wolfgang Jäger, *Wer regiert die Deutschen? Innenansichten der Parteiendemokratie* (Osnabrück, 1994), 27.
15. Wolfgang Rudzio, "Informelle Entscheidungsmuster in Bonner Koalitionsregierungen," in *Regieren in der Bundesrepublik II: Formale und informale Komponenten des Regierens in den Bereichen Führung, Entscheidung, Personal und Organisation*, eds. Hans-Hermann Hartwich and Göttrik Wewer (Opladen, 1991), 130.
16. Klaus Hildebrand, *Von Erhard zur Großen Koalition 1963-1969* (Stuttgart, 1984), 295; Schönhoven (see note 5), 171-172.
17. Heribert Knorr, *Der parlamentarische Entscheidungsprozeß während der Großen Koalition 1966 bis 1969* (Meisenheim am Glan, 1975), 227.
18. Andrea H. Schneider, *Die Kunst des Kompromisses: Helmut Schmidt und die Große Koalition 1966-1969* (Paderborn, 1999), 95-96.

19. *Frankfurter Allgemeine Zeitung,* 12 October 2005.
20. Michael Sauga, "Die Macht des Stellvertreters," *Der Spiegel,* 12 December 2005.
21. This included most of the serving SPD ministers who were responsible for monitoring the developments within one or two CDU-led departments. See Schönhoven (see note 5), 174-175.
22. Mainhardt Graf von Nayhauss, "Berlin vertraulich," *Bunte,* 15 December 2005.
23. Heribert Prantl, "Die neue Merkel," *Süddeutsche Zeitung,* 11 January 2006.
24. Karl A. Otto, *Vom Ostermarsch zur APO: Geschichte der außerparlamentarischen Opposition in der Bundesrepublik 1960-1970,* 3rd ed. (Frankfurt/Main, 1982).
25. For an overview of the issues involved see Shaun Bowler, David M. Farrell and Richard S. Katz, eds., *Party Discipline and Parliamentary Government* (Columbus, 1999).
26. There were fifty-one members of the coalition parties who voted against Merkel. While the secret ballot prevented an identification of the dissidents, no one doubted that the bulk of them belonged to the SPD.
27. For a more detailed comparative analysis of chancellor elections in the Bundestag see Helms (see note 8), 81-83.
28. Schneider (see note 18), 18.
29. *Die Welt,* 10 December 2005.
30. Party cohesion among the CDU/CSU and SPD parliamentary parties fell below the levels recorded for earlier legislative periods, and both "intra-party control," especially by the SPD parliamentary party, and parliamentary control of the Bundestag as a whole significantly intensified. Both majority parliamentary party groups had a rather strong impact on the content of government bills through their work in the committees. They also made ample use of the traditional instruments of parliamentary control, such as parliamentary questions and debates. See Thomas Saalfeld, *Parteisoldaten und Rebellen. Eine Untersuchung zur Geschlossenheit der Fraktionen im Deutschen Bundestag (1949-1990)* (Opladen, 1995), 129; Schneider (see note 18), 58-60.
31. Elisabeth Noelle, "Große Koalition in Politikverdrossenheit," *Frankfurter Allgemeine Zeitung,* 23 November 2005. However, it should not be forgotten that the grand coalition topped the list of preferred coalition scenarios for several months until the last week of the election. It was only then that a CDU/CSU-FDP coalition emerged as the most desirable option. See Forschungsgruppe Wahlen (see note 6), 43.
32. There has been a more recent general shift of preferences concerning the relationship between effective governing and scrutiny, as can be seen from the public debate surrounding the reform of the German federal system and the powers of the Bundesrat in particular. See Roland Lhotta, "Zwischen Kontrolle und Mitregierung. Der Bundesrat als Oppositionskammer?," *Aus Politik und Zeitgeschichte* 53 (2003), B 43: 16-22.
33. Franz Horner, "Die Große Koalition," in *Der Weg der Bundesrepublik. Von 1945 bis zur Gegenwart,* ed. Franz Schneider (Munich, 1985), 77-101; Gerhard Lehmbruch, "Die Große Koalition und die Institutionalisierung der Verhandlungsdemokratie," in *Eine lernende Demokratie: 50 Jahre Bundesrepublik Deutschland,* eds. Max Kaase and Günther Schmidt (Berlin, 1999), 41-61; Schmoeckel und Kaiser (see note 4); Schönhoven (see note 5), 689-697.
34. Schönhoven (see note 5), 69-70. For an illuminating overview of the competing views on electoral reform at the start of the grand coalition see Werner Kalte-

fleiter, "Die Große Koalition. Verfassungspolitische Aufgaben und Probleme," *Aus Politik und Zeitgeschichte* 17 (1967), B 18-19: 12-18.

35. Arnulf Baring, *Machtwechsel. Die Ära Brandt-Scheel* (Stuttgart, 1982), 111-112.

36. See, among others, Thomas Saalfeld, "The German Party System – Continuity and Change", in *The Berlin Republic: German Unification and a Decade of Change*, eds. Winand Gellner and John D. Robertson (London, 2002), 125-126.

37. Heidrun Abromeit, *Der verkappte Einheitsstaat* (Opladen, 1992), 58.

38. *Frankfurter Allgemeine Zeitung*, 10 January 2006.

39. That the Merkel government's first federal budget remained just within the outer limits of the constitution was thanks to an amendment to Article 115 passed by the first grand coalition in 1969, allowing governments to exceed the normal limits of public borrowing if necessary to avert a serious disruption of the macroeconomic equilibrium.

40. *Frankfurter Allgemeine Zeitung*, 17 February 2006: 11.

41. *Die Welt*, 11 January 2006; *Neue Zürcher Zeitung*, 11 January 2006.

42. Wolfgang C. Müller and Kaare Strøm, "Conclusion: Coalition Governance in Western Europe," in *Coalition Governments in Western Europe*, eds. Wolfgang C. Müller and Kaare Strøm (Oxford, 2000), 589.

Chapter 4

From High Hopes To On-Going Defeat

The New Extreme Right's Political Mobilization and its
National Electoral Failure in Germany

Lars Rensmann

Introduction

In the last two decades new extreme Right parties have gained considerable political successes in many West and East European countries.[1] Within the context of this international development, researchers have also observed a rise or "fourth wave" of right-wing extremism in Germany.[2] However, the electoral performance of extreme Right parties has been rather poor: successes are sporadic, restricted to regional elections, and limited overall. Far from entering the national parliament (Bundestag) in any election, German extreme Right parties have also failed to survive more than two legislatures in any state parliament (Landtag), which indicates severe political consolidation problems and the inability of these parties to create loyal voters. In addition, rather than being co-opted into the political process, with a concomitant softening of ideology, the extreme Right remains strictly isolated politically, similar to the situation in Great Britain and the United States.[3] Yet, especially in the postcommunist East (the five states (Länder) of the former German Democratic Republic (GDR)), there are extreme Right actors in Germany that have established and consolidated themselves in different socio-political arenas apart from conventional party politics and competition. Moreover, the new right-wing extremism in contemporary Germany shows some very distinctive organizational and ideological features. These include an affirmative relation to the Nazi past and a particular radical tradition, as well as an especially strong, wide-spread, and partially violent "informal" subculture and youth culture—a phenomenon that has long escaped political science and party research.[4]

Considering this background, the success of German extreme Right parties in state elections in 2004—the Deutsche Volksunion (DVU) scored 6 percent in the state of Brandenburg and was re-elected into parliament, the "revolutionary" National Democratic Party of Germany (Nationaldemokratische Partei Deutschlands, NPD) entered parliament in Saxony with a considerable 9.2 percent share of the vote—possibly points to an ending of the split between subcultural and conventional electoral politics. In particular, the NPD's unexpectedly good performance in Saxony was euphorically celebrated by right-wing extremists nation-wide and across different parties and organizations as a general "victory of the national spirit." This regional success seemed to imply an electoral boost for the extreme Right that possibly could carry them into national parliament for the first time. The extreme Right's high hopes even induced a new cooperation between the NPD and DVU, with the latter withdrawing from the electoral competition to benefit the former. Nevertheless, despite noticeable gains the Bundestag election in 2005 ended in yet another defeat for extreme right parties.

Looking at the interplay of supply side and demand side factors, this chapter explores the transformations and continuities of extreme Right parties in the German party system, their performance in the 2005 general election, and the reasons for their on-going *national* electoral failure. This failure is evident in spite of new mobilization agendas and strategies, on one hand, and, on the other, windows of political opportunity at the turn of the century linked to new public issues, shifting socio-cultural cleavages, and increasing voter volatility, which allow for new spaces in the established party system. However, I also discuss if and how the extreme Right may nonetheless remain a challenge to the democratic political system.

A Difficult Legacy: Extreme Right Parties in the German Party System

The extreme Right in Germany[5] could never escape the shadows of the Nazi past. In general, the catastrophe of Nazism has discredited socially and politically extreme Right governments in post-Holocaust Germany. Even though right-wing extremist attitudes are not more or less popular than in other European countries, the social acceptance of extreme Right parties is significantly lower.[6] Extreme Right parties and organizations have been under legal and political pressure ever since the inception of the Federal Republic and Konrad Adenauer's strict course against right-wing extremist organizations. In addition to such political and cultural restrictions, structural limits ingrained in electoral rules like a high legal electoral threshold[7] have helped to prevent extreme Right parties from entering the national parliamentary arena and from consolidating as legitimate players in the party system. On the demand side of the electorate, the considerable proportion of potential voters (9 percent) with extreme Right views is mostly tied to catch-all parties (two-thirds of voters with extreme Right attitudes in a country still with *comparably* low volatility vote for the Christian Democratic Union/Christian Social Union, CDU/CSU, or Social Democratic Party of Germany, SPD), or can be found among the group of non-voters.[8]

On the supply side, the extreme Right party landscape in Germany has suffered continuously from its fragmentation. Internal and ideological struggles have been constant features of the extreme Right party scene, a divide that runs counter to these parties' appeals for national unity, thereby restricting their political impact.[9] The lack of internal cohesion within the extreme right and even within the parties corresponds to a lack of organizational structure, as well as professional political personnel and charismatic leaders who could facilitate modernized images and agendas to attract new voter segments. Instead, even those few German extreme Right parties that tried hard to modernize their public image, like the Republicans (Die Republikaner, REP) since the late 1990s, largely have failed to dissociate themselves from the smell of Nazism. Different from other *new* extreme Right parties (NERs) in Western Europe since the mid-1980s,[10] extreme Right actors in Germany are either unable or, for the most part, unwilling to distance themselves from this stigma of being an "old" fascist or Nazi party. Instead, being tied to this history and political ideology serves identity-generating functions for members, but is disastrous for any long-term public outreach and aspirations for broader political legitimacy, especially in the German context.[11]

Even though some parties focused on regional campaigns and had temporary electoral success on the state level, their generally poor parliamentary performance and overtly displayed political incompetence[12] almost systematically prevented re-elections. As a consequence of all these factors, these parties could never win a seat in the Bundestag. They have not been able to play any role in post-war electoral politics on a national level, with the notable exception of the general election in 1969, in which the NPD lacked only 0.7 percent in order to enter the Bundestag.

Table 1: Extreme Right parties' electoral results in Germany, 1949-2005

	1949	1953	1957	1961	1965	1969	1972	1976
AUD	-	-	-	-	0.2	-	-	0.1
DG	-	-	0.1	0.1	-	-	-	-
DKP-DRP	1.8	-	-	-	-	-	-	-
DRP	-	1.1	1.0	0.8	-	-	-	-
DVU	-	-	-	-	-	-	-	-
NPD	-	-	-	-	2.0	4.3	0.6	0.3
REP	-	-	-	-	-	-	-	-
UAP	-	-	-	-	0.0	0.1	-	0.0
WAV	2.9	-	-	-	-	-	-	-
Total	4.7	1.1	1.1	0.9	2.2	4.4	0.6	0.4
	1980	1983	1987	1990	1994	1998	2002	2005
AUD	-	-	-	-	-	-	-	-
DG	-	-	-	-	-	-	-	-
DKP-DRP	-	-	-	-	-	-	-	-
DRP	-	-	-	-	-	-	-	-
DVU	-	-	-	-	-	1.2	-	-
NPD	0.2	0.2	0.6	0.3	-	0.3	0.4	1.6
REP	-	-	-	2.1	1.9	1.8	0.6	0.6
UAP	0.0	-	-	-	-	-	-	-
WAV	-	-	-	-	-	-	-	-
Total	0.2	0.2	0.6	2.4	1.9	3.3	1.0	2.2

Source: Official Electoral Data; Steffen Kailitz, Politischer Extremismus in der Bundesrepublik Deutschland (Wiesbaden, 2004), 55

The Profile of Extreme Right Parties in the Electoral and Political Process

The oldest, most visible, important and radical political actor of the extreme Right party family[13] today remains the NPD. Founded in

1964, it almost disappeared after its initial successes in the late 1960s and the defeat in 1969. By the 1990s the NPD had become largely an "irrelevant force comprising competing and opposing wings within the party."[14] Its long-time chairman Günther Deckert was sentenced to prison for Holocaust denial, which did not help the party, although it always remained active on the margins. But, after Udo Voigt took over party leadership in 1996 with a narrow victory over Deckert by 89 to 86 votes, the party saw reinvigorated efforts to embark on a new course to unite the party and broaden its appeal.[15] The new leadership reaffirmed an anti-system, national-*socialist* agenda based on the Nazi concept of people's community (*Volksgemeinschaft*), addressing issues such us unemployment of German workers and focusing on potential voters of the "proletariat." Be that as it may, the party radicalized even further under Voigt's leadership in the 1990s and openly endorsed, attracted and integrated neo-Nazis, who increasingly suffered from legal prosecution and a series of bans in the mid-1990s that had affected seventeen neo-Nazi organizations.

The party's program is based on extreme ethnic nationalism and xenophobia (expressed in the demand that all foreigners should leave Germany); a persistent antisemitism linked to "national anti-capitalism,"[16] which blames Jews for all social problems and attacks the "failure of liberal Jewish capitalism;" and on Holocaust revisionism, i.e., the ongoing downplaying or denial of Nazi crimes against European Jews. According to author Richard Stöss, the new party programs indicate a move from a German nationalist orientation and system adaptation to an anti-system party.[17] However, this interpretation is questionable. Although the party clearly radicalized in the last years, throughout the party's existence electoral politics consistently was seen only as a tool within the vision of a radical system change and "national revolution."

Of particular importance is the party's strategic re-orientation after 1997 under Voigt, who declared a new three-fold strategy inspired by concepts of its extremely militant youth organization, the Young National Democrats (Junge Nationaldemokraten, JN).[18] The NPD today declares to fight a "battle over people's minds" (ideological influence and cultural hegemony), "battle on the streets" (mobilization of extreme right social movements and cooperation with militants), and a "battle for voters" (participation in the electoral process).[19] This new strategic concept has enabled the party to develop grassroots mobilization, take a hold in the new, young subcultural extreme right which has consolidated in the East, and create regional and local strongholds. With its young and dedicated members,[20] the NPD thereby has begun to overcome previously severe organizational problems, at least in some of its new Eastern strongholds. Many of the party's 5,300 (2005) members are active, and the monthly paper *Deutsche Stimme* has now a circulation of 10,000.[21] However, until recently in Saxony, the party could not succeed in a state election even in the East.

The second relevant extreme right party DVU, founded in 1986 and renamed in 1987 by Gerhard Frey, has possibly more financial resources, but also even more organizational problems. Frey, a wealthy media businessman and real estate manager, has continuously been the party's chairman. However, the party always has remained a "phantom" party, and, according to the terminology of party sociology, does not even qualify as a party because, beyond Frey and his extremist media, there is practically no organizational substance. Within the extreme Right, therefore, the DVU often is accused of not being interested in the "national fight," but solely in making money.[22]

In his analysis of the DVU's ideology, Cas Mudde shows that the DVU's ideological profile is based on old-style German ethnic nationalism ("Germany for the Germans!") and xenophobia ("alien" equals "anti-German"). The party also facilitates a paranoid view of the world: "The DVU sees the world as full of anti-German conspiracies, which is in part the result and the cause of its (open) anti-Americanism and (more hidden) antisemitism."[23]

Pursuing a slightly more moderate political image than the "revolutionary" NPD, the DVU has nonetheless built ties to the most extreme edges of the Right and neo-Nazis, such as the Holocaust denier David Irving and the Russian extremist Vladimir Zhirinovsky.[24] Although it is often considered less extreme than the NPD, the party still shows an affinity to Nazi ideologies and has affirmative relationship to the Nazi past,[25] which is especially evident through their "historical revisionism." The party's membership peaked in 1992 at 26,734, dropping steadily thereafter. It is currently at roughly 11,000.[26] This aging membership, however, is built primarily from the readership of Frey's extreme Right newspapers. His weekly *Deutsche National-Zeitung* is in decline, but with 40,000 sold copies every week, it is still the most circulated extreme Right paper in Germany.

Even though the DVU has had "several (surprising) electoral successes in its short existence, these were obtained with an existing but not functioning organizational structure."[27] Similar to previous performances in state parliaments in Schleswig-Holstein and Bremen and especially in Saxony-Anhalt, where in 1998 the DVU had its best electoral result ever (12.9 percent), one quarter of the politically incompetent parliamentary faction defected within the first year,[28] leaving many disillusioned voters.

Finally, there are the Republicans, founded in 1983, that constitute maybe the only party in Germany that can be classified as a modernized, *new* extreme Right party (NER).[29] Distancing itself from the conventional, fascist extreme Right and eventually even from the extreme Right as such, the party seeks to attract less radical voters who are disillusioned with mainstream conservatism. Particularly since Rolf Schlierer became party chairman, its image returned to a more national-conservative appearance.[30] According to Mudde, the primary ideological feature of the party is and always has been German nationalism, voiced mainly in ethnic terms such as *Volksgemeinschaft* and *Heimat* (homeland).[31] Mostly centered on Germany and the German ethnic community elsewhere, the party also holds an extremely xenophobic view on the world in which foreigners within and outside of the country are seen as a hostile threat, rather latent antisemitism and historical revisionism.[32] Although the party is seeking to address new issues and strives for mainstream acceptance, its program and constituency are still predominantly right-wing extremist.

In spite of initial successes in the European elections (7.1 percent) and in Berlin (7.5 percent) in 1989 by employing extremely xenophobic campaigns,[33] and a re-election in Baden-Württemberg (10.9 percent in 1992 and 9.1 percent in 1996), where it temporarily hoped to find a sufficient number of loyal voters, the party could not establish itself in the party system. Even the 2.1 percent result in the first postunification national election in 1990 was disillusioning. Clearly, the peak of the party's success was in the late 1980s and early 1990s. The declining membership (down to fewer than 8,000 members), lack of media attention, on-going electoral failures and the inability to find new mobilization issues are indicators of general decline. Several sub-units are still quite active, but since the late 1990s it is no longer the strongest party of the extreme Right.

Lacking the ability or willingness to adapt to the political system, German extreme Right parties generally tend to act as an opposition of principle offering alternatives *to* but not *within* the system.[34] Thus despite periodic successes as "protest parties," all extreme Right parties have clearly remained politically marginalized and never left the peripheries of the party system. Exposed to a consistent *cordon sanitaire* and (with few temporary exceptions) generally discredited as political agents, there has been no successful electoral party of the extreme Right that could find a relevant place in the German party system. Although there is potential, these parties have so far largely failed in the electoral process, Piero Ignazi argues, foremost because of a "lack of legitimacy, linkage to the past, and inner structural weakness."[35]

Windows of Opportunity? New Mobilizations and Agendas, the Consolidation of "Informal" Right-Wing Extremism, and Successful State Elections

Until the mid-1990s, extreme Right parties performed better in West (especially in Bavaria and Baden-Württemberg) than in the East German Länder—this applied to both national elections and state elections. The REP succeeded to overcome the 5 percent electoral threshold in the 1992 and 1996 elections in Baden-Württemberg, while the DVU succeeded in 1991 in Bremen and in 1992 in Schleswig-Holstein. This pattern changed only with the 1998 election in the eastern state of Saxony-Anhalt, in which the DVU gained a remarkable 12.9 percent and was the strongest of all parties among voters under the age of thirty.[36]

The landmark election of 1998 first highlighted the new regional success at the ballot boxes in the East, and paved the way for the DVU's re-election in Brandenburg (6.1 percent) and the surprising success of the NPD in Saxony (9.2 percent) in 2004. The NPD's spectacular turnout at Saxony's ballot-boxes, finishing just next to the Social Democrats, was the first electoral success of an extreme Right party with a clearly neo-Nazi orientation since the prohibition of the Socialist Imperial Party (Sozialistische Reichspartei, SRP) in 1952.[37] The initial success of the DVU in Saxony-Anhalt and its follow-ups elsewhere in East Germany also signal an important change regarding the political opportunities, electoral fortunes, mobilization strategies, and targeted potential voters of the extreme Right. There are three factors that possibly indicate a silent transformation toward more favorable political conditions in the long run, as well as corresponding changes of the political strategies of extreme Right parties at the turn of the century.

1. Newly evolving socio-cultural cleavages in relation to issues national identity, Europeanization and globalization offer chances for new extreme mobilizations addressing and utilizing these new cleavages; produce corresponding changes in the self-understandings of the major catch-all parties, including the CDU, towards immigration, globalization and social reform; provide space for new political arenas, especially in the still less democratically consolidated East.

2. There is an increased awareness within extreme Right parties like the DVU and the NPD that a consolidated "informal" and subcultural right-wing extremism in the East can be used as a political resource; that right-wing orientations are more widespread in the East, hence the neue Länder should be special targets of mobilization.

3. There is a revived attempt to foster long-term cooperation among the fragmented extreme Right actors, though there are no signs of any ideological moderation, renewal or de-radicalization.

These first signs of possible political transformation processes and new opportunities for the extreme Right resonate particularly in the NPD, which aggressively adapts Zeitgeist topics and employs new mobilization strategies based on the "uncivil society" of local grassroots activities and informal subcultures. The party also has forced new forms of cooperation with other extreme Right actors, including the competitor DVU and so-called "free fellowships" (*freie Kameradschaften*, i.e., autonomous neo-Nazi groups). Today, the NPD seeks to link the generally rather unsuccessful electoral politics with the rather widespread and relevant extreme Right subculture and youth culture which is still flourishing in specific regions in the East. At any rate, the three factors mentioned above indicate slightly transformed political conditions and interaction processes.

1. In light of the postnational transformations and socio-cultural modernization associated with globalization and Europeanization, many authors observe another restructuring of political orientations and cleavage patterns that may induce party system changes. All over Europe, the emergence of a new politics of national and regional identity has a significant impact on the readjustment of Left-Right locations.[38] According to Mary Kaldor, there is a new politically relevant divide between cosmopolitanism versus nationalism, between globalization/Europeanization versus anti-globalization/Euroscepticsm. Thus, a new cleavage has arisen: "between those who favor a new diversity of transnational, national, and local forms of sovereignty and those who want to build fractional territorial fiefdoms."[39] This new cleavage often runs counter to conventional Right/Left divisions and opens space for new parties and re-alliances, although this new cleavage is linked to, and partially overlaps with old class cleavages or a "new social cleavage."[40] Despite other ideological differences, supporters and actors of the radical Left and radical Right share an opposition to globalization and Europeanization, which is also fairly widespread in the electorate.

In addition to the fact that all major democratic parties in Germany endorse Europeanization and globalization, the turn of the century and new immigration laws have also signaled a changing view on ethnicity and immigration. Emphasizing general party competition, Ruud Koopmans and Hanspeter Kriesi argue that part of the extreme Right's weakness in the party system had been due to an "ethnic-exclusivist discourse of citizenship and nationhood close to the extreme right's ideal" among dominant democratic parties.[41] To a considerable extent this has changed, and with it the discursive opportunity structure[42] for extreme Right mobilization in Germany. Even the conservative Christian Democrats no longer deny that Germany is a country of immigration and needs immigration.[43] This may provide new opportunities for actors opposing immigration, which is also a quite widespread attitude among the populace.[44]

Finally, 9/11, the war in Iraq, the American "war on terror" and the more general conflict in the Middle East are new issues that have polarized the political climate and resonate with voters. Twenty-six percent believe that "Jewish influence" on U.S. politics was the central reason for the military intervention in Iraq;[45] 30 percent of young adults under the age of thirty believe that "the U.S. government itself could has commissioned the attacks of September 11;"[46] and 35.1 percent fully agree to the statement that Israel wages a "war of annihilation against the Palestinians."[47]

While sticking to their radical ethnic-nationalist, fascist and neo-Nazi ideologies, the DVU and especially the NPD have tried to adapt their programs and most recent electoral campaigns in reaction to these new cleavages and Zeitgeist issues. On the one hand, classical extreme Right and Nazi topics, such as the alleged Allied "bombing holocaust" in Dresden or the Rudolf Hess memorial march, do remain important. On the other hand, hot topics like welfare reform, globalization, war and the Middle East[48] have become central campaign issues. With unemployment and anti-globalization sentiments on the rise, new mobilizations focus particularly on the "social question," which these parties turn into a "national question" betrayed by corrupt "anti-German" politicians, multi-national capitalism, and immigrant workers. The goal is to mobilize the "ethnic community" against fears of socio-cultural diffusion and social deprivation associated with individualization, modernization, and globalization.[49]

The NPD and DVU also mobilize a revived "ethno-pluralism" ("Germany for the Germans!," "Palestine for the Palestinians!") and other forms of xenophobia and group-focused enmity.[50] But today, they often also focus on popular issues such as prejudice against Israel and anti-Americanism. The quite widespread opposition to globalization, for example, is endorsed and addressed as a national struggle against "Israelization and Americanization." Globalization is identified with America's "one-world ideology" and also personified as a Jewish activity and linked to antisemitic discourse about "Jewish multi-national capitalism," "Jewish conspiracies," and an alleged global rule of "Wall Street." Particularly the NPD declares that "America" is currently the main enemy of all nationalists and it facilitates aggressive anti-Americanism.[51] Two days after 9/11, NPD chairman Udo Voigt blamed America for its wrong-doings and announced that his party will "be at the top of a new German peace movement and lead all opponents to globalization."[52] While this scenario was surely too optimistic, the NPD participated in peace demonstrations across Germany, locally endorsed by the Party of Democratic Socialism (PDS),[53] and mobilizes against "U.S. imperialism" by using Leftist slogans ("Fuck the U.S.A.").

The DVU represents a similar position, though the language and rhetoric is more moderate. In reference to the 9/11 attacks, DVU leader Frey maintains that they were the "desperate acts of Arabs, who, sacrificing their own lives, protested against Bush's key role in the Palestinians' annihilation."[54] However, although these extreme Right parties adopt and radicalize rather popular slogans, they have not been successful so far with these attempted mobilization efforts.

More promising and effective are the new nationalistic mobilizations against the "neoliberal" welfare reforms, which hit unemployed workers and recipients of welfare (legislation called Hartz IV). In several Eastern cities, so-called "Monday demonstrations" expressing social protest were dominated by the NPD and other right-wing extremists. The successful parties of the extreme Right in the 2004 elections of Brandenburg and Saxony, the DVU and NPD, have been especially effective in mobilizing blue collar workers (10 percent and 14 percent) and wide-spread opposition to social cut-backs linked to the government's welfare reform (see Table Two). They also scored high among males, adolescents and young adults under the age of thirty (14 percent and 18 percent). It is remarkable that 25 percent of men who are eighteen to twenty-four years old voted for the neo-Nazi party NPD in Saxony. Fully 57 percent of NPD voters said the welfare cuts of Hartz IV were a crucial motive for their decision.[55] This shows the party's ability to address particularly–though not exclusively–young and uneducated males in the East. Be that as it may, while the new mobilization issues have helped extreme Right parties gain ground on a regional level, more general success is so far limited. Although they are clearly responding to new agendas, overall the extreme Right parties have yet been unable to really exploit new cleavages and social concerns.

2. The consolidated, subcultural right-wing extremism in Germany, which is particularly widespread in the East, has long been (and to a considerable extent still is) a rather separate realm from (electoral) extreme Right parties, as Rainer Erb points out.[56] Seeking links to these lose networks of "uncivil society," however, the NPD increasingly is using this mobilization resource, as well as more widely shared right-wing extremist attitudes in the former GDR with its antidemocratic, authoritarian heritage.[57] In parts of the Eastern Länder of Saxony, Saxony-Anhalt, Mecklenburg-Pomerania, Thuringia

Table 2: Electoral Turn-out of the DVU in Brandenburg and the NPD in Saxony in 2004 and Turn-out among Selected Social Groups

	DVU (Brandenburg)	NPD (Saxony)
Electoral Results	6.1%	9.2%
Men	9%	11%
Women	4%	7%
Age 18-29	14%	18%
Age 30-44	7%	12%
Age 45-59	6%	9%
Age 60 and older	2%	3%
Blue-collar workers	10%	14%
White-collar workers	4%	6%
Public servants	0%	7%
Self-employed	5%	9%
Farmers	11%	5%

Source: Forschungsgruppe Wahlen Mannheim, Reports 118/119, quoted in Richard Stöss, Rechtsextremismus im Wandel (Bonn, 2005), 91

and Brandenburg, there is not only a strong extreme Right socio-cultural environment with parties, youth centers, racist rock music and dress codes,[58] but this subculture also faces weak democratic institutions and a dearth of alternatives. This socio-cultural environment attracts adolescents even without initial political interest.[59]

Different from the DVU, which is only present in electoral campaigns, in many Eastern regions the NPD is a permanently active party which has successfully relocated its headquarters in the East. The party has strong organizational roots in specific Eastern regions and communities, is present in community councils and institutions of civil society (e.g., community councils or neighborhood initiatives for schools and against asylum-seeker homes) and has developed strong ties to the local subcultures and militant *"freie Kamerad-schaften."*[60] Hence the NPD's effective organizing on a local and communal level, which originated in the late 1990s,[61] today strongly benefits from the systematic inclusion of extreme Right youths, subcultures and social movements ("informal" right-wing extremism) in the neue Länder. In addition, subunits associated with the party imitate organizational models and grassroots activities invented by the Left,[62] from lawyers' collectives to organized assistance for prisoners to social work in neighborhoods.[63] Activists also take part in or found environmental groups, soccer clubs, or school boards.[64] All of this is an expression of the three-fold strategy of a battle over parliaments, minds, and the streets. In particular, it is a long-term struggle for cultural hegemony and ideological infiltration. Through its grassroots activities, the party has established a link between the electoral politics of the organized extreme right and subcultural right-wing extremism. It has gained credibility among average people in the East, on one hand, and, on the other, among local extreme Right subcultures by showing that parliamentary politics and seats are not ends in themselves but serve as a public forum and political as well as financial mobilization resource for the movement that advocates a "national socialist revolution." However, while the NPD now effectively concentrates its resources on specifically targeted Eastern states, it decreases its mobilization opportunities in the West.

3. Finally, the NPD and DVU signed a "pact for Germany" in 2004, announcing cooperation in all upcoming elections.[65] This may establish an unprecedented unity among two major parties of the otherwise fragmented extreme Right. Therefore Eckhard Jesse's thesis that both tactical and fundamental differences make cooperation between these parties impossible is no longer valid.[66] This could possibly raise these parties' electoral chances in the long run. In this process it becomes increasingly questionable, though, whether the DVU can still be classified as "less radical" than the NPD.

Furthermore, the NPD's overt endorsement and integration of the most militant neo-Nazi cadres of the extreme Right into the leadership, as well as splinter groups that either find "refuge" in the NPD or cooperate with the party, intend to overcome previous splits and create a spirit of unity within the extreme Right. But this strategy reinforces the lack of broader appeal and further radicalizes a party that is essentially neo-Nazi anyway. Despite all these seemingly more favorable demand-side conditions, new supply-side activities among extreme Right parties, and the modest electoral gains in the former socialist Eastern Germany, the hopes for the national election have ended more-or-less in yet another defeat.

The Electoral Campaigns and Performances of Extreme Right Parties in the *Bundestagswahl* of 2005

Like other small parties, for the extreme Right the early general election in 2005 and the minimal time to prepare a campaign caused great logistical difficulties. The fading Republicans were largely unnoticed by the public and played no role despite reviving their anti-immigration stances and nationalist agenda. The NPD also received little media attention and could not deliver anything but a fairly limited program and campaign agenda.

The major campaign slogans, such as "Work-Family-Fatherland: Vote for the Original" (referring to a similar slogan used by a Christian Democratic politician), were rather moderate in nature and incorporated almost exclusively the new mobilization issues mentioned above, while lacking any coherent political program. Portraying itself as the only force for a "strong community" and the only "real opposition" against all other "system parties", the social cutbacks of Hartz IV, "the war in Iraq and Palestine," "globalism," and "foreign workers" replacing German workers,[67] the NPD clearly tried to appeal to a broader spectrum of disenchanted voters and non-voters. Opposition to Turkey's EU membership and the anti-European call for a reintroduction of the German Mark were side issues that fit into the new or revived nationalistic focus on antiwar, antiglobalization, anti-European, anti-Israel ("against the Israeli occupation–solidarity with Palestine") and anti-American sentiments. However, these issues remained linked with the conventional racist xenophobia, opposition to any immigration and Muslims in Germany, and a paranoid as well as antisemitic look at the world consistently perpetuated by the NPD.

Although the NPD was barely able to pursue a campaign at all, the party quadrupled its votes, from 0.4 percent in 2002 to 1.6 percent in 2005. The REPs achieved 0.6 percent, repeating their overall electoral result of 2002, while still losing 14,000 votes. In total, the extreme Right increased its turnout from 1.0 percent to 2.2 percent (see Table Three).

Table 3: Electoral Results of the NPD on the National and State
Level in the General Elections in 2002 and 2005

	NPD (2002)	NPD (2005)
Schleswig-Holstein	0.3%	1.0%
Bremen	0.5%	1.4%
Hamburg	0.2%	1.0%
Lower Saxony	0.3%	1.3%
Hesse	0.4%	1.2%
Berlin	0.6%	1.6%
North Rhine Westphalia	0.2%	0.8%
Rhineland-Palatinate	0.4%	1.3%
Bavaria	0.2%	1.3%
Baden-Württemberg	0.3%	1.1%
Saarland	0.7%	1.8%
Saxony	1.4%	4.9%
Saxony-Anhalt	1.0%	2.5%
Thuringia	0.9%	3.7%
Brandenburg	1.5%	3.2%
Mecklenburg-Pomerania	0.8%	3.5%
Total	0.4%	1.6%

Source: www.bundeswahlleiter.de; Der Tagesspiegel, 20 September 2005

In spite of these considerable gains especially in the neue Länder, the turnout of 1.6 percent at the ballots is clearly not what the NPD had hoped for. The support by the DVU hardly paid off, and the envisioned united "people's front" remained rather at the margins. The NPD scored high in their regional strongholds like Saxonian Switzerland (Sächsische Schweiz, 7.1 percent), but even here the result was much lower than in the state election the year before. It is argued here that the national electoral performance is due to the interaction of several structural difficulties the party faced, the role of other party competitors (especially the Left Party), and the NPD's inability really to exploit the new cleavages and voids in the party system because of the party's revolutionary neo-Nazi ideology and militancy.

The one-year-early election in 2005, which took the entire political landscape by surprise, proved to be especially dramatic for the NPD's electoral campaign in several other respects. Until the Fall of 2006, the party intended to prepare ground in the West and to increase its budget with public money by surpassing the 1 percent threshold in the 2006 state elections in Rhineland-Palatinate, as well as in its former stronghold of Baden-Württemberg. With the additional financial support of Gerhard Frey, the wealthy leader of the

DVU, and on the basis of the surprising electoral success in Saxony, the NPD initially declared a "march on Berlin" in 2006, meaning an electoral turnout of more than 5 percent.[68]

While the party leadership never fully believed in such an early national success at the ballots, it clearly hoped for massive public attention as well as for another regional electoral success in the election in the Eastern state of Mecklenburg-Pomerania, which was originally designated to take place on the same day as the federal election in Fall 2006. Because of the early election, the NPD soon recognized that 5 percent nationwide was an unattainable goal and therefore further concentrated its national electoral campaign resources on its particular (Eastern) strongholds in Saxony, hoping to popularize its message there and possibly gain three direct mandates, which would have also carried them into the Bundestag.[69] But even this strategy was utterly unsuccessful. The NPD did not even come close to a direct mandate and also lost significant support in Saxony compared to the state election in 2004. In turn, the campaign almost fully collapsed in the West.

Another crucial factor for the lack of success in light of potentially more favorable conditions (such as higher voter volatility, new issues, and new cleavages in the electorate) was the political performance and campaign by the Right's left-wing competitor. Most of the protest votes against social reform, globalization, and the war in Iraq were received by a newly created list and first-time runner called the Left Party (PDS/Die Linke), an electoral merger of a left-wing grassroots organization (Wahlalternative Arbeit und soziale Gerechtigket, WASG) with the former head of the Social Democrats and federal minister of finance, Oskar Lafontaine, as front-runner, on one hand, and the Party of Democratic Socialism, the successor of the GDR's authoritarian-socialist ruling party SED, with the prominent socialist Gregor Gysi as front-runner, on the other. Since unification, the PDS had sustained a solid electoral strong-hold in the East, while the WASG with its Western roots was able to attract parts of the electorate in the West. With the prominent politicians Lafontaine and Gysi in the top ranks, the new party list received enormous political and media attention in the months before the election. It immediately scored high in the polls, soon gained political momentum, and effectively utilized it. Successfully portraying itself as the crucial and only relevant oppositional force against the ruling parties, the "elite," and neoliberal reform, the Left Party rapidly turned into *the* voice of the disenchanted. The NPD, in turn, no longer played any role in the media and had soon lost any momentum. The Left Party was obviously more popular, more credible and by far more respectable and moderate, while it employed similar populist slogans against globalization, "American war," "foreign workers," and the government's cutbacks of welfare and unemployment benefits. During the election campaign, the NPD's chairman, Udo Voigt, claimed: "German workers will clearly vote against the old communists' cheap attempt to neutralize them."[70] This was certainly not the case. The new Left Party was not only able to draw in most socially frustrated voters representing the anti-modernization and antiglobalization segments of the electorate. The party also successfully mobilized especially those East German voters who are dissatisfied with (the reality of) liberal democracy and who harbor feelings of nostalgia for life in the Communist GDR, and share ethnocentric, national-protectionist attitudes—the political targets of the extreme Right.[71]

Finally, the party's more moderate, allegedly fashionable or popular campaign slogans appeared like a half-hearted camouflage carried by neo-Nazi cadres in uniforms. The NPD is unwilling to detach itself from its neo-Nazi core and "national-revolutionary," anti-system position and has, therefore, limited outreach. In addition, the only time the party made it into the pre-election news caused a credibility gap between the party and its electorate. While the NPD aggressively agitates against "foreign wage-dumpers," it became public that the party newspaper is printed in Poland and Slovakia. The party's major campaign event in Dresden, where the NPD expected 10,000 visitors, was cancelled thereafter. In sum, the NPD was totally unprepared for the early national election, had a strong competitor on the Left, completely lacked resources to mobilize on a national level and was soon forced to concentrate on regional strong-holds (where it was partly successful), and it failed to attract new voters because of credibility problems and neo-Nazi radicalism.

The NPD tried to gloss over the disappointing results by (correctly) claiming that this was the party's best performance since the Bundestag elections in 1969, when it had reached 4.3 percent and was just short of the 5 percent electoral threshold that would have taken the party into national parliament. However, in this historic case, too, there were initially much higher hopes for an electoral success paving a road to Bonn after promising previous regional electoral successes. In 1969, the defeat and disillusionment led to an almost complete organizational and electoral collapse in the decades to come.[72]

Today, there are no indications that this is going to happen again. Though still on the margins, the NPD probably will not collapse. After all, the result of the election is rather ambivalent: while the party, like the extreme Right in general, suffers from another electoral defeat, is far from any national success in the near future, and even experienced some dramatic losses in Saxony compared to 2004, there is an overall increasing nationwide support (5.5 percent of all male adults under twenty-five across the country voted for the NPD). More important, the NPD can build upon consolidated strongholds in the neue Länder (particularly in parts of Saxony, Mecklenburg-Pomerania, and Thuringia). Here the NPD has found loyal voters and further long-term potential to get into state parliaments, the party's neo-Nazi character notwithstanding. I will now evaluate the further prospects of extreme Right parties in the political and electoral process, and discuss why they will remain a matter of concern.

A Trade-Off between Electoral and Subcultural Politics? Why the Extreme Right Continuously Fails in the National Electoral Process but Still Remains a Challenge

Public fears and the NPD's confident announcements about national electoral victories and a "march on Berlin" were clearly premature and unfounded. The NPD, like all parties of the extreme Right family, continuously fails to achieve any significant national breakthrough, though it did have significant gains. The REPs, to the contrary, are slowly dissipating.

We do find considerably widespread extreme Right, nationalistic and xenophobic views in parts of the electorate and a consolidated extreme Right subculture (especially in the East). But despite the windows of opportunities that are consequences of this subculture, increasing voter volatility, and new socio-cultural cleavages and issues (which may enhance these parties' political chances), the Bundestag election of 2005 has demonstrated once more that parties of the extreme Right are yet overall unable to effectively mobilize on a national level and to fill any possible new void in the party system.

There are several factors contributing to this situation. First and foremost, there is the legacy of the discredited Nazi dictatorship that deprives the extreme Right of any legitimacy. A *cordon sanitaire* is in effect and is upheld by all democratic parties, institutions and actors. Electoral rules also shape the extreme right parties' limited political opportunity structures and influence their electoral fortunes. A high national legal threshold across the whole country limits the chances of minor extremist parties to enter parliament.[73] In addition, other protest parties and left-wing competitors—in particular the PDS/Left Party—are much more successful, moderate and respected agents that address new issues, social frustration, and corresponding loopholes in the context of party system changes. Furthermore, the identification with major catch-all parties is still relatively high compared to other European democracies.

The main obstacle for a more successful electoral performance on a national level remains the extreme Right itself. Its more-or-less affirmative relationship to the Nazi past (especially among the NPD and the DVU) is self-marginalizing. Even if though they address Zeitgeist topics and create communal grassroots networks, they have failed to modernize and moderate, rather radicalizing their extremist agenda. Although there is a new level of cooperation between different actors, there is still a lack of cohesion and consolidated party organization, as well as a lack of credibility, substantial programs, and any sort of charismatic leadership. Therefore, it is unlikely that they may be able to exploit the new cleavage of national and social protectionism against Europeanization and globalization[74] for electoral gains in the near future.

Nevertheless, it is certainly no longer true that favorable conditions for the extreme Right in Germany, like the immigration debate of the early 1990s, have dissipated.[75] Since the turn of the century, there are indicators of new opportunities and loopholes in the party system, new cleavages and issues from which the extreme Right may benefit in the long run. It is also noteworthy that Germany's "informal" right-wing extremism (an ensemble of racist rock music, youth and everyday culture, day-to-day violence, social movements and various local and grassroots activities), which has consolidated over more than a decade and is a threat in itself, is no longer simply a separate realm from extreme Right party politics.

Instead, there are indicators of new cooperation between political parties and this informal right-wing extremism, which mutually nurture each other. As Ami Pedahzur and Leonard Weinberg point out, it is not clear at all if there will be an inevitable trade-off between an "uncivil society" of sub-cultural extremist grassroots politics and long-run electoral success. Parties and "informal" right-wing extremism do not necessarily replace each other but, as cooperating partners that mobilize resources and support for one another, may improve the prospects of the extreme Right in elections and in society, thus posing a threat to liberal democracy inside and outside parliament.[76] Particularly the regional strongholds in the East and the increasing attraction among young voters indicate that right-wing extremism remains a present and a future challenge.

Notes

1. For recent comparative overviews see Roger Eatwell and Cas Mudde, eds. *Western Democracies and the New Extreme Right Challenge*, (New York, 2004), 3ff; Pippa Norris, *Radical Right: Voters and Parties in the Electoral Market* (Cambridge, 2005); Cas Mudde, ed. *Racist Extremism in Central and Eastern Europe*, (New York, 2005); Martin Schain, Aristide Zolberg, and Patrick Hossay, eds. *Shadows over Europe: The Development and Impact of the Extreme Right in Western Europe* (New York, 2002); Lars Rensmann, "The New Politics of Prejudice: Comparative Perspectives on Extreme Right Parties in European Democracies," *German Politics and Society* 21 (2003): 93-123.
2. Richard Stöss, *Rechtsextremismus im Wandel* (Bonn, 2005), 86ff; Hajo Funke and Lars Rensmann, *Rechtsextremismus in Deutschland* (Berlin, 2005), 17ff.
3. See Mark Potok, "The American Extreme Right: The 1990s and Beyond," in *Western Democracies and the New Extreme Right Challenge*, eds. Roger Eatwell and Cas Mudde,(New York, 2004), 41.
4. Ami Pedahzur and Leonard Weinberg systematically address this aspect. Taking Germany as a special case study, they innovatively conceptualize the ensemble of extreme Right youth culture, violent subculture, networks and highly

institutionalized organizations, social movements and grassroots activities as "uncivil society." See Ami Pedahzur and Leonard Weinberg, "Modern Democracy and its Enemies: The threat of the extreme right," *Totalitarian Movements and Political Religions* 2 (2001): 59ff.

5. See Frank Decker, *Der neue Rechtspopulismus* (Opladen, 2004), 149.

6. See Terri Givens, *Voting Radical Right in Western Europe* (Cambridge, 2005); Richard Münch, *Das Projekt Europa: Zwischen Nationalstaat, regionaler Autonomie und Weltgesellschaft* (Frankfurt/Main, 1995), 79ff.

7. Norris, see note 1, 26.

8. Stöss, see note 2, 94ff.

9. Armin Pfahl-Traughber, *Rechtsextremismus in der Bundesrepublik* (Munich, 2001), 38.

10. See Piero Ignazi, *Extreme Right Parties in Western Europe* (Oxford, 2003), 20ff.

11. To be sure, no postwar German extreme Right party can escape from positioning itself in relation to the history of Nazism. By clearly distancing itself from this legacy, it risks using its credibility and identity among loyal core members and voters, by affirming Nazism in one way or another–which has generally been the case–the party loses its chances to become a legitimate political force and attract new voters. The alternative for extreme Right parties is formulated by Alexandre Dézé: "Either adapt themselves to the system, hence running the risk of losing a part of their original identities and of the support of their most orthodox members, or distinguish themselves from the system, thereby running the risk of being excluded from it, or of being marginalized." German extreme Right parties tend to do the latter. See Alexandre Dézé, "Between adaptation, differentiation and distinction: Extreme right-wing parties within democratic political systems," in *Western Democracies and the New Extreme Right Challenge*, eds. Roger Eatwell and Cas Mudde (London, 2004), 20.

12. Norbert Lepszy and Hans-Joachim Veen, *'Republikaner' und DVU in kommunalen und Landesparlamenten sowie im Europaparlament* (Sankt Augustin, 1994).

13. On the concept of party family employed here see Peter Mair and Cas Mudde, "The Party Family and its Study," *Annual Review of Political Science* 1 (1998).

14. Lee McGowan, *The Radical Right in Germany: 1870 to the Present* (London, 2002), 177.

15. Ibid.

16. Hans-Gerd Jaschke, "Die rechtsextremen Parteien nach der Bundestagswahl 1998: Stehen sie sich selbst im Wege?," in *Die Parteien nach der Bundestagswahl 1998*, ed. Oskar Niedermayer (Opladen, 1999).

17. Stöss, see note 2, 132.

18. Unlike the DVU, for example, the NPD is not lacking organizational sub-units such as a youth and a university organisation.

19. See Eckhard Jesse, "Politischer Extremismus heute: Islamistischer Fundamentalismus, Rechts- und Linksextremismus," *Aus Politik und Zeitgeschichte* B 46 (2001); Stöss, see note 2, 135.

20. The average age of members is thirty-seven, which is much younger compared to catch-all parties; see Toralf Staud, "Vormarsch in der Provinz," *Die Zeit*, 28 July 2005.

21. Funke and Rensmann, see note 2, 15.

22. Stöss, see note 2, 140.

23. Cas Mudde, *The Ideology of the Extreme Right* (Manchester, 2003), 79.

24. Ibid., 65.
25. Decker, see note 5, 147.
26. Stöss, see note 2, 141; Funke and Rensmann, see note 2, 15.
27. Mudde, see note 23, 64.
28. Ibid.
29. See Michael Minkenberg, *Die neue radikale Rechte im Vergleich* (Wiesbaden, 1998).
30. REP chairman Franz Schönhuber moved the party to the radical edges of the extreme right during the 1980s and early 1990s. Under his leadership, the party displayed authoritarian, anti-pluralist, anti-system and völkisch-nationalist positions; see Ignazi, *Extreme Right Parties in Western Europe*, 72.
31. Mudde, see note 23, 41, 44.
32. Ibid., 58.
33. Stöss, see note 2, 83.
34. Dézé, see note 11 21.
35. Ignazi, see note 10, 82; see also Hans-Georg Betz, "Rechtspopulismus: Ein internationaler Trend?," *Aus Politik und Zeitgeschichte* B 9-10: 11f.
36. Although, the party soon lost credibility because the parliamentary faction collapsed within months due to a lack of inner cohesion and the incompetence of its members. Stöss, see note 2, 88f.
37. Ibid., 90.
38. For changing Left-Right locations see Michael Laver, ed. *Estimating the Policy Position of Political Actors* (London, 2001).
39. Mary Kaldor, "Cosmopolitanism versus Nationalism: The New Divide?" in *Europe's New Nationalism: States and Minorities in Conflict,* eds. Richard Caplan and John Feffer (Oxford, 1996), 56. See also Lisbet Hooghe, Gary Marks and Carole J. Wilson, "Does Left/Right Structure Party Positions on European Integration?," *Comparative Political Studies* 25 (2002); Ulrich Beck and Edgar Grande, *Das kosmopolitische Europa* (Frankfurt/Main, 2004), 258ff.
40. On the empirical basis of a comparative voter analysis, Pippa Norris convincingly argues that we should "look skeptically upon the idea that the rise of the radical Right is purely a phenomenon of the politics of resentment among the underclass of low-qualified workers in inner-city areas, or that it can be attributed in any mechanical fashion to growing levels of unemployment and job insecurity in Europe. The socioeconomic profile is more complex than popular stereotypes suggest." Norris, see note 1, 257; see also Rensmann, see note 1, 116ff.
41. Ruud Koopmans and Hanspeter Kriesi, *Citizenship, National Identity and the Mobilization of the Extreme Right: A Comparison of France, Germany, the Netherlands and Switzerland* (Berlin, 1997), 20. For a similar line of argument see Michael Minkenberg, "The New Radical Right in the Political Process: Interaction Effects in France and Germany," in *Shadows over Europe: The Development and Impact of the Extreme Right in Western Europe,* eds. Martin Schain, Aristide Zolberg, and Patrick Hossay (New York, 2002).
42. Koopmans and Kriesi, see note 41, 16.
43. The Kohl government continuously had declared that Germany is no country of immigration; Decker, see note 5, 151; Minkenberg, see note 41, 264f.
44. Nationalistic, racist and extreme Right attitudes reach far beyond the NPD's electorate and even their potential voters. This is especially valid among young adults and uneducated voters. For an excellent research overview see Klaus

Ahlheim and Bardo Heger, *Der unbequeme Fremde: Fremdenfeindlichkeit in Deutschland – empirische Befunde* (Schwalbach, 1999); Corinna Kleinert and Johann de Rijke, "Rechtsextreme Orientierungen bei Jugendlichen und jungen Erwachsenen," in *Rechtsextremismus in der Bundesrepublik Deutschland*, eds. Wilfried Schubarth and Richard Stöss (Bonn, 2001). On the one hand, not every voter of an extreme Right party is a right-wing extremist. On the other hand, many nonvoters and voters of established democratic parties share extreme Right attitudes. Until today, few voters who share extreme Right attitudes vote for extreme Right parties. See Kai Arzheimer, "Wahlen und Rechtsextremismus," in *Extremismus in Deutschland: Erscheinungsformen und aktuelle Bestandsaufnahme*, ed. Bundesministerium des Innern, (Berlin, 2004), 77ff.

45. The American Jewish Committee, *German Attitudes Towards Jews, the Holocaust, and the U.S.* (New York, 2002).

46. Quoted in Jochen Bittner, "Blackbox Weißes Haus," *Die Zeit*, 24 July 2003.

47. See Aribert Heyder, Julia Iser and Peter Schmidt, "Israelkritik oder Antisemitismus? Meinungsbildung zwischen Öffentlichkeit, Medien und Tabus," in *Deutsche Zustände*, ed. Wilhelm Heitmeyer (Frankfurt/Main, 2005), 151.

48. See Lars Rensmann, "Nahost-Konflikt und Globalisierung als neue politische Mobilisierungsfelder in der extremen Rechten und Linken," *Zeitschrift für Genozidforschung* 6 (2005): 77ff; Lars Rensmann, *Demokratie und Judenbild: Antisemitismus in der politischen Kultur der Bundesrepublik Deutschland* (Wiesbaden, 2004), 241-276.

49. Michael Minkenberg, "The Renewal of the Radical Right: Between modernity and anti-modernity," *Government and Opposition* 35 (2000).

50. See Wilhelm Heitmeyer, "Gruppenbezogene Menschenfeindlichkeit," in *Deutsche Zustände 3*, ed. Wilhelm Heitmeyer (Frankfurt/Main, 2005).

51. In the NPD periodical *Deutsche Stimme* (German Voice), this new ideological focus is explained: The U.S. is portrayed as a main enemy because "this racially mixed artificial nation, driven by a desire for profit and the old-Israeli spirit of being the 'Chosen People'", has "decided to fight two world Wars against Germany and thus put the entire European continent on the wasteland of history." America is also a major enemy because "America is the ideologue and executor of the multicultural and dollar-capitalist 'one world' ideology." While the political center is allegedly "insane," the NPD finds "in parts of the German left" a kind of radical "anti-Americanism which makes one enthusiastic." *Deutsche Stimme*, January 2006.

52. Press Declaration of the NPD , 13 September 2001.

53. Neo-Nazi groups have welcomed 9/11 as an attack on the "symbol of Jewish world power," as stated by the *National German Workers' Party*'s periodical *NS-Kampfruf*. At any rate, many extreme Right and neo-Nazi intellectuals, some associated with the NPD ,endorse the 9/11 terror attacks and the antisemitic and anti-American motivation behind them more overtly than others. Reinhard Oberlecher of the neo-Nazi think tank *Deutsches Kolleg* describes the attacks as an overdue response against "Judaeo-American civilization." According to him, "destroying the United States of America including their global Jewish power apparatus as well as the expiry of the Jewish state" form part of the "general process of anti-capitalist world revolution." See Reinhold Oberlercher, "Der Untergang des judäo-amerikanischen Imperiums," *Sleipnir* 36, 2001; All quotes

from Federal Office for the Protection of the Constitution, *The significance of anti-Semitism,* 13.

54. *Deutsche Nationalzeitung,* 14 December 2001.

55. See Report Infratest Dimap, quoted and summarized in Viola Neu, *DVU-NPD: Perspektiven und Entwicklungen* (Sankt Augustin, 2004), 9.

56. These are developments "from below." In contrast to the older, formerly hegemonic German right-wing extremism which was fixated on hierarchical organization, Rainer Erb argues that "the modernised, younger, movement-oriented right-wing extremism of today connects its different elements in a lose, network-like structure without formal hierarchies." Rainer Erb, "Ideologische Anleihen, Geschichtsbilder und Symbole rechtsextremer Jugendgruppen–'Neonazis' und 'Skinheads,'" in *Rechtsextreme Ideologien in Geschichte und Gegenwart,* ed. Uwe Backes (Cologne, 2003), 301f.

57. Even right-wing extremist activities and violence had long formed a part of life in the GDR, but all these activities and incidents had been played down. See Lee McGowan, *The Radical Right in Germany: 1870 to the Present* (London, 2002), 189.

58. For a recent case study of those youth cultures see Ralph Gabriel, Ingo Grastorf, Tanja Lakeit and Lisa Wandt, *Futur Exakt: Jugendkultur in Oranienburg zwischen rechtsextremer Gewalt und demokratischem Engagement* (Berlin, 2004).

59. See Bernd Wagner, *Rechtsextremismus und kulturelle Subversion in den neuen Ländern* (Berlin, 1998).

60. Stöss, see note 2, 90; Funke and Rensmann, see note 2, 17ff. Partly supported by and partly separate from the NPD, the violent far Right has developed new organisational modes of operation, without central, rigid or formal structures. Small, locally based groups, the so-called *freie Kameradschaften,* have been set up and are operating at a local or regional level; see Fabian Virchow, "The groupuscularization of neo-Nazism in Germany: The case of the Aktionsbüro Norddeutschland," *Patterns of Prejudice* 38 (2004): 56-70. In some East German states we find not only forms of subcultural right-wing extremism but also Neo-Nazi cells and organized *Kameradschaften* in almost every small town or city.

61. See Rainer Erb, "Die kommunalpolitische Strategie der NPD Ende der Neunziger Jahre," in *NPD: Herausforderung für die Demokratie?,* eds. Heinz Lynen von Berg, Hans-Jochen Tschiche (Berlin, 2002).

62. Eckhard Jesse, "Von der Linken lernen? Vier rechtsextremistische Intellektuelle im Vergleich," in *Rechtsextreme Ideologien in Geschichte und Gegenwart,* ed. Uwe Backes, (Cologne, 2003), 261–88.

63. Erb, see note 56, 300.

64. For a full account see Toralf Staud, *Moderne Nazis: Die neuen Rechten und der Aufstieg der NPD* (Köln, 2005); Hajo Funke, *Politik und Paranoia: Rechtsextremismus in der Berliner Republik* (Berlin, 2002).

65. In order to avoid any competition, the NPD was running in the 2005 general election, the DVU will run in the European elections in 2009. In the meantime, the DVU will participate in five of the next state elections, the NPD will participate in two other state elections.

66. Jesse, see note 19, 5.

67. See http://www.npd.de, September 2005; *Deutsche Stimme,* September 2005.

68. Staud, see note 64.

69. Staud, see note 20.

70. Quoted in *Telepolis,* 22 June 2005.

71. On the performance of the Party of the Left see the contributions by Jeffrey Kopstein and Dan Hough in this special issue.
72. Steffen Kailitz, *Politische Extremismus in der Bundesrepublik Deutschland,* (Wiesbaden, 2004), 54f.
73. Norris, see note 2, 119.
74. On the success of other European extreme Right and populist parties which more effectively utilize new national identity politics and the electoral divide between national-protectionist and pro-globalization/pro-European views see Susanne Frölich-Steffen and Lars Rensmann, "Populistische Regierungsparteien in Ost- und Westeuropa: Vergleichende Perspektiven der politikwissenschaftlichen Forschung," in *Populisten an der Macht: Populistische Regierungsparteien in West- und Osteuropa,* eds., Susanne Frölich-Steffen and Lars Rensmann, (Vienna, 2005).
75. Ignazi, see note 10, 73.
76. Pedahzur and Weinberg, see note 4, 70.

Chapter 5

Angela Merkel
What Does it Mean to Run as a Woman?

Myra Marx Ferree

Question: Do you intend to run as a woman?
Answer: Do I have any choice?

(Representative Patricia Schroeder, D-Co)

The year 2006 marks almost a century after women worldwide began to gain the right to vote. It is still only half a century after it became internationally commonplace for the ideal of democracy to include both women and men as participants.[1] Yet as this year begins, we not only see Angela Merkel in office as Germany's first woman head of government, but a variety of women leaders emerging around the globe. On January 15, Michelle Bachelet was elected president of Chile, one of the most conservative countries of Latin America, and the next day, Ellen Johnson Sirleaf was inaugurated as the first president of Liberia. Japan is poised to open its imperial succession to women, after a favorable report from its government.

That these are newsworthy events underlines the reality that women are still far from commonplace in positions of national leadership. But the political context into which Chancellor Merkel leads her government has changed dramatically, both domestically and internationally. This transformation is ultimately rooted in the achievements of the women's movements of many nations, whose long-term efforts detached the meaning of citizenship from the family-centered right of an independent head of household, the *pater familias*, and made it a relationship that all individuals had with their governments.

Developing the idea of citizenship as based in the personhood of the individual regardless of gender has been a slow and still incomplete process. Laws establishing women primarily as mothers and wives, dependents with special disabilities and limited rights, have been undone only gradually.[2] Separating the welfare of dependent women and children from the absolute authority of the family patriarch has demanded concrete political struggles. Detaching the meaning of political authority from its literal roots in patriarchy is an even more precarious and partial process, but the signs that it is underway are unmistakable.

This long-term process of degendering politics provides a significant backdrop for any contemporary woman's rise to and exercise of power, including that of Angela Merkel. Unlike the women who held political authority on the basis of their family relationships, whether as hereditary monarchs or "over the dead bodies" of their politician husbands or fathers, she and other women making political news today around the world are rising through their own campaigns and with their own agendas. This could not have happened without women's movements driving the world toward a more gender-inclusive understanding of politics. Considering Angela Merkel as an individual woman as well as a symbol of women's greater role in politics raises the question of how her position should be understood in relation to the state of gender relations in the 21st century. Without in any way claiming her as an exemplar or advocate of feminism, I nonetheless argue that the opportunities and obstacles facing her need to be analyzed in feminist terms.

What women's movements have done since the 19th century and continue to do today is threefold: they change political expectations; they redefine political interests; and they remake political networks. Each of these changes is an essential precondition for allowing women, whether feminist or not, to rise in politics as individuals rather than heirs of a male relative. None of these effects could materialize from thin air—all require political agency and imply active struggles. Both women and men, in complex constellations of interests, have taken part on both sides. Nor are any of these battles over yet, even though there have been important and cumulative victories. This feminist context is fundamental for understanding Angela Merkel, since she has no choice but to "run as a woman". Her very presence both rests on past gains and changes future opportunities for women in several ways.

First, women like Angela Merkel who step onto the political stage make all women visible as citizens, with interests that are sometimes distinctive and sometimes overlapping with those of men, and create legitimacy for women acting politically. John Stuart Mill over a century ago sang the virtues of such faits accomplis when he pointed out the expansion of women's education was the most powerful rebuttal to the claim that women could not be educated.

Second, any woman's political activity challenges the conventional distinction between "public" and "private." This "separation of spheres" ideology assigns women the roles conventionally understood as domestic, private, supportive and nurturing–and thus as the antithesis of the political. While ideology is not reality, and certainly not all women are wives and mothers or define themselves in terms of these roles, the association is politically potent. Women's presence evokes this association, but also challenges its exclusionary and demeaning political interpretation. Whether they embrace or reject motherhood, politically active women undermine assignment of all women to "their place."

Third, women in politics often create alternative associations and networks. This work goes on both inside and outside of states, parties, unions and other institutional settings–not only in autonomous women's groups. Mary Katzenstein has pointed out that struggle to change institutions from the inside out, not just to set up parallel women's organizations, has been the distinctive addition to the women's movement's strategic repertoire in the late 20th century.[3]

What does this long-term transformatory struggle have to do with Angela Merkel, a female politician who rapidly rose through the ranks of the Christian Democratic Union (CDU), a party with a distinctly non-feminist agenda and a lower than typical share of women members and representatives? The conventional wisdom is that she did not even "run as a woman," at least not until the last sprint toward the election, not explicitly making any appeal to vote for her on gender grounds. Yet this judgment fails to recognize that she has never had any other choice than to "run as a woman" unless she were not to run at all. Within a gendered political system, in which power is still very much associated with manhood, Merkel never has had the privilege of having her gender taken for granted and made invisible. Unlike male politicians, whether she has wanted to embrace or distance herself from the women's movement, she has always had to face questions and challenges about her position on gender politics, both past and future.

Changing Expectations

To think of gender simply as one of many attributes that Angela Merkel has as a person detracts from recognizing the political opportunity structure itself as gendered. Interpretations of behavior are made through a gendered lens, as her biographer Evelyn Roll, pointed out:

> If Angela Merkel is convinced of the inevitability of a process, she moves on unsentimentally. But that is remarked on differently for her than it would be for a man. And should she seek a compromise, which would be called political talent in a man, the newspapers call her hesitant. If she gets her own way, she's called the iron lady whose path is littered with the corpses of her male opponents.[4]

The gendered implications of power and citizenship are already the outcome of long term struggles by and for women, and her choices and chances, in turn, will have an impact on these opportunities, whether she want to have such an effect or not. Even a press release from SPD politician, Renate Schmidt, concedes: "Angela Merkel was not elected because she is a woman, but it also has not hurt her. This can be explained by the increasing normality of this in Germany, to which the women's movement has contributed."

Because Merkel has no choice but to run as woman, govern as a woman, and negotiate with foreign leaders as a woman, the way that women are understood in today's political culture has an impact on her no less than her position as symbol and role-model has on the opportunities opening for other women. Just as British Prime Minister Margaret Thatcher is invoked as a comparison for Angela Merkel, regardless of any actual similarities between them or Merkel's own resistance to such analogies, it will be inevitable for Merkel to be invoked, for better or worse, as model for thinking about future women in politics. Real cultural change in expectations about women in politics, of which the past century has seen a great deal, comes out of just such concrete, complex and consequently ambivalent individual struggles and accomplishments, not from some disembodied force.

In fact, it would be difficult to overestimate the visibility of Merkel's gender in the past election. Although the media noted, sometimes approvingly and sometimes not, that Merkel herself was not making a political issue of her gender, the press was happy to rush in and fill that gap. If she had perhaps hoped that her gender would be treated as irrelevant, such a wish was certainly naive.

On the positive side, there were continual hopes expressed that she would serve at last to break the "glass ceiling" that held women from top jobs. It was pointed out that the glass ceiling was set higher up for women in the U.S. and even other EU countries than in Germany, and having Angela Merkel as head of government was construed as having a potential effect on breaking that ceiling outside of politics. Alice Schwarzer, the publisher of the magazine *Emma* and consistently anointed by the press as "the" representative of the women's movement, was omnipresent on the media stage. Being asked continually to assess Merkel's "meaning for women," Schwarzer separated herself from Merkel's policy positions but still pointed out the symbolic value of any woman in a leadership role: "just imagine that in America an African American was running for the White House. What effect would that have on Blacks? Exactly. And the feelings among us German women are just like this—ambivalent excitement."[5] In the U.S. as well, her candidacy was welcomed as a symbolic alternative to the posturing of the current American regime, with some suggesting that President Bush may also have come to be "the biggest reason why female leaders suddenly seem so relevant. He has debased the currency of machismo."[6]

On the negative side, Merkel was chastised by the press for her unwillingness to embrace her gender explicitly as a defining feature of her candidacy, to speak "as a woman" to women as voters and to mobilize them on her behalf across party lines. Whether such a "gender gap" strategy could work in an electoral system in which no popular votes are cast for the individual candidate for chancellor is an open question, but it certainly deserves a degree of skepticism. Nonetheless, as the election neared, Merkel responded to the demands for such a public acknowledgment of her gender, giving interviews to not only to mass-circulation women's magazines such as *Brigitte* and *Cosmopolitan* but also to the feminist magazine *Emma* that celebrated her identity as a woman and implicitly recognized the significance of Schwarzer's support.

Women Representing Women and Femininity

Merkel's positive acknowledgement of her position as a female pioneer represents an interesting shift in political norms regarding gender. Women long have been considered particularly unelectable if they were in any way perceived to represent women, a "special interest" rather than the "general" interest for which men (understood to be genderless) stood. Most press calls for Merkel to be more explicit about her gender identity framed their demands in terms of her thus "missing an opportunity" to appeal to women rather than being appropriately cautious about deterring voters from supporting the supposedly "narrow" concerns of women. Assuming these calls were not hypocritical appeals to Merkel to commit political suicide, one would have to conclude that in the minds of journalists at least, being a woman was an "extra" rather than a sign of being more limited and "less qualified."

The legitimacy of considering being female a disqualification for executive office dropped as women mobilized in the 1970s–not time alone but the women's movement made this belief less tenable.[7] As women have increasingly run for and been elected to public office, the fait accompli effect has taken hold. Women increased from less than 10 percent of the Bundestag in the 1970s to 32 percent in 2005, and women heads of government from Margaret Thatcher in the U.K. to Gro Harlem Brundtland in Norway have had a large and unmistakable presence on the world stage. Moreover, even in the course of this German electoral campaign the polls showed signs of an additional fait accompli effect. Early in the campaign, 56 percent of women (and 37 percent of men) were willing to say in principle that they approved of a woman being Chancellor, but by the end of the campaign 84 percent of women and 70 percent of men said they thought this was fine.[8]

Media interest in Merkel as a woman candidate brought predictable attention to her hairstyle, makeup and dress as well as to her family life, and on all these grounds she was assessed as deficient but trying to meet expectations. A more fashionable haircut and clothes served not only to define her as more feminine but also as accommodating to West German norms of femininity. Paradoxically, because the less conventionally feminine self-presentation she offered in her earlier years was attributed to her "German Democratic Republic (GDR) experience," the naturalness of the equation between female character and feminine style was somewhat undermined. While for Western women politicians, discussions of appearance are used signal their office-worthiness, Merkel's looks became a less presumptively reliable guide to what kind of woman she is "underneath." Becoming more feminine in style thus could be used to signal her willingness to accept West German norms in other matters as well, and not as a demonstration of her lack of seriousness.

The press also found itself needing to justify its interest in her appearance as non-sexist, which would not have been the case when sexism was simply the norm. Journalists insisted that the press had shown similar interest in whether Gerhard Schröder dyed his hair, and tried to construct an image of a new androgynous political norm, one that supposedly governed the behavior of politicians as well as of the media. Thus it was asserted that it was now okay for politicians to cry, presenting Schröder in particular as a testosterone-charged stud (with four wives as evidence) and yet as being just as able to cry or be vain (see the hair dye issue) as any woman.[9] Martin Benninghoff mocked the idea that gender had anything to do with Merkel's campaign at all; in his view, she is the "Alpha female" (*Alphaweibchen*) who can beat the "sharks" at their own game and make the chest-thumping masculinity of the men look merely foolish.[10]

Although Merkel's gender was not presented as a disqualification, observers did portray it as a vulnerability, adding to their doubts as to whether she would emerge as Chancellor at the end of the party negotiations. The long period of postelection bargaining among the German parties inadvertently provided a window for women politicians in other EU countries to express their own sense of identification with Merkel. When accused of meddling in the German political process, they insisted that they were only reacting to her symbolic role as a woman pioneer and perforce role-model, not endorsing a party or policy for the government. Although her party's failure to win a strong electoral mandate was laid at her feet, her success in assembling a government, over opponents within her party as well as without, and actually emerging as the first female Chancellor in Germany's history then became a separate, and in some ways more notable, accomplishment than her party's electoral showing.

Overall, Merkel's candidacy emerged on a global stage in which it was still perceived to be surprising but no longer inherently illegitimate or even deeply controversial for a woman to head a major government. Women's capacity to direct the affairs of state has become a fait accompli, and even though some voters and some of her own colleagues were understood as having difficulty with this, their resistance to her on the basis of gender was portrayed as a sign of their backwardness.

The Intersectionality of Gender

Of course, Merkel is not only a woman. As commentators never tire of pointing out, she is an Easterner of a certain generation, an "89er" rather than a "68er" who, at a transformative political moment, saw more democratic promise in capitalism than in socialism. She is Protestant in a party still largely dominated by Catholics, a natural scientist in a parliament dominated by lawyers and managers. Already her multiple outsider status is being invoked to treat her as a placeholder for the "real" politicians, to explain and justify the prediction that the grand coalition that she heads is doomed to be short-lived and ineffective. These expectations, like the belief that even as party leader she would never actually become the CDU's candidate for chancellor, may well underestimate her individual political talents. Only a few months after the election, her personal popularity has risen to the top of the chart of German politicians.

This may not only be the result of a personal skill, but of the complex meanings of gender. The inevitable co-existence of multiple identities for any one individual, and the varied meaning of any one of them depending on the structural location on other dimensions, has become known in the social sciences as "intersectionality." An intersectional analysis, for example, notes that for women in the former GDR, the role and identity of housewife was alien, while the particular demands of a double day for women under socialism were not felt in the Federal Republic of Germany (FRG), where entry into a male-dominated occupation and access to full-day childcare and schools represented a vision of liberation. Certainly all women or all men do not share the same interests, or even experience the costs and benefits of their specific position in the same way.

Looking at Angela Merkel in such an intersectional way highlights the way her own upbringing provided specific experiences of gender, but also rejects simplistic political attacks on her as "not able to represent women" because she did not have children nor live through the generational transformation that West German women did after 1968. Merkel's autobiography is no less infused with gender meaning than that of a woman raised in the West who sacrificed all or some of her career goals to her children. However, the gendered meanings of growing up in the GDR are definitely different than those of a West German.[11]

The GDR trumpeted women's liberation as its "accomplishment" even as the FRG committed itself to restoring the *pater familias,* or *Familienvater,* to his "proper" place of patriarchal authority.[12] While East Germany did not even come close to real emancipation, it did make marriage less a matter of the economic dependence of women on men, particularly for raising children.[13] This freed women to pick husbands with less attention to their earning capacity and to have children or not, depending on their own wishes. The GDR also took away political rights, making all citizens dependent on the authority of the state as father-of-all, and made access to better jobs depend on political conformity more than on gender per se. Divorced and remarried to a fellow scientist, Joachim Sauer, but also blocked from advancement for her politics, Merkel fits the GDR model of semi-autonomy for both women and men.

Merkel faced discrimination in her career choices because of her father's position as Protestant pastor, not because she was a woman seeking an education in the sciences. For her, science was a refuge from political discrimination rather than a bastion of gender discrimination. Disappointment in the reformability of socialism nonetheless did not prevent her from engaging in political activism in the heady days of 1989, joining the social movement group *Democratischer Auf-bruch.* Although gender distinctions were present in this and other groups emerging during the unification process, the fluidity and unbureaucratic nature of social movements generally offer women more opportunity than formally organized parties and groups do. Moreover, a framing of those in authority as corrupt old men also offers more political credibility to those who are moral young women, an advantage that Merkel was able to exploit not only in the context of the *Wende* but also in the wake of the CDU's own scandals. It is worth noting that both Bachelet in Chile and Johnson Sirleaf in Liberia came into office with the mantel of reform and opposition against corruption. This expectation of women's moral rectitude and less self-serving behavior is part of the gendered opportunity struc-ture of politics that pastor's daughter Merkel has been able to use to get into office, but will also offer chances for her to take stands inter-nationally (in confronting the US over Guantanamo, for example) that resonate well with a wide spectrum of German voters.

For Merkel, her gender is important but not in the way it would have been in the FRG. As her supporter, Susanne Mayer, wrote in *Die Zeit*:

> If Angela Merkel had been a typical East German woman, she would have been a mother and already defeated by the shortage of kinder-garten spots and lack of full-day schools in Bonn. Had she been a typ-ical West German woman, she would have trumpeted her fury over these shortfalls and alienated everyone. Angela Merkel is a unified German childless model of success.[14]

During the election, her distinctiveness as a non-mother set up an interesting conflict between Merkel and those who appealed to West German norms of appropriate womanhood to discredit her. Since sexism has lost its simple legitimacy, this attack had to come from other women who presumably would be insulated from this charge by virtue of their gender. One mode of critique was to argue that her non-motherhood made her incapable of representing women, an argument that was interesting for what it implied about the visibility and legitimacy of women as an interest group. Since the primary spokesperson chosen for this attack was Doris Schröder, Schröder's fourth wife, and he had recently and notoriously dismissed the strug-gle for women's interests as a fuss about nothing (*Gedöns*) the cyni-cism in this strategy was hard to overlook.[15]

Feminism as an Implicit Asset

If Merkel's lack of credentials as a mother were advanced as if they were a damning argument by some, other women from the western Länder argued that she lacked credentials as a feminist, as if this identity were not otherwise treated as political leprosy. Of course, in some ways her position as a woman raised in the GDR automatically disqualified her from this label, since she could hardly claim to be a 68er. In the U.S. the feminist label is not nearly as narrow or negative as it is in Germany, but it still would be implausible to expect a serious woman major party candidate (such as Hillary Clinton) to embrace it. Instead, those who would like to see a more feminist candidate look for smaller indications, noting for example that Merkel, unlike many women from the new Länder, embraced and used the grammatically feminine "in" ending.[16] Comparably, in Chile, it was noticed that Michele Bachelet inverted the usual order and addressed "*chileanas y chileanos.*"

Another behavior that some were willing to interpret as a "hint" of Merkel's feminist sympathies was the fact that her closest and most trusted advisors within the party are women (e.g., Beate Baumann, Eva Christiansen, Hildegard Müller, Annette Schavan). It is more than likely however that such a female-centered network represents less of a clue to her politics than an indication of just how untrustworthy as allies and confidants she has probably found her male colleagues to be. Merkel has herself chided Alice Schwarzer for claiming her as a latent feminist, noting that "she is likely to be disappointed. I am after all in the CDU." Schwarzer, however, back in 2000, already had countered this argument, saying "no one expects her to be a true feminist, since she is a woman of the CDU. But such women, from [Elisabeth] Schwarzhaupt to [Rita] Süssmuth, have already provided sufficient evidence that a sort of feminism-lite is possible."[17] However, just this willingness to see a gender-political advance in a nonfeminist party victory was also frequently condemned by other feminists: "Forget symbols and milestones—whoever wants Merkel as a chancellor is going to get the really existing CDU/CSU. This is the consequence Frau Schwarzer is unwilling to draw."[18]

But having a feminist effect on the gender norms of politics does not require a woman to actually espouse feminist policies. It may be more telling to note that Merkel is well aware of the male norms and expectations that demean and attempt to exclude her; as Alice Schwarzer pointed out, Merkel had even favorably reviewed *Backlash*, Susan Faludi's bestseller about political and media attacks on women, in 1993 in the pages of Schwarzer's feminist magazine, *Emma*. Merkel also began her government career with an appointment to head the Ministry of Family, Women, Seniors and Youth, where she could not possibly have avoided working with civil servants dedicated to women's advances. While it indeed seems unlikely that Merkel is in any meaningful sense a feminist, she is clearly not allergic to contact with feminism or incapable of trusting and promoting other women around her.

Women's Networks and Gender Solidarity

This ability to be part of a network of women, not a lone woman who is trying to pretend to be as man-like as possible to fit into prevailing definitions of legitimate political authority (the Thatcher strategy), is one critical way in which Merkel's gender matters. As a woman chef quoted in one of the many forums on expectations for Merkel-as-woman argued, "I expect Frau Merkel, as I expect any woman in a position of leadership, to provide other competent women networks of support and to cover their backs. It would be naive to assume that Frau Merkel's gender does not play a role and will not play a role."[19] As threatening as her building a "girls' club" seems to be to some men and media who remark upon it, it is indeed remarkable that German political culture has changed enough to create a route from being a woman heading the ministry for women to being a woman chancellor (*Frauenministerin* to *Kanzlerin*) and to accumulate a pool of talented and experienced women at the top on which Merkel can draw for personally loyal advice.[20]

This significant influx of women into cabinet positions, state executive roles, and among parliamentary leaders arose as a consequence of decades of feminist struggle. The idea of party quotas for women was first embraced in Germany by the Green Party (at 50 percent) and was spread, in diluted form, through processes of party competition. Twenty years later, the idea that women would be absent from a party list seems sexist and wrong across the entire spectrum. As all parties adopted their own, weaker quota rules, however reluctantly, the previously unquestioned norm of maleness began to topple. In that sense, no matter how unfeminist her political positions, Merkel is an heir of Green politics in Germany and of the women's movement worldwide.

The quota model has become a powerful global norm, taken up in the African Union, India and many of the countries of Europe as a means of making their democracies more truly representative of all the voters. By dismantling the implicit male norm for who belongs in government, the quota approach opens up more opportunity to women, even women who, like Merkel, were initially appointed by men who seriously underestimated and patronized them. The ability of women to take advantage of such opportunities, however, depends on their own initiative, not only as individuals, but as part of a network of women who take each other seriously and support their advances. That Merkel can be so evidently part of such a network is both evidence of the accomplishments of those who have gone before and also another symbolic blow against the belief that woman are less able or appropriate in positions of authority.

In sum, Angela Merkel necessarily did run as a woman, both symbolically and personally. Both general expectations about women in politics, and specific expectations tied up with her individual biography and political skills play a particular role in the meaning that her historic position carries. Whether or not women were more likely to vote for her (all else being equal, which will demand more multivariate analysis of the polling data), she definitely benefited from the efforts of women over the past century and from the specific feminist struggles of the past thirty years to change politics in more inclusive directions. The general challenge to machismo as a political style– exemplified not only in criticisms directed at Gerhard Schröder but at the resistance to President Bush's "cowboy" style of governance–contributed to her success, and offers her opportunities to walk the thin line between being an "Iron Lady" and a presumed pushover. She is also inevitably going to contribute in her turn to changing the symbolic associations of gender and politics, as the intense media attention to her has already shown. Paradoxically, one of the most powerful evidences that such a change has happened already is the extent to which her gender can actually become unremarkable as she goes about the work of exercising political authority, though the regularity of such attention to her gender is the surest sign that change is still has a long way yet to go.

Notes

1. Francisco Ramirez, Yasmin Soysal and S. Shanahan, "The changing logic of political citizenship: Cross-national acquisition of women's suffrage rights, 1890 to 1990," *American Sociological Review* 62, no. 5 (1997): 735-745.
2. Sabine Berghahn, "Ist die Institution Ehe eine Gleichstellungsbarriere im Geschlechterverhältnis in Deutschland?" in *Verharrender Wandel: Institutionen und Geschlechterverhältnisse*, eds. Maria Oppen and Dagmar Simon (Berlin, 2004): 99-138.
3. Mary Katzenstein, *Faithful and Fearless: Moving Feminist Protest inside the Church and Military* (Princeton, 1998).
4. Susanne Gaschke, "'Was Merkel so anders macht:' Interview with Evelyn Roll," *Die Zeit*, 25 August 2005. "Wenn Angela Merkel von der Unumkehrbarkeit eines Prozesses überzeugt ist, leistet sie sich keine Sentimentalitäten mehr. Nur wird das bei einer Frau anders kommentiert als bei einem Mann. Sucht sie den Kompromiss–bei Männern gilt das als politische Begabung–, liest man über Merkel in den Zeitungen, sie sei zögerlich. Setzt sie sich durch, ist sie die eiskalte Lady, an deren Wegesrand sich die Leichen von gemeuchelten Männern türmen."
5. Thomas Widmer, "'Ihre größte Schwäche: Sie ist eine Frau:' Interview with Alice Schwarzer," *Weltwoche*, 26 May 2005.
6. Tina Brown, "You've come a long way, ladies." *The Washington Post*, 13 October 2005.
7. Myra Marx Ferree, "A Woman for President? Changing Responses, 1958-1972," *Public Opinion Quarterly*, 38, no.3 (1974): 390-399.
8. Udo Ludwig and Cordula Meyer, "Weil sie kein Mädchen ist," *Der Spiegel*, 26 September 2005.
9. Matthais Geyer and Dirk Kurbjuweit, "Die Mechanik der Macht," *SPIEGEL ONLINE*, 21 November 2005.
10. Martin Benninghoff, "Höhi! Das Alphaweibchen lacht," *Die Zeit*, 4 October 2005.
11. Myra Marx Ferree, "Patriarchies and feminisms: The two women's movements of unified Germany," *Social Politics*, 2, no. 1 (1995): 10-24.

12. Robert Moeller, *Protecting Motherhood : Women and the Family in the Politics of Postwar West Germany* (Berkeley, 1993).
13. Myra Marx Ferree, "The rise and fall of 'mommy politics': feminism and German unification," *Feminist Studies*, 19, no. 1 (1993): 89-115.
14. Susanne Mayer, "Weil sie eine Frau ist?/PRO," *Die Zeit*, 25 August 2005. "Wäre Angela Merkel eine typische Ostdeutsche, dann wäre sie Mutter und hätte schon in Bonn in Ermangelung von Kita-Plätzen und Ganztagsschulen die Segel streichen müssen. Wäre sie eine typische Westdeutsche, hätte sie ihre Empörung darüber herausposaunt und sich alle zu Feinden gemacht. Angela Merkel ist ein gesamtdeutsches kinderloses Erfolgsmodell."
15. Cora Stephan, "Im Dschungel: Da konnten die Männchen noch so zetern: Von nun an führt eine Frau die Horde," Die Welt, 13 October 2005.
16. Barbara Sichterman, "Angela Merkel," *Die Tageszeitung*, 28 May 2005.
17. Alice Schwarzer, "Der Merkel-Effekt," *EMMA* Mai/Juni 2000.
18. Ulla Meinecke, "Eine Kanzlerin?," *Die Tageszeitung*, 3 September 2005.
19. Uta Felgner, "Stimmen zu Deutschlands erster Kanzlerin," *Berliner Morgenpost*, 11 October 2005.
20. Mathia Krupa, "Girls ja, Camp nein: Angela Merkel hat durchaus einflussreiche Unterstützerinnen–doch ein Frauennetzwerk gibt es nicht," *Die Zeit*, 28 August 2005.

Chapter 6

Merkel's EU Policy

"Kohl's Mädchen" or Interest-driven Politics?

Dorothee Heisenberg

With every new German chancellor, analysts are driven back to their keyboards to assess whether or not Germany will choose continuity or change with respect to postwar foreign policy traditions. German policies towards the European Union (EU)[1] have always been at the intersection of domestic and foreign policy, and, over time, EU policy has become more important and has moved into the chancellor's office to a much larger degree than other foreign policy areas.[2] This chapter will examine new Chancellor Angela Merkel's words and deeds in the first months of her term, and contrast them with outgoing Chancellor Gerhard Schröder's EU policies. The aim is to answer the question whether a Merkel-led government will prioritize European integration and the success of the EU as an integral part of its policies almost irrespective of Germany's interests, or whether Germany will continue the transition toward a more pragmatic EU policy. This renewed emphasis on domestic interests comes at a time when the German public is more skeptical about the benefits of European integration to Germany. According to the latest Eurobarometer poll taken in Fall 2005, 46 percent of Germans believe that Germany has not benefited on balance from being a member of the EU. Thus, putting EU priorities ahead of domestic economic priorities will be difficult in any case.

There is an unusual amount of agreement in the literature about Germany's role historically in the EU. Germany was an essential part of the "Franco-German motor" as well as being very Atlanticist in the foreign policy arena. This was important because it meant that European integration rarely conflicted with fundamental U.S.

interests and allowed the U.S. to take an approach of benign neglect to integration. Moreover, Germany's Atlanticist leanings as well as its "hands off" approach to its own economy (arguably up until the 1980s) meant that it could be a bridge to the UK. Finally, its "reflexive multilateralism" coupled with its role as the facilitator of grand bargains in the EU through side payments and general checkbook diplomacy meant that Germany was the indispensable partner in EU integration progress.

Germany's acceptance of its role as primary contributor[3] to EU endeavors is the focus of this chapter, because the issue shows a willingness to put aside "national interest"–understood in a way even realists could support, not relying solely on rhetorical flourishes about the importance of the EU. To state this hypothesis more explicitly, one might expect Merkel to provoke more conflict in EU budget battles than Schröder did, as Germany's domestic finances continue to deteriorate, a development that compelled Schröder to be tougher than Helmut Kohl. I also examine the policy differences between Schröder and Merkel (to the extent that they are already evident) toward the Stability and Growth Pact, which requires domestic economic sacrifice for the sake of meeting EU obligations.

Finally, one simplifying assumption should be clarified: although all German governments are formed with coalitions, I assume the chancellory sets EU policy. This assumption is not always completely warranted, and was especially problematic in the years when Hans-Dietrich Genscher of the Free Democratic Party (FDP) was Germany's foreign minister, but in the last decade it has proved to be a decent working assumption.[4] It remains to be seen if the Christian Democratic Union-Social Democratic Party (CDU-SPD) grand coalition will maintain that trend. Methodologically, however, any exception to that trend (i.e., giving SPD Foreign Minister Frank-Walter Steinmeier–Schröder's former chief of staff–more importance for shaping EU policy) would lead to greater continuity with the Schröder government's EU policies. Thus, if we see Schröder-Merkel EU policy divergences, then these differences clearly must come from Merkel herself.

Germany's EU Budget Policies

In retrospect, it seems fair to characterize the Kohl years as the high water mark for Germany's willingness to subordinate domestic interests to greater European integration. Although the Single European Act was perceived positively by virtually all German policymakers despite less progress on the institutional side than Kohl had wanted, the Maastricht Treaty (TEU) showed that the government was willing to go against perceived national interests, elite consensus and public opinion in order to further EU integration. With opinion polls in 1996 showing 58 percent of the German public against the creation of the EURO, Kohl insisted on keeping to the timetable and ignored opportunities to delay the advent of the single currency. As the EU's largest net contributor, Kohl also funded a significant part of the new structural funds (Delors II) in the TEU. Jeffrey Anderson's analysis of Germany's role vis-à-vis the EU in the areas of competition policy, trade policy, the Common Agricultural Policy (CAP), and the structural funds concludes: "... it is still possible to interpret Germany's approach to the EC/EU in terms consistent with the preunification period ... Germany's exaggerated multilateralism and culture of restraint have endured."[5] Anderson does acknowledge the deterioration of the domestic consensus regarding the EU due to the budgetary strains arising from unification, but notes that during the Kohl years these did not translate into uniform changes in Germany's approach. In large part, the lack of policy changes during the Kohl years was attributed to ideational/generational factors that were somewhat unique even within the government.[6]

The Schröder Years

Gerhard Schröder's 27 September 1998 victory over Kohl was hailed as a generational change and a significant break from the longest postwar government of Germany. The stability of the SPD coalition with the Greens was perhaps the biggest question mark, but also in question was the "68er" generation's commitment to the EU.

Even before Schröder was formally sworn in on October 27, he had visited Paris to show his ongoing commitment to the Franco-German alliance. He also visited British Prime Minister Tony Blair in an effort to shore up his claims of a "new middle" (*Neue Mitte*) and to signal a new willingness to include Britain in the stewardship of the EU. However, he also made clear to the electorate that Germany's EU Council presidency, which would begin 1 January 1999, would reflect the budgetary realities of the German state after unification, and that Germany would work to lighten the EU load on German finances. Speaking to the Bundestag on 10 December 1998 Schröder stated:

> We can not and will not solve the problems of Europe with a German checkbook. Without more fairness over contributions, the people of our country will distance themselves from Europe instead of being won over to further integration ...When countries such as Luxembourg, Denmark and Belgium ... are receiving revenue, while we by far are the largest revenue contributors, then there is something (wrong with the calculations).[7]

Schröder's main target was the EU's medium term financial perspectives (2000-2006), particularly the monies that were being negotiated to accommodate the planned enlargement to the Central and Eastern European applicants. Germany had paid approximately U.S. $13 billion into the EU's accounts (see Table One) and Schröder's aim was to reduce this contribution at the special Berlin Council meeting on Agenda 2000. At the Berlin summit on 24-25 March 1999, Schröder failed to get the significant reduction in Germany's net payments to the EU for which he had hoped, but considered it a success given that an agreement on the financial perspectives had been reached at all after the marathon nine hour negotiations on the 25th. As Table One shows, Germany was able to reduce its payments and reverse the trend of the country paying more as a percentage of GDP to achieve unity at summits.[8] Thus, although Schröder failed in his quest to reduce Germany's contribution by one third, it was the first time that its contribution declined even a bit. By contrast, in the previous negotiations of December 1992, Kohl had achieved the budget compromise by "[reaching] into a deep pocket to finance a sharp rise in spending over the following seven years."[9] This time, Germany's partners were struck by Schröder's intransigence on the budget. It should be added that the statistics in Table One make clear that Germany had a very reasonable case for reducing its net contribution–

Table 1: EU Net Payers and Net Receivers 1998 and 2003

Country	Net Contribution per person (ecu) 1998	Net Contribution per person (euro) 2003	Net Contribution per GDP (ecu) 1998	Net Contribution per GDP (euro) 2003	forecast (euro) 2008-13
Germany	121.6	92.7	0.52%	0.36%	0.54%
Netherlands	152.9	120.7	0.72%	0.43%	0.55%
Britain	38.9	46.6	0.18%	0.16%	0.23%
Italy	22.6	13.8	0.12%	0.06%	0.41%
Sweden	78.3	106.8	0.33%	0.36%	0.50%
France	6.8	32.1	0.03%	0.12%	0.37%
Austria	24.7	41.5	0.11%	0.15%	0.38%
Finland	-19.4	4	-0.09%	0.01%	0.23%
Denmark	-37.8	39.6	-0.13%	0.11%	0.31%
Luxembourg	-1875.7	140.5	-5.41%	0.28%	
Belgium	-176.3	74.5	-0.81%	0.28%	
Ireland	-622.3	-391.2	-3.28%	-1.40%	
Portugal	-283.2	-334.8	-3.13%	-2.66%	
Greece	-387.9	-306.2	-3.92%	-2.22%	
Spain	-154.9	-214.6	-1.24%	-1.21%	

Negative signs mean net receipt of funds from the EU budget. Highlighted countries are the "group of six" net payers.

Sources: For 1998 data: "Welcome, whoever you are," The Economist, 3 October 1998–based on Center for European Policy Studies and Eurostat data. For 2003 data: www.european-democracy.org/archives/2005/06/13/finance-in-perspective. For 2008-13 forecast: "Of Principle and Pragmatism," The Economist, June 25, 2005"–based on Commission data. Following the deal in December, Germany's share is likely understated.

hence the partners' surprise at Schröder's stance can only be understood in the context of a significant change from past behavior.

Interestingly, before the 1999 summit, three dominant themes about the EU budget had been discussed: Britain must give back some of its budgetary rebate that had been negotiated in 1984;[10] France must accept changes to the CAP; and EU funds should not be used to subsidize unfair tax competition.[11] These themes are highlighted here because six years later they would reappear in practically the same form.

When Angela Merkel began her campaign after Schröder's announcement of an early election in May 2005, the European Union budget was already in crisis. Following the failure of the Summit on the Constitution in December 2003, Schröder had used the EU budget as a veiled threat to Poland and Spain, saying, "there were 'certain parallels' between the constitutional and the budget talks."[12] The Luxembourg presidency had not been able to bridge the gap between six net payer states, (Germany, the Netherlands, Sweden, Austria, France and the UK) on the one hand, which wanted to cap the EU budget at 1.00 percent of member states' GDP, and the Commission and other net receiver countries, which argued that with the expansion of the EU in 2004, the EU budget had to grow rather than shrink. The Commission's plan proposed an initial 1.00 percent budget rising to 1.24 percent in seven years. The German newsmagazine *Focus* cited the Finance Ministry as completely against the proposal.[13]

The budget was to have been approved at the 16-17 June 2005 summit but all sides showed no signs of compromise. The primary problems were that the UK refused to give up any of its rebate, and wanted instead to cut the CAP. France, by contrast, said that CAP spending had already been negotiated and cut in the 2002 agreement, and that it would not consider further reductions until that agreement expired in 2013. Schröder's position was consistent with his earlier budget negotiations: it made sense for Germany to be the EU's largest contributor before the economic malaise from German unification had dropped Germany from second richest EU member state according to per capita GDP in the 1980s to 11th place. Poland, taking on the role of spokesman for the other new members, argued it was bad faith for the EU to cut structural funds to the new member states after having let them join with the expectation of receiving aid.

The lack of agreement on the budget at the summit was overshadowed by the shock of the recent referendum failures on the constitution in France and the Netherlands, and, thus, it in and of itself did not create the deep crisis atmosphere. However, the failure to agree at the 11th hour as was usual certainly contributed to a sense of disaster. Moreover, whereas Luxembourg was considered an honest broker, the British presidency which began on July 1 was considered particularly self-interested, and most observers doubted that an agreement on the budget would even be possible.

The platform of Angela Merkel's CDU focused inward more than outward, but she did agree with Schröder on the importance of strict limits on the EU budget.[14] Her tenuous victory in September 2005 left many questions about the general themes of her domestic economic policies in a grand coalition, but no great change in Germany's demands about the EU budget were expected. Thus, it was somewhat of a surprise to find that Merkel was the catalyst to a budget deal at the 16-17 December 2005 summit. "EU Budget: Merkel Emerges as Heroine of Financing Deal," "The German Wallet Saved the EU Budget" were typical headlines after another marathon summit.

In the meeting, Merkel had restrained French President Jacques Chirac on his demands that nothing change except the British rebate, and had received commitments from France and Italy to increase their contributions. She had cajoled a small dent in the British rebate, but it had been her willingness to contribute 1.045 percent of Germany's GDP into the EU budget which made it possible to obtain an agreement. Perhaps the biggest change from Schröder was in negotiation style and largesse. *The Economist* recorded her success:

> But perhaps the most intriguing implications of the budget deal concern the role of Germany ... At previous summits ... Gerhard Schröder, and Jacques Chirac ... agreed on a joint position beforehand, and presented it to the rest ... The dynamics of [this] summit proved very different. There was no Franco-German démarche. Instead, Ms Merkel held meetings with everyone in sight, in parallel with the official talks chaired by the British ... Like her Christian Democrat predecessor as chancellor, Helmut Kohl, she agreed that Germany would finance the lion's share of the increase in the size of the EU budget. And in the end, the final compromise owed more to her proposals than to Britain's original one.[15]

Scarcely a week after the summit victory for Merkel, her government began to use the EU budget victory to combat unfair tax competition. "It cannot be that some countries demand more funds from the EU budget while on the other hand fail to improve their own tax basis,"[16] said German Finance Minister Peer Steinbrück. As unfair EU tax competition had a place in the laboriously negotiated grand coalition document,[17] it was evidence that a Merkel government intended to pursue the issue of tax harmonization, using goodwill from the summit to prepare the way. It remains an open question whether Merkel's negotiation style can get an agreement on this controversial issue during her tenure, as Britain and Ireland now have countries in Central and Eastern Europe to support their position that taxes remain subject to member state vetoes.

Germany's Stability and Growth Pact Issues

The other EU policy that had an important impact on Germany's domestic financial commitments was the Stability and Growth Pact (SGP) that threatened extremely large fines for any country in which an excessive deficit of more than 3 percent of GDP persisted. Ironically, it had been Finance Minister Theo Waigel in 1996 who had proposed the pact, and Germany had been adamant that the fines be automatic rather than requiring political will to implement. Germany had been isolated in that position, however, so the final pact was subject to a political process. In retrospect, this was fortunate because by 2002, Germany was on the receiving end of the excessive deficit procedure, and over the next years would be in violation of the pact.

The final breakdown of the Stability and Growth Pact came in a 25 November 2003 meeting of the Economic and Financial Affairs Council (ECOFIN), when Germany and France defied the other (mostly smaller) EU member states and achieved a majority vote to hold the excessive deficit procedure in abeyance. In essence, this meant stopping the clock on fines and other consequences of not meeting SGP goals. The arguments of the Chirac and Schröder governments was that fiscal policy remained at the member state level and that the Commission was trying to expropriate competences from the nations that had not been formally given.

Austria, the Netherlands, Finland and Spain did not agree and sued the Germans and French before the European Court of Justice, arguing that the Council had not followed the proper procedure. Leaving aside the question of whether the Germans and French had the correct macroeconomic policy (which many observers argued they had), what is key in the context of Schröder's leadership is that he was willing to alienate the smaller member states to such a significant degree. The SGP crisis happened at the same time as the EU constitutional crisis, and in both negotiations, Schröder's approach was that the small countries should have less importance than the Franco-German motor. During the final three months of 2003, Schröder made a number of comments about enhanced cooperation, closer cooperation with France and even allowed Chirac to stand in for him at the October 16 EU summit. The closer cooperation between France and Germany to the exclusion of Britain and the smaller EU member states had certainly been revitalized by the Iraq conflict, but with the constitutional debate and SGP issues it became unnecessarily divisive.

Part of the discussion in the November 2003 European finance ministers' meeting was whether Germany was willfully ignoring its SGP commitments or whether it was being penalized for a situation outside of its control. There was a valid argument that the primary economic justification of the pact had been to prevent member states from increasing the "numerator" and did not ever mean to impact situations where the "denominator" imploded. However, Schröder was never able to fully convince his Council colleagues that his budgets took SGP overshooting seriously and that Germany genuinely intended to live within the pact. Moreover, the small countries had felt threatened by ideas involving a "directoire" of the EU or "pioneer groups" and, thus, when the conflict in the ECOFIN came about, there was little goodwill left with which to bargain. Schröder's similar disregard for the Commission also helped to undermine the necessary trust that might have averted the SGP crisis.

By contrast, in the first four months of the Merkel government, she has gone out of her way to show the Commission and the European Parliament respect, meeting with Jose Manuel Barroso and the President of the European Parliament on the same day as her inaugural meeting with Chirac. It is certainly too early to tell whether she will ultimately maintain close relations to the smaller member states, but if the EU budget summit is an indication, it could be a pattern that closely resembles her erstwhile mentor's, Helmut Kohl.

On the specific issue of the SGP, the CDU was clear about taking the commitment seriously, and explicitly wrote it into the coalition contract that Germany would meet the SGP by 2007 at the latest. Obviously, Merkel's coalition contract is purely rhetorical at this point, but given that her first domestic budget targeted a deficit of 3.3 percent as compared to the 4 percent Schröder left, there are reasons to believe she takes the pact as a more serious constraint. This is all the more unusual because the SGP was watered down following the European Court of Justice's ruling in July 2004 that the member states do, in fact, control fiscal policy. The Commission seemed to have taken Merkel's attempts to lower the deficit as a mitigating factor when it merely warned Germany that it was in breach of the SGP in March 2006 and gave it until 2007 to bring its deficit under 3 percent.[18]

Conclusions

With four months of the grand coalition, it is certainly too early to make definitive judgments about the Merkel-led government's EU policies. There are a few pointers that suggest that she is more committed to working with the smaller countries to achieve consensus and less likely to find ideas of enhanced cooperation or "directoire" notions appealing. She has shown, moreover, that she is willing to forego short-term economic gains in, for example the EU budget or domestic stimulus packages, for the sake of longer term payoffs like tax harmonization. It will be difficult to make too many short-term economic concessions, however, because German public opinion is increasingly restive with respect to the attractiveness of the EU for Germany. If Merkel's leadership style can produce results at the EU level, however, that could translate into higher domestic marks for both the EU and the Merkel government. For the EU, a reprise of Kohl-esque leadership would only be welcome news.

Notes

1. For consistency, throughout this chapter the term European Union (EU) is used to subsume all the other appellations of the collection of integrating states in Europe. Histories of the EU include Alan S. Milward, *The European Rescue of the Nation State,* 2nd ed. (London, 2000); Desmond Dinan, *Ever Closer Union: An Introduction to European Integration* (Boulder, 2003); Derek Urwin, *The Community of Europe: A History of European Integration Since 1945* (New York, 1994): John Gillingham, *European Integration, 1950-2003* (Cambridge, 2003); and Neill Nugent, *The Government and Politics of the European Union,* 5th ed. (Durham, 2003). Works on Germany in Europe specifically include Jeffrey Anderson, *German Unification and the Union of Europe: The Domestic Politics of Integration Policy*

(Cambridge, 1999); Thomas Banchoff, *The German Problem Transformed: Institutions, Politics, and Foreign Policy, 1945-1995* (Ann Arbor, 1999); Simon Bulmer and William Paterson, "Germany in the European Union: Gentle Giant or Emergent Leader?," *International Affairs,* 72, no. 1 (1996); and Peter Katzenstein, *Tamed Power* (Ithaca, 1997).

2. Bulmer and Paterson , see note 1
3. Germany ranked first in absolute amount and second in per capita amount after the Netherlands. See "Welcome, whoever you are," *The Economist,* 3 October 1998.
4. James Sloam, *The European Policies of the German Social Democrats* (New York, 2005). One weakness of Sloam's otherwise excellent book is that it does not systematically address Foreign Minister Fischer's high-level role in EU policy. However, for the purposes of the budget and the SGP issues that this chapter addresses, Fischer's impact was not definitive.
5. Anderson, see note 1, 104
6. On Kohl's isolation on European monetary union, see Wayne Sandholtz, "Choosing Union: Monetary Politics and Maastricht," *International Organization* 47 (1993) and Dorothee Heisenberg, *The Mark of the Bundesbank: Germany's Role in European Monetary Cooperation* (Boulder, 1999).
7. "Being European Paymaster," *Agence France Presse,* 29 December 1998. In the original, the quote was mistranslated as "false with the reckoning."
8. "Twenty-hour talk marathon ends in compromise," *Financial Times,* March 27 1999.
9. Ibid.
10. "German surrender over British rebate; Blair Wins GBP 2Bn Reprieve in Deal to Save Berlin Summit," *Daily Mail,* 22 March 1999.
11. "Germany stirs up row with plans for fiscal harmony," *The Guardian,* 28 December, 1998.
12. "Failure to agree a new EU constitution shows that the goodwill of new members cannot be taken for granted," *Financial Times,* 2 January 2004.
13. "Battle of the Billions," *BBC Monitoring International Reports,* 28 January,2004.
14. "New leaders do not guarantee a new Europe," *Financial Times,* 21 July 2005.
15. Ibid.
16. "German finance minister urges fairer tax competition within EU," *EUObserver,* 30 December 2005.
17. "At the European level, we will demand stronger rules against unfair tax competition," *Gemeinsam für Deutschland. Mit Mut und Menschlichkeit. Koalitionsvertrag von CDU, CSU und SPD,* 82. Available at http://www.cdu.de/doc/pdf/05_11_11_ Koalitionsvertrag_Langfassung_navigierbar.pdf.
18. "EU to Berlin: Reduce deficit or pay penalty; Warning softened by praise for Merkel," *International Herald Tribune,* 1 March 2006.

Chapter 7

The Change in Government and Transatlantic Relations

Jackson Janes

Since the end of World War II, German-American relations have been marked by a total of ten American Presidents and eight German Chancellors. During that half century, those relations evolved from one of conqueror over the vanquished in 1945 to one that in 1989, President George Herbert W. Bush described as a partnership in leadership. Today, almost seventeen years after the Berlin Wall fell, German-American relations represent a mixture of partnership, competition, and a vast network of political, economic and cultural ties that together make up one of the most intensive bilateral relationships on the globe. A cornerstone of the Euro-Atlantic framework, German-American relations remain of critical importance to both sides of the Atlantic. However, the reasons behind this importance have been in continuous transformation, as the interests and the needs of the United States and the Federal Republic of Germany have responded to the demands of a changing environment during the past five decades, especially since the end of the Cold War.

The divided Germany and divided Europe that emerged out of the ashes of 1945 have emerged united and uniting in the twenty-first century, together forming an enormous and unique economic and political force on the world stage. The basis of the transatlantic bargain during the Cold War–the U.S. protected Western Europe from the Soviet forces while European nations became loyal allies of the United States in NATO, the UN, and in a whole range of other institutional settings–has been shifting gradually during the last decade. German unification, the end of the Soviet Union, the incremental formation of a European Union currently with twenty-five members and an expanded NATO membership has altered the geopolitical map of

Notes for this chapter can be found on on page 135.   121

Europe in fundamental ways. While there remains an enormous asymmetric balance across the Atlantic when it is measured by the projection of military force and power, the presence on the world stage of the European Union, the world's largest single internal market with almost 500 million citizens in a political and economic system in which increasing numbers of other nations want to participate, all make the transatlantic relationship a substantially different equation than it was a half century ago.

Throughout this evolution, the story of German-American relations was always a special one. The transformation of Nazi Germany into the Federal Republic was a long term commitment by both German and American leaders, determined to recast the basis of democracy and to forge a firm foundation for a Germany to be fully dedicated to helping rebuild itself and the Europe destroyed during the war. It was also a relationship that was based on understanding and bearing witness to the full legacy of the Holocaust in order to prevent such a horror from ever happening again. Finally, it was based on the belief that Germany's division was not permanent and that Germany and Europe should one day overcome it. All those objectives have been met due, in no small measure, to a continuous and constructive cooperation between Germany and the United States.

Relations over the Atlantic in general are always defined by more than the national leadership and its specific worldview and policy preferences. They are shaped as much by crises, conflicts and confrontations as by cooperation, coordination and a web of shared institutions pointed toward common goals. The incentives for the latter course in policy-making can be driven by self-interests and by recognition that a shared burden can be lighter than carrying it alone. The ways in which confrontations or conflicts are managed depends greatly on the degree of trust underlying the relations between those who are in charge of policy-making. Especially today, when contact between individuals has become far more direct and frequent, leaders and the decisions they make in steering the ship of state can reflect a far more intimate relationship than in the past. When governments change and a new set of leaders emerge on the scene, they are challenged to establish a channel of communication with their counterparts that can be of central importance to both their foreign and domestic policy-making processes. The history of relations between Germany's chancellors and U.S. presidents illustrates that equation and how the choices made on each side of the Atlantic shaped it during the last half century. Overall, it has been a largely successful venture, especially considering the course of the first half of the twentieth century. But there has been a need for adjustments on both sides of the Atlantic all along the way in light of the ever-changing environment.

Angela Merkel has taken the helm of the German ship of state at a time when Germany and the United States need to clarify once again the parameters of partnership and interdependence, cooperation and competition, and the sharing of both burdens and responsibilities in a world that looks very different from that of the recent past. While all her predecessors in office were confronted with their own challenges in forging relations with the United States, Chancellor Merkel has new challenges and choices as she begins her tenure in Berlin. As Germany's first female Chancellor with a biography that reflects the story of German unification like no other leader before her, she brings a unique mixture of skills to a tough job at a critical time for the republic she now leads. How will she compare with her predecessors remains for future historians to contemplate. However, as she begins her term, a look back at the track record is quite useful.

The Record of Relations

The story of the last five decades in German-American relations testifies to more continuity than abrupt changes, largely due to the constraints imposed by the framework of post World War II geopolitics and by self-imposed norms and institutions that both Germans and Americans have placed on that framework. German and American foreign policies on the whole were matched in terms of their mutual needs and capabilities. Germany's commitments to a heavy emphasis on European integration and multilateral ties would mark its path for the four decades leading to unification in 1989.

During his fourteen years in office, Germany's first chancellor, Konrad Adenauer, dealt with three Presidents—Harry Truman, Dwight Eisenhower and John Kennedy—and steered Germany through the first decade of the Cold War into a close relationship with the United States, choosing to direct early efforts toward unification by enveloping it in a firm commitment to NATO, the fledgling European integration movement and many other international bonds all of which would testify to the Federal Republic's intention of being a loyal ally. This strategy also included strong relations with Paris as evidence of Germany's desire to build bridges over the legacy of centuries of European wars, yet an equally pronounced commitment to intimate relations with Washington. Bonn had a vested interest in the constraints it imposed on itself as well as those which were in place due to the legacy of World War II and the emerging European communities in which it wanted so urgently to be included as a way back into the community of nations. As a result, Germany chartered a course that emphasized a multilateral approach to its foreign policy, a belief in shared sovereignty within the European framework, and a willingness to apply all its political and economic resources to achieve those goals. Adenauer knew the price for this and was quite willing to pay it—including joining NATO as soon as it was politically possible and being a core signatory of the Rome Treaty establishing the European Community. These two pillars remained the basis of German foreign policy under Adenauer's successors.

The construction of the Berlin Wall in 1961 generated tensions between Adenauer and Kennedy, underlining how reaction to critical events can be both catalysts for cooperation and conflict. Adenauer and a cross section of the West German leadership at the time— including Willy Brandt—were disappointed at the reluctance of Kennedy to confront the Soviets with force to stop the building of the division through Germany. Yet, it was only a year later that Kennedy arrived in Berlin to give his unforgettable "Ich bin ein Berliner" speech that forever would endear him in the hearts of Germans. The timing and the message of that speech, followed by Kennedy' assassination the following year, generated a strong foundation for German-American relations, a benchmark to which West Germans would point for years to come even in times of tensions across the Atlantic. Fifty years after that speech, a special exhibition about the Kennedy era was presented in Berlin in 2002. The contrast of the lasting affection for Kennedy—despite the division of the Berlin Wall—with the negative attitudes toward his successor, George

W. Bush, is a reminder of how important the images of the American presidency in Germany are and how quickly they can change.

Following Adenauer, relations between chancellors and presidents had their ups and downs. Ludwig Erhard and Kurt-Georg Kiesinger got along with their counterpart, President Lyndon Johnson, who was largely preoccupied with Vietnam and turbulent domestic affairs. Willy Brandt and Richard Nixon were on less friendly terms, especially as Brandt began to engage in his Ostpolitik initiatives, making both Nixon and his National Security Advisor and then Secretary of State, Henry Kissinger, nervous about his relations with both Eastern Europe and Moscow. Following Brandt, Helmut Schmidt got along with President Gerald Ford but thought far less of Jimmy Carter and Ronald Reagan, seeing them as less sophisticated when it came to understanding the nature of international politics. Arguments over how to deal with the Soviets was a constant staple of German-American debates, primarily because the two nations shared such a large stake in the subject. Nevertheless, the premises of German foreign policy for the Federal Republic did not change. Deeper integration in Europe and strong links across the Atlantic remained the cornerstones.

Indeed, it was Schmidt who actually had demanded a response to the installation of Soviet SS 20 missiles in Eastern Europe in the late 1970s, an action that Ronald Reagan later ordered and that generated a huge peace protest wave in Germany. Schmidt's successor Helmut Kohl carried through with Reagan on that policy when he became Chancellor in 1982 and spent the next sixteen years in office cooperating with three presidents in shaping German-American relations. The pinnacle of that long tenure was German unification in 1990 and it was also the apex of German-American relations in the post-World War II era. George H.W. Bush and Helmut Kohl came to represent the bonds of trust and commitment across the Atlantic that led to the end of the division of Germany and eventually of Europe throughout the next decade. This did not exclude transatlantic tensions over Germany's position in Operation Desert Storm in 1991, or over Germany's role in the Balkans as Yugoslavia disintegrated. However, Chancellor Kohl's personal relations with Bush and then President William Clinton remained close as the map of Europe continued to evolve and the Soviet Union's demise signaled the end of the Cold

War. However, structural transformations were beginning to change the reference points of the transatlantic relationship.

The end of that East-West standoff did not generate an immediate successor conflict that generated a clear mandate for the transatlantic alliance. In fact, it signaled a trend toward domestic preoccupation on both sides of the Atlantic. Europe became immersed in its own affairs as the EU moved forward with more treaties and a common currency. In the United States, President Clinton was elected with a primary focus on economic issues at home and an expectation that the end of the Cold War meant the reaping of a huge peace dividend. Yet, events around the globe in Africa, Middle East, the Balkans and the first attempt in 1993 at destroying the World Trade Center in New York kept reminding policy-makers that the world was still a dangerous place for too many people.

By the time Gerhard Schröder became Chancellor in 1998, President Clinton was mired in domestic scandal and an impeachment process, but the two leaders quickly established a good rapport. The discussion of new directions of political reform in Europe resonated with Clinton who enjoyed the discussions he had with his Social Democratic counterpart in Berlin and elsewhere in Europe. The fact that there was a set of hard decisions to be made in the Balkans to deal with Serbia and Kosovo was a challenge for Clinton and Schröder. Yet, in the end, Germany joined the United States in a NATO-led attack on Belgrade without a UN mandate–a decision that would have been unthinkable less than a decade earlier.

By the time Clinton left office, German-American relations seemed to be on an even keel. In the summer of 2000, Gerhard Schröder delivered the speech awarding President Clinton the esteemed Charlemagne prize in Aachen, Germany, and lauding him for his friendship with Germany and Europe.[1] Recalling President Kennedy's "Ich bin ein Berliner" speech, Schröder said that while Kennedy had "won the hearts of all Germans by professing to be a Berliner," through his commitment to the continent Clinton had "become a European." This high benchmark set the stage for the shock Germans then had when the next president acted and talked in a very different manner.

A few months later in 2001, the initial encounter between Gerhard Schröder and George W. Bush was less relaxed, with initial signs of discord over certain policies dealing with climate change, arms control, national missile defense and other issues. But the events of September 11 put those concerns on hold as the world reacted to the attacks in Washington and New York. Schröder's initial response–unlimited solidarity with the U.S.–seemed to reflect the mood of the German nation to identify with the wounded Americans. The moves to help the United States in responding to the attacks suggested that the U.S. could rely on solid support throughout Germany and Europe in the effort to stop terrorism.

Yet by the summer of 2002, things were beginning to go seriously wrong. Schröder and Bush met in Berlin that May to discuss the simmering problems of terrorist threats and also the issue of whether Iraq was a source of that terror. Bush's rhetoric was already causing negative reactions in the German public but his speech in the Reichstag seemed to make a reasoned argument to join in the effort to fight terrorism as a shared responsibility. While there appeared to be agreement on how to proceed, the next few months saw the unraveling of the relationship between the two men and their governments as the United States prepared for war against Baghdad.

That conflict was more than the story of confrontation over the decision to remove Saddam Hussein from power. And it was more than the story of two leaders, Bush and Schröder, who lost confidence and trust in each other. Rather, it was a signal that the changes which had been occurring across the Atlantic since the end of the Cold War and the trauma experienced by the United States following 9/11 were having consequences in the ways through which German-American relations were being perceived, shaped and discussed. It was also about the changing range of choices German chancellors and American presidents confronted in dealing with foreign policy and relations across the Atlantic. This has as much to do with changing geopolitical constellations as with domestic politics in the post-post-Cold War period.

On one level, the transatlantic security bargain gradually has lost its central role for Germany and the United States: Soviet troops no longer threaten Germany's borders. American forces in Germany have been reduced drastically because they are needed elsewhere. In turn, the value of Berlin and of Germany as a military ally to the United States began to diminish, in part due to the enormous expansion of American force projection around the world. For Americans, the Fulda Gap–the location in the middle of Germany that witnessed the massing of troops because it was considered the most likely invasion route if Warsaw Pact forces ever came west–was now in many places around the world.

At another level, the transformation of the domestic framework in both countries, particularly the unification of Germany and the relocation of the capital to Berlin, as well as the shift in foreign policy priorities in the United States, came with an increased polarization at home and abroad. Public arguments over the Atlantic concerning the death penalty, the International Criminal Court or climate change became a larger and nosier part of the German-American dialogue. The importance of international institutions, such as the United Nations as an example of the rule of law and legitimacy among nations, is much greater in Europe than in many corners of the American political debate. The forces behind the European integration process were acting as a strengthening centripetal force on the member states of the European Union, even if there remain serious arguments about how that process should be steered–exemplified by debate over the constitutional proposals. Along with many of their European neighbors and energized by the dislike of President Bush, Germans increasingly emphasized the need for more autonomy from America. Meanwhile, American critics of Europe and Germany saw the transatlantic dialogue as a hindrance to needed policies and decisions. In short, the constraints of the Cold War's web of interdependence seemed to be loosening while the choices and alternatives to the old web remained unclear.

While the American administration was stressing the need for a "coalition of the willing," the European response was on the need for consensus. The clash over principles and policies seem to escalate around the Iraq war. At the time, CDU leader Angela Merkel was voicing her opinion that the war to remove Hussein was justified, winning her much criticism from her German domestic audiences and much approval from the Bush White House. But, the longer term impact of the transatlantic clash over Iraq would generate serious questions about the meaning of security, the definition of terrorism, the use and legitimacy of force in responding to it, and how we identify the global threats and responses to them.

Enter Angela Merkel

In light of this background, how will the Federal Republic of Germany's eighth chancellor shape the German-American dialogue? How much does personality count in managing change in the transatlantic relationship? How much structural adjustment is still ahead of us? And how much change and continuity will we see in the Merkel government's foreign policy?

Following the first visit of Chancellor Merkel to Washington in early 2006, the stage appeared to have been reset for the German-American dialogue. While there was a clear effort to change the tone of that dialogue, there was also recognition that there would be continuity in key areas of German foreign policy. Issues that will require careful coordination and collaboration in the coming months will begin to test the staying power of the dialogue between Washington and Berlin. Part of that test will be shaped by the domestic arenas on both sides of the Atlantic, and another part of it will be seen in the immediate foreign policy challenges and decisions that lie ahead.

During the press conference following Chancellor Merkel's visit to Washington in early January, it was amusing to hear the President mention how one thing he has in common with the Chancellor is that neither one of them was elected with a landslide majority, a moment of unusual candor from George W. Bush.[2] The observation does point at the difficult task for both leaders in crafting a consensus at home while trying to do the same among allies. Just as President Bush is facing increasing criticism of his policies and decisions, and not only from the Democratic Party, Chancellor Merkel will be facing tough scrutiny both from the opposition and also from some of her own coalition members.

Germany is in the midst of reshaping its consensus on economic and social policies at home and facing the consequences of an increasingly competitive world market in which it has consistently been a winner. The equations of the social and market dimensions of German society are being rebalanced to keep up with changes in German society, such as its demographic dips in population, immigration inflows and challenges to its traditional strength as a manufacturing nation. What worked during the last five decades in managing these tasks may not work the same way in the twenty-first century. Discussing those issues is tough. Making tough decisions is Merkel's challenge, but needs to be done without overly exacerbating a sense of winners and losers in the process—a challenge for any political leader. Despite the fact that Merkel's coalition has a large majority in the Bundestag and the Bundesrat, policy-making may still be particularly hard within the coalition she now leads, given the strains within each of the parties as well as between them in making this grand coalition work. A much needed economic recovery can be stymied by political gridlock, something that would prevent the reforms Germany needs if it is to lift itself and Europe out of the economic malaise of the recent past. The chancellor can first measure her progress in the spring of 2006 when she faces three state elections, which will give her an idea as to how the public perceives her policies and her persona. Similarly, President Bush is anticipating the November 2006 Congressional elections as a measure of where his policies will leave the Republican hold on Washington two years before he leaves office. Neither leader can be assured of positive outcomes.

Given the intensity of the domestic political debates in Germany and the United States, it will not be surprising if they also impact the German-American dialogue. The chancellor has referred to the increasing importance of the global marketplace, which increases competitive clashes and the risks of protectionism—issues that will impact domestic and foreign policy decisions on both sides of the Atlantic. The race for the aerospace market between Boeing and Airbus is an often cited example of this transatlantic competition. Germany's central role as the largest economy in the European Union and the enormous importance of the EU for German economic interests will continue to make the transatlantic relationship a field of competitive challenges, often marked by disputes over regulatory policies. Issues involving trade policies with other countries and regions, particularly in Asia, will be long-term competitive agenda items. On the other hand, the enormous amount of investment moving in both directions across the Atlantic—reflecting over half the global trade flows—will require increasing efforts to deal with subsidies, export controls, and environmental regulations if that flow is to grow further. Germany's role in the major organizations dealing with these questions, from the European Union to the WTO, the World Bank or the IMF, to name only a few, remains a critical one for the U.S.

Part of the debates in Germany will also include a growing need to think through its foreign policy roles and responsibilities and to make that a part of a national dialogue. After the final resolution of the election and Merkel's appointment as chancellor, there was a good deal of German discussion (and concern) that American expectations of the chancellor and Germany might exceed capabilities. However, Merkel herself has said that Germany must accept its responsibilities as well as its limits. Among the responsibilities, she has committed Germany to continuing its presence in Afghanistan, Kosovo, Bosnia and elsewhere outside the traditional European theater. She has stated that Germany will continue to make its contribution to the NATO Response Force, even though defense spending will not increase significantly as long as the domestic arguments about economic policies remain paramount. While there is no expectation that she will set different parameters for German military forces with regard to Iraq, she has indicated that assistance to the Iraqi government will continue in various other forms such as debt relief and training programs.

Merkel has also stated that she envisions NATO to be the primary forum for discussion of issues and decisions in the future, before action is taken by the membership. She has publicly criticized the neglect of NATO as such a forum in the recent past and has called for a new debate to determine the Alliance's mission, its obligations and its limitations. At the same time she has called for a stronger channel of communication between NATO and the European Union, illustrated by her visit to both organizations on her first trip as chancellor to Brussels. How that evolves depends on the willingness of both sides to find common ground, process and resources. Merkel has also indicated that she sees continuing need to seek reform of the United Nations and has not backed away from a more prominent role for Germany within the Security Council, without immediately putting it on the front political burner. All of these directions represent more continuity than change in German foreign policy, with most of these precepts clearly outlined during Schröder's tenure. The fact that Merkel's foreign minister, Frank-Walter Steinmeier, was Schröder's chief of staff for seven years in the chancellery, suggests that he embodies such continuity. Yet, there is no doubt that as Chancellor Merkel confronts new challenges in office, both her style and substantive debates will define whether and how she will differ from her predecessor.

Merkel needs to confront the issue of German influence and power as it pursues its foreign policy goals. Given the key position and role Germany has within Europe and in the path of European integration, as well as its global engagement, Germany has been able to pursue a successful foreign policy primarily by forging consensus and coalitions through the many institutional and multilateral tools it used. It was also based on a set of mutual expectations shared by both European partners and the United States. That consensus-building process has been weakened in the recent past in part due to the fragmentation of the foreign policy process within Germany and in the European Union. Germany's ability to generate a consensus within the EU has been reduced by its weakened ability to deliver resources exemplified by the inability to meet its own obligations through its debt and budget constraints. Its ability to forge a consensus with the United States has also been weakened by both significant change of course in American foreign policy, but also by the choices Germany made in response to that change, be it with regard to the war in Iraq, the effort to secure a permanent seat on the UN Security Council or a number of other issues resulting in friction across the Atlantic. How Merkel can manage these developments and steer a foreign policy course in an environment which presents an increasing proliferation of issues and actors involved at many levels will be a significant challenge.

An immediate test case is the response to Iran's nuclear ambitions. During the coming years, this issue will dominate a good deal of the discussion on both sides of the Atlantic. How we think about this challenge—and there may be more proliferation problems in the future—will be important in defining how close the Euro-Atlantic alliance will remain. Again, it will also be an opportunity for defining how our domestic debates can be more closely linked on these issues in the future. This issue can be an opportunity for Berlin and Washington to find common ground. Yet, it also represents the danger of another clash if the potential for military action against Iran comes part of the dialogue. Another area which will require close collaboration is the path of the Israeli-Palestinian negotiations following the election victory of Hamas and the unresolved question of a post-Sharon Israel. Germany's special role in this troubled region will make coordination between Washington and Berlin particularly important. The larger circle of the Middle East nations makes that part of the world a long-term shared agenda for Europe and the United States.

The long-term battle against terrorism will also mark Merkel's agenda. She has made it clear that we need to talk through our policies and perspectives, overlapping and divergent, without losing sight of shared values. She also stressed the need to restate a common commitment to those values but also to ask ourselves what that means in the new environment of a new century. That includes talking about concerns relating to the policies we follow in battling the dangers of terrorism, including the treatment of prisoners in that battle, and how and when both sides need to pool resources in sharing information and intelligence. Merkel has not wasted time in testing those waters with references to her concerns about the future of the Guantanamo prisons or the controversy over renditions of prisoners in European networks.

Merkel and Bush found common ground in talking about securing both freedom and security. Getting the policy mix right will be a goal both sides share, but will also require that attention is paid to respective debates about how to get there successfully. Some of our instruments in dealing with these challenges need to be retooled. This will involve making sure that there is a common vocabulary when the two sides talk—a serious problem in the past few years across the Atlantic. Indeed, many may think that they mean the same thing in discussing issues like terrorism, freedom or security, but often the partners have been talking past each other. During the past decade, there have been a series of developments that have changed the ways Germany and the United States relate to each other. As Germany unified, the European Union expanded, and the United States emerged in the twenty-first century as both all-powerful and still vulnerable, the web of interdependence has been transformed. No longer dependent on the protection of the American military to help defend its borders from Soviet tanks, Germany is now helping others to defend themselves. In addition, the central importance of the European Union for German domestic and foreign policy planning is expanding. For historical and current reasons, Germany needs the EU. The question is whether that need can be balanced with the connections with Washington at a time when U.S. foreign policies are increasingly aimed well beyond Europe. Indeed, there are many areas in which Germany and the United States find common cause, and still others that they can disagree on without risking a total meltdown of the relationship. Resolutions of such controversies will be based on respect, trust and a sense of common purpose, articulated by the leadership on both sides of the Atlantic.

During Merkel's tenure as chancellor, German-American relations will have numerous opportunities to mark milestones of post-World War II success stories. The sixtieth anniversary of the Berlin airlift will occur in 2007, the year during which Germany will have the rotating presidency of the European Union and will host the G-8 summit. One year later, the same anniversary of the Marshall Plan takes place and in 2009, six decades of the Federal Republic of Germany can be celebrated along with the twentieth anniversary of the fall of the Berlin Wall. Those reminders of the success stories in the early years of the postwar German-American relationship should not be occasions for nostalgic looks back in history, but rather catalysts for discussions about how we can continue to build on them in a very different environment today.

Angela Merkel has stated clearly that she sees a stronger Europe and a stronger transatlantic relationship as two sides of the same coin. While that has been the mantra of many chancellors before her, she has a unique opportunity to help define actively what it means today. In setting the priorities and the course of German foreign policy while engaging in an honest and candid dialogue with Washington, Angela Merkel will be building on a mixture of continuity and change within the German debate about its European and global roles and responsibilities. She will be addressing the interests and needs Germany claims for itself as well as those that it shares with other nations, especially with its European neighbors and with the United States. While the parameters of interdependence across the Atlantic continue to be transformed, the bonds within the European Union will continue to exert a comprehensive pull and push on all its members, redefining relations among them and with the United States. Germany's voice as one of the main architects and engineers in this ongoing construction process will be of central importance. That voice now is Angela Merkel's. Many across the world, but particularly in Washington, will be listening intently to what she says.

Notes

1. Laudation of Chancellor Gerhard Schröder at the awards ceremony of the Charlemagne Award for President Bill Clinton, June 2, 2000 at: http://www.karl-spreis.de/html/frame.html
2. See the text of the joint news conference at : http://www.whitehouse.gov/ news/releases/ 2006/01/20060113-1.html

Chapter 8

Honecker's Revenge

The Enduring Legacy of German Unification in the 2005 Election

Jeffrey Kopstein and Daniel Ziblatt

At first glance, any analysis of contemporary Germany would seem to require only minimally thinking about the former German Democratic Republic (GDR). For most East Germans, life in the GDR is increasingly a distant memory and unification has been a resounding success. Whether judged by productivity growth, aggregate incomes, air and water quality, or political freedom, East Germans have benefited enormously from joining the united German state. East and West Germans share similar patterns of work and leisure, they are represented by the same trade unions and employer associations, and they divide their votes among the same palette of political parties. In fact, the shadow of the communist past appears so far removed that Erich Honecker, the former General Secretary of the Socialist Unity Party (SED), is more likely today to be the object of quiet laughter or pity rather than fear or hatred.

Yet, a core lesson of Germany's federal election in September 2005 is that the communist past has in fact an enduring legacy in East Germany, a legacy that substantially shapes politics in unified Germany. Fifteen years after unification, the crucial difference in German politics still lies in the East. Indeed, at one level, the Bundestag election of September 2005 simply demonstrated, as did the 2002 result, the presence of an east-west divide in German party politics. As in 2002, any party that hopes to win at the federal level must perform well in the very different circumstances of the East.

But beyond observing that parties must win the "East" to capture the prize of national office, a particularly ironic and less frequently

---

noted feature of Germany's east-west electoral divide can explain what is perhaps the most puzzling outcome of the federal election of 2005: the failure of the two major parties to garner at least 70 percent of the vote for the first time since 1949. To some, the decay in Germany's party system indicated by the simultaneous fall in support for *both* major parties simply seems to be an aligning of German trends with those in other democracies, such as France, Canada, Italy, and Great Britain. Corruption scandals, the importance of the mass media as opposed to party organizations in mobilizing voters, disputes over welfare reform, and declining rates of unionization all, according to most accounts, have reduced the importance of political parties in established democracies.[1] The latest developments in Germany, so the argument goes, are part of a broader trend, reflected in public opinion beginning in the 1970s and fortified by the breakthrough of the Greens in the 1980s, in which Germany is no longer so different from other advanced democracies.

As compelling as this logic is, our chapter offers an alternative argument: the decay in Germany's party system reflected in the decline in support for both major parties is a direct outgrowth of German unification in 1989-90. Absent unification, Germany's previously robust party system would have remained entirely intact. Decisive in this regard is the presence of two distinctive but now overlapping electorates. One electorate was produced by fifty years of capitalism and the other by fifty years of communism. In arguing this we build on the work of Herbert Kitschelt who first identified this pattern in a seminal article forecasting postcommunist party systems.[2] For Kitschelt, the central question was whether party systems in the postcommunist world would be more or less "coherent" (defined as a system of clearly articulated party positions). The case of unified Germany suggests that two party systems that are coherent in different ways can, in combination, produce decay when unified.

In what follows, we first place the changes in Germany's party system in cross-national perspective. We then propose the argument that Germany's party system decay is a direct result of the 1989-90 unification and the long term legacy of the communist experience in East Germany. In the final part, we reflect on the broader significance of our argument for German politics.

The Decay of Germany's Party System: Evidence and Existing Explanations

In the federal parliamentary elections of 2005, the two largest parliamentary groupings, the Social Democratic Party (SPD) and the Christian Democratic Union/Christian Social union (CDU/CSU), failed jointly to receive 70 percent of the vote for the first time since 1949. Why is this simultaneous decline of the two major parties at the center of the Germany party system so surprising and important? When viewed in historical and comparative perspective, it is arguable that the decline of Germany's two leading parties is an indicator of larger problems in the party system itself. First, since the 1950s, West Germany's party system has been one marked by unusual stability, continuity, and high degrees of institutionalization. As Figure One indicates, the so-called "two-and-half party system" (CDU/CSU, SPD, and the Free Democratic Party (FDP)) emerged in the 1950s via an unprecedented *concentration* of political competition in which smaller parties were eliminated, the seat share of the two leading parties grew rapidly, and a nearly bipolar party system was established.

Figure 1: Percentage Change in SPD and CDU/CSU's Total Share of Seats from Previous Election

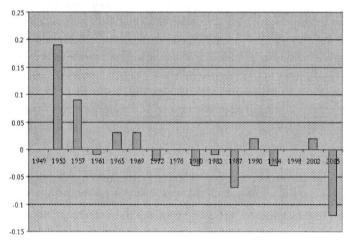

Source: Bundeswahlleiter, 2005

The concentration of the party system into two major parties was one of the hallmarks of democratic consolidation and was the result of a series of fusions on the Right (between catholic and conservative parties) and on the Left, indicating that the historical legacy of Weimar–to the surprise of many of the participants themselves–could be overcome.[3] As Figure One also demonstrates, during the 1980s, the trend towards ever-greater concentration was undermined by the emergence of the Greens on the electoral stage. Yet, despite the appearance of the new Green party on the scene, the biggest single drop-off in support for the two major parties occurred in 2005, a moment when no new major party, except for the renamed Party of Democratic Socialism (PDS)/Left coalition–had appeared on the scene. In short, the most precipitous decline of Germany's two main parties in postwar history occurred in the absence of a serious electoral threat, making the election of 2005 historically unprecedented.

But does this simply bring Germany in line with other advanced democracies, marking Germany's transition to a "normal" democracy? Indeed, at first glance, this appears to be the case. When viewed comparatively, West Germany's party system has been unusually stable among advanced democratic states. Whether measured in terms of electoral volatility, voter turnout, or the institutionalization of the parties themselves, Germany's party system has been consistently stable and marked by high levels of continuity. In the wake of Weimar and the failure of democracy in the interwar period, that Germany's two leading parties could consistently garner such a major proportion of the vote was taken to be a major indicator of political success. In Figure Two, we see when viewed in cross-national perspective, across the entire postwar period, the two leading parties in Germany consistently received a major share of the vote, outperforming similar democratic states.

Moreover, it is likely Figure Two in fact understates the stability of the German party system. Whereas those that counted as the "leading parties" changed in Sweden, the Netherlands, France, and Canada, the same two parties–the CDU/CSU and the SPD–were always on the scene in Germany.

The comparative data might simply be telling us that Germany's party system is converging with other democracies, succumbing to similar pressures of party system decay. But such an argument does

Figure 2: Share of Votes Receved by Two-Top Scoring Parties in
Parliamentary Elections, Late 1950s-Late 1990s

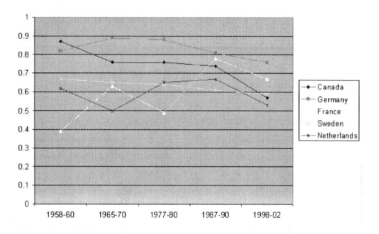

Source: Lijphart Electoral Archive, 2005

not tell us precisely why this is happening. In addition, there is evidence that strongly suggests that Germany's particularly robust parties would have remained intact had it not been for unification. For
one thing, Germany's major parties had survived scandals that had
decimated similar parties in other contexts. In this regard, it is worth
comparing the impact of two revealingly analogous corruption scandals on the Christian Democrats in Italy and Germany. Both came
to light immediately after the end of the Cold War and both
involved the intersection of private money, public contracts, and the
financing of political parties. Whereas the Italian Christian Democrats were wiped out electorally by these scandals, the most that can
be said for their impact on the CDU is that, after the humiliation of a
several old party stalwarts, such as Helmut Kohl and Wolfgang
Schäuble, it moved into respectable opposition.[4]

The Christian Democrats were also able to survive the move of
the Social Democrats to the center of the political spectrum during
the 1990s. Here the interesting comparison is with the British conservatives, who were crippled by Tony Blair's deft movement away
from the Left. To this day, Conservatives have yet to find a viable
ideological alternative and remain in disarray. By contrast, the CDU

when confronted with a similar though perhaps less emphatic move to the center by former Chancellor Gerhard Schröder's SPD, stood by its position at the center of Germany's political spectrum, did not engage in self-destructive internal infighting over the fundamental direction of the party (this, despite keen competition among the provincial party bosses for control of the party), and remained poised to take back power when the SPD faltered.

Although reeling from its loss in the current election, there is no sign that the Social Democrats are ready to self-destruct. They, too, remain ready to capture a large swath of votes should another election be called. What is disorganizing German party politics is not a decreasing coherence of internal party organization. Rather it is the unwillingness of German voters to vote for either of these two parties in large enough numbers to grant either of them governing status with parties that are ideologically close enough to enact coherent public policies.

The East-West Divide

What then has driven German's party system into relative disarray? Our central argument is that there is a fundamental *disjuncture* between Germany's party system and its electorate. While party systems may not be "frozen," as Seymour Martin Lipset and Stein Rokkan long ago argued, they do reflect the cleavages out of which they develop.[5] As a result, it is not surprising that the contemporary German party system reflects postwar West German society and only awkwardly fits the context of a unified Germany. In other words, taken as a whole, Germany's electorate is deeply divided between East and West; the failure of the leading parties to sustain their nearly oligopolistic support reflects this new reality. Consider the final results of the 2005 election broken down between East and West, as seen in Table One below

What these numbers reveal is that had West Germany been on its own, a stable and familiar CDU-FDP coalition would have been possible, with an equally plausible Red-Green alternative waiting in the wings. The Left Party would not have crossed the 5 percent threshold. From the standpoint of politics, things would be very much "the way they used to be" in pre-1989 West Germany. In the East, on the other

Table 1: Election Results in West and East Germany 2005

West German Election Results, 2005	East German Election Results, 2005
SPD: 35.1%	SPD: 30.5%
CDU: 37.5%	CDU: 25.3%
Greens: 8.8%	Greens: 5.1%
FDP: 10.2%	Left Party: 25.4%
Left: 4.9%	Others: 5.8%
Others: 3.5%	

Source: Bundeswahlleiter, 2005

hand, neither the CDU nor the SPD could have constructed a viable coalition without the presence of the Left Party which actually outperformed the CDU–a reality totally unfamiliar in the history of Western Germany. Whereas in the West, the most stable coalition would have been a bourgeois dominated CDU-FDP, in the East the most stable coalition would have been a "red-red," SPD-Left Party dominated government. In other words, the two parts of Germany each have the potential for a coherent party system but taken together they do not. What is the basis for these two distinctive party systems?

Two Underlying Social Structures

In his work on party systems, Herbert Kitschelt identifies two primary cleavages that drive party politics. As summarized in Figure Three below, one cleavage concerns the preferred mode of the distribution of resources in society. Citizens either prefer markets or state distribution of resources. The second cleavage concerns a narrow or broader notion of citizenship. Citizens either prefer a liberal-cosmopolitan or a strong conservative-particularist orientation to political membership.

In the transition to capitalism, those favoring market modes of resource distribution find affinity with those oriented toward liberal-cosmopolitan orientations to membership and authority. Those favoring state redistribution, such as the Tory socialists, also tended to be conservative and even particularist in their notions of citizenship. In this type of polity, though voters are generally distributed along the "early modern" axis of competition, Kitschelt argues that the bulk of voters are found in the lower left quadrant. In advanced

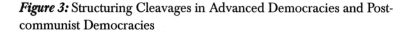

Figure 3: Structuring Cleavages in Advanced Democracies and Post-communist Democracies

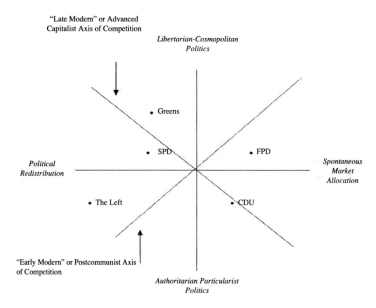

capitalist societies, by contrast, the primary cleavage structure shifts; as capitalism becomes the status quo, those favoring market modes of resource distribution become more conservative and particularist in political orientation and those favoring state-redistribution, such as social democrats, articulate more inclusive conceptions of political membership and cultural policy. Though voters are located along the "late modern" axis of competition in this type of polity, the bulk of voters are now found in the upper-left quadrant.

Kitschelt's model is a simple one in which social structure determines cleavage structures. But the argument does point to a sharp electoral dilemma facing Germany's leading political parties. On the one hand, it is the latter, developed capitalist form of cleavage structure that was characteristic of most of Western Europe, including West Germany in 1989 and today. It is thus not surprising that the western-based parties that developed their ideologies in this context today still find themselves along this "late modern" cleavage. Based on the parties' stances taken during the 2005 campaign, Figure Three places the main German political parties along the two

143

ideological dimensions.[6] Since political parties are not infinitely flexible and are constrained by their past positions, that the major German political parties remain largely along a West German cleavage makes sense. Moreover, what is striking is that when one looks at the 2005 campaign, one sees clearly the failure of FDP and Greens as well as—to a lesser extent the CDU and SPD—to move away effectively from this cleavage to mobilize eastern voters.

By contrast, as Kitschelt argues, the nature of early postcommunist social structures, as found in East Germany and the rest of Eastern Europe, was much more akin to that of the early capitalist era than that found in contemporary Western Europe. As we see in Figure Three, it is the Left Party—rooted in the East—that finds itself along this "early modern" axis, and as a result, outperforms all the western parties in the East with the exception of the SPD. But, two crucial questions remain: first, why did it take so long after 1990 for the distinctive eastern cleavage to emerge? And, second, what is the structural basis of Eastern distinctiveness? With regards to the first question, as a recent study by Kai Arzheimer and Jürgen Falter[7] argue, the East-West electoral divide is not so new and has, in fact, been present throughout the 1990s, characterized by three persistent attributes: lower voter turn-out, greater electoral volatility, and a gradual rejection of western parties. While the frenzied unification period of 1990 may have resulted in support for the CDU, the PDS/Left Party has been making consistent gains ever since. In that sense, the electoral behavior of eastern voters has differentiated them from western voters since 1990. Though the divide is deep and persistent, it is in 2005 that the two party systems have most clearly manifested themselves.

A second important question is the following: What is the basis of this distinctive cleavage in the East? Broadly speaking, as economic historians of East Germany have noted pointedly, capitalism and industrialism are very different.[8] Although East Germany was by Western standards over-industrialized, on the eve of its transition to capitalism, it completely lacked a capitalist middle class. Much of the human capital geared toward success in a communist economy was devalued overnight because of the rapidity of the transition. West German production could easily cover existing East German demand, and wages in the East outpaced productivity growth, ensuring that private investment remained low even when the infusion of public funds remained high. The result was a largely stagnant social structure that much more resembled the "early modern" than the "late modern" model. Unlike the other countries of postcommunist Europe, which were forced overnight to develop their native capitalist classes, this was not the case in East Germany. It is not surprising then that the prevailing moral economy and political orientations of the communist period should have hung on with a tenacity in East Germany that exceeded their postcommunist neighbors in either Poland or the Czech Republic.

The strength of the divergent orientations on economic and cultural issues between East and West Germans has been demonstrated convincingly and repeatedly by survey researchers. On cultural issues, as is the case in other postcommunist contexts, East Germans are systematically less religious and less cosmopolitan than their West German counterparts.[9] On the question of preferences for different modes of resource distribution, Alberto Alesina and Nicola Fuchs-Schündeln show in an exhaustive study of household panel data from East and West Germany, using a wide range of control variables, that living under communist institutions has rendered East Germans much more favorable to redistribution and state intervention in the economy than West Germans.[10] These findings remain robust even when controlling for economic position and incentives. Alesina and Fuchs-Schündeln find that although the fifteen years since unification have witnessed change in East German economic preferences, this change is taking place very gradually. Based on current trends, they calculate that it will take between one and two generations for East and West German preferences to converge completely.

Seen in terms of Kitschelt's model, while East Germans have quickly and easily come to develop a party system with the same palette of political parties as in the West, the East German social structure and its underlying values have generated a political cleavage structure that is much more in line with the early modern than the late modern period. The result, therefore, is an overall party system that is coherent in the West and coherent in the East but incoherent as a whole when combined into one country.

The strategic consequence for political parties confronting this split electorate is that they face a series of dilemmas: electoral appeals directed to western voters offend eastern voters, as only most prominently seen in the missteps of figures such as the Bavarian Minister President Edmund Stoiber whose populist appeals to Westerners inevitably offended East Germans. Conversely, electoral messages aimed to mobilize eastern voters fail to excite western voters. Small parties have dealt with the dilemma in a sensible fashion: the FDP and Greens appeal to Western voters and largely make no effort at mass appeal in the East, receiving together less than 8 percent of the vote in the new Länder. Similarly, the Left/former PDS, despite Oskar Lafontaine's efforts to broaden the appeal of the party, failed to make any headway in the West. Indeed, the Left Party felt so constrained that they had to draw upon a second "tenor," East German stalwart Gregor Gysi, in order to conduct a second campaign, as it were, in the East. As the SPD and the CDU/CSU pursue their national ambitions, they find they are stuck on the horns of a dilemma that has weakened the core of Germany's party system.

Conclusion

As Gerhard Schröder exited the unusually tumultuous political stage in the fall of 2005, one fact was clear–the normally highly composed world of German party politics had become quite a messy affair. Pundits excitedly discussed the possibility of such exotic governing coalitions as the so-called "Jamaica Coalition" of Greens, CDU, and Liberals (FDP), or the possibility of a "traffic light coalition" of SPD, Greens, and FDP. Unusual in German postwar history, this jumbled state of affairs that generated a grand coalition will not simply dissolve under the apparently stable partnership of the two largest parties in Germany. Rather, German politics has become fundamentally more complex, reflecting a new postunification political reality that has taken fifteen years for analysts and politicians to recognize. The disjuncture of a party system created in postwar West Germany and an electorate created in a divided Germany is a phenomenon that will shape German politics in important and possibly unanticipated ways.

Nevertheless, we can ask: what are the most important potential implications of "Honecker's revenge" for German politics? First and most immediately, Germany's leading parties must come to terms with the new electoral reality facing them. Just as the "South" has shaped a generation of Republican-Democratic Party battles in the United States, the Social Democrats and Christian Democrats must develop electoral strategies that effectively manage the East-West electoral divide. It was, after all, the U.S. Republican Party's effective deployment of a "Southern strategy" beginning in the early 1970s that has generated that party's domination of American politics for nearly a generation. Whichever party—CDU or SPD—can adopt a compelling "eastern" strategy might find itself in a similar position. Although after 1949 the Federal Republic pursued an aggressive strategy of creating a rough material equality between various Länder, changing international economic conditions and the unmanageable costs of unification indicate that the post-1989 Berlin Republic will in one respect return Germany to its prewar condition: a country of marked regional economic disparities. This transformation of one important feature of West Germany by the act of unification will have long-term consequences for party politics.

The second implication of "Honecker's revenge" for German politics is that it is unclear whether the "solution" settled upon for the time being—a grand coalition—will deal effectively with the divide. Even though Germans have elected their first Eastern (and female) chancellor, the current grand coalition seems as much of a holding action to preserve what is left of the party system of the Bonn Republic as it is an adaptation to the conditions of the Berlin Republic. Neither the Greens, nor the FDP, nor the Left Party/PDS constitute opposition parties that most Germans feel could rule the country reasonably. Germany is thus left in a grand coalition without a "shadow cabinet" or an opposition that the broad public could turn to should the CDU-SPD government falter. Seen in this way, Germany's current grand coalition will suffer from the same weaknesses as all "consosciational" arrangements in which most large interest groups are included in the spoils arising from the division of power.

The final implication of "Honecker's revenge" is that compared to its eastern neighbors, East Germany's initial "comparative advantages" that included a generous western "sponsor" may turn out to hinder the political and economic transitions that have been homegrown and hence more successful in countries like the Czech Republic and Poland. From the standpoint of development economics,

East Germany is now saddled with high wages, lagging productivity, and low levels of private investment. The postcommunist countries bordering Germany, by contrast, as full members of the European Union have benefited from their low wages and (comparatively) low taxes within a highly competitive and integrated continental market. Sixteen years after unification, it appears obvious to most Germans, East and West, that no amount of public transfers from the West to the East will succeed in kick-starting the East German economy in the way that has already occurred in Germany's East-Central European neighbors.

Even more important than the economic advantages of backwardness, however, is the sense of "ownership" that Poles, Czechs, and Hungarians have over their postcommunist transformations, something completely lacking in East Germany. For all of the missteps and failures of the postcommunist transition in East-Central Europe, the citizens of these countries can still plausibly tell themselves that what happened in 1989 was a restoration of popular sovereignty. Even the choice to join the European Union was not experienced as a loss of control over their collective fates but as a choice for Europe. In Germany, by contrast, half way through the second decade after unification, most East Germans, even the majority who still believe that there was no alternative to a single Germany, have not regained a sense of control over their lives. Honecker's revenge is the reflection of this sustained collective sense of difference in the still divided party landscape of united Germany.

Notes

1. Ronald Inglehart, "Postmaterialist Values and the Erosion of Institutional Authority," in *Why People Don't Trust Government*, eds. Joseph S. Nye, Philip D. Zelikow and David C. King (Cambridge, 1997); Russell Dalton, ed., *Parties without Partisans: Political Change in Advanced IndustrialDemocracies* (Oxford, 2001).
2. Herbert Kitschelt, "The Formation of Party Systems in East-Central Europe," *Politics and Society*, 20, no.1 (1992): 7-50.
3. Gerhard Lehmbruch, *Parteien Wettbewerb im Bundesstaat* (Wiesbaden, 2000).

4. For an account of the dynamics of adaptation inside the CDU after the fall of Kohl, see Ludger Helms "Is there Life after Kohl? The CDU Crisis and the Future of Party Democracy in Germany," *Government and Opposition*, 35, no.2 (2000): 419-438. It is of course worth noting that between Italy and Germany there were important differences in the nature and scope of the political scandals as well as public expectations of acceptable behavior. Nevertheless, that the CDU survived its own crisis essentially unscathed points to the durability of the German party system.

5. Seymour M. Lipset and Stein Rokkan, eds., *Party Systems and Voter Alignments: Cross-National Perspectives* (New York, 1967).

6. Andranik Tangian, "German parliamentary elections 2005 in the mirror of party manifestos," Hans Boeckler Foundation, Discussion Paper Nr. 139E, January 2006.

7. Kai Arzheimer and Jürgen Falter, "Goodbye Lenin? Bundes- und Land-tagswahlen seit1990: eine Ost-West-Perspektive" in *Wahlen und Wähler. Analysen aus Anlaß der Bundestagswahl 2002,* (Wiesbaden, 2002), 244-283.

8. Jeffrey Kopstein, *The Politics of Economic Decline in East Germany,* 1945-1989 (Chapel Hill, 1997).

9. Robert J. Barro and Rachel McCleary, "Religion and Political Economy in anInternational Panel," NBER Working Paper No.8931, 2002.

10. Alberto Alesina and Nicola Fuchs-Schündeln, "Good Bye Lenin (or Not?): The Effect of Communism on People's Preferences." NBER Working Paper No. 11700, 2005.

Chapter 9

From the Outside In

Angela Merkel as Opposition Leader, 2000-05

Clay Clemens

Angela Merkel made headlines for being the first woman and first citizen of formerly communist East Germany to head a major political party in the Federal Republic. Yet, her leadership was path-breaking not only for who she was, but also for what she sought to do: run the Christian Democratic Union (CDU) seemingly without many of the assets deemed vital for that job. Even one of Merkel's key strengths–"the capacity to radically call into question trusted systems"–seemed more likely to hurt than help in a party noted for, at most, incremental change.[1] Still, by 2006, she had been chair longer than all but two of her CDU's six predecessors–its postwar founder Konrad Adenauer and the eternal Helmut Kohl–as well as seven straight Social Democratic (SPD) counterparts. As head of the opposition, she had pushed her party to adopt major programmatic change, and, in spite of a disappointing election, was elected chancellor in late 2005. Merkel had worked her way from the outside in, despite, and partly thanks to being an agent of change.

Admittedly, at first glance, there might have appeared to be harder tasks than heading the pragmatic, middle-class CDU, with its long record of electoral success.[2] Yet, despite the integrative forces of Cold War anticommunism and social-market economics, it had long been an unwieldy alliance of clashing political traditions: Christian social-ism, liberalism and conservatism. It was rooted in Germany's Catholic milieu, but had strong Protestant and secular admixtures, as well as an appeal that crossed regional and class lines. This "polyarchy" of rival power centers–autonomous Land-level party associations, vocal inter-est group affiliates, an assertive Bundestag caucus–defied attempts at streamlining, even after modern extra-parliamentary structures evolved.[3] In this "complicated coalition," differences could be resolved only by reliance on consensual means: observing the norm of proportionality, assigning divisions of labor, respecting discrete policy domains, seeking lowest common denominator solutions, and "satisficing." As a result, leaders (even Adenauer) often were limited to the role of power broker.[4] Yet, due to its own self-image as Germany's natural party of government, the CDU also paradoxically demanded that its chair wield a strong hand and come across as a credible chancellor, so as to help the party gain or retain power. By contrast, the rival SPD placed a higher premium on chairs who could provide guidance with regard to policy substance and convey a sense that it stood for lofty principles.[5]

Given the CDU's pragmatic preoccupation with power, its leaders had the best chance of success while also holding high elective office, but that was no guarantee. Serving simultaneously as chancellor had not helped two chairs, Ludwig Erhard (1966-67) and Kurt Georg Kiesinger (1967-71). Nor had heading the CDU's joint Bundestag caucus with the Bavarian Christian Social Union (CSU) been a decisive boon to party chiefs Rainer Barzel (1971-73) and Wolfgang Schäuble (1998-2000). Plainly, there were other keys to power, best demonstrated by Kohl, who lasted a quarter century as chair (1973-1998). To be sure, in his first decade while in opposition, he faced two rebellious CDU general-secretaries, restive Bundestag peers, and autonomous Land party leaders (especially minister-presidents) who made it hard to steer Union policy in Bonn's other legislative chamber, the Bundesrat. Initially seen as weak for letting decisions drag on, he faced calls to step down even after a successful 1976 Bundestag campaign, and did in fact defer to CSU chief Franz Josef Strauss as the Union's joint candidate for chancellor in 1980. As late as 1982, CDU rivals still sought to block him from that post. Yet even without much charisma, voter appeal, or, after initially dabbling with it, programmatic innovation, Kohl prevailed. The explanation for his success lay mainly in a biography that tied him closely to his party, a tactically folksy style that forged myriad personal contacts, and a neutrality on programmatic issues that kept foes divided. Above all, he maintained an array of organizational assets: a bond with members, an "early warning system" among functionaries, a loyal regional base in his native Land, Rhineland-Palatinate, aides implanted at federal headquarters, relationships forged with key intraparty interest associations, an entrenched role atop the Bundestag caucus, and allies high up within each Land-level party. On top of all of this came a strategy that helped his Union regain power in 1982 and hold it for sixteen years, during which the CDU (again, despite internal struggles) was an instrument of his power.[6]

There seemed little likelihood of fully replicating Kohl's formulae, which were tailored to a specific time period, and partially discredited by his own later fall from grace. Worse, leading the CDU after his era also seemed sure to be even more challenging, given that unification in 1990 had eliminated the integrative power of anticommunism, while making an already heterogeneous party even more so.[7] Broader forces were eroding the viability of social market economics. Defeated in 1998, the Union was in opposition at the federal level for the first time in sixteen years, and soon beset by its worst scandal ever. Kohl's first successor as chair, Schäuble, fell within eighteen months. There seemed little reason to assume that the job could be mastered by Merkel, with her unconventional biography, almost apolitical style, narrowly based program, and modest organizational assets.

Merkel's Curriculum Vita

Merkel was born in her mother's native Hamburg, but raised in the German Democratic Republic (GDR) district of Brandenburg. Her father, a Protestant pastor, had gone east with hopes of helping his church build bridges between Christians and the communist state (an idealism he retained, resisting pressure to aid the secret police). Merkel recalled growing up with "a very atypical view of the GDR" due to contacts with western cousins. Moreover, even if being a pastor's daughter brought her more privileges than penalties, at home some topics were discussed outdoors to foil wiretaps, while at school she felt singled out and pressured to excel.[8] Ultimately, Merkel qualified to study physics at the university in Leipzig, and then obtained a laboratory position at the GDR Academy of Sciences. Despite holding office in a Communist youth group, she grew more critical of the regime than her father, but never joined the tiny dissident movement, settling instead for a niche in an apolitical profession, scientific research.

When the Wall fell in 1989, Merkel joined the crowds surging through it for a glimpse of prosperous, democratic West Berlin, quickly resolving to help revolutionize the GDR. Feeling out of place among pacifist-environmentalist dissidents and the re-founded Social Democrats, she joined a tiny new group, Democratic Awakening (DA), and became its spokesperson.[9] When her DA allied with the larger "East-CDU"–long a Communist front, but now seeking a new image–she worked for the pro-reunification ticket that, backed by Kohl, swept to victory in the March 1990 election. Merkel served as an aide to the prime minister of a democratized GDR that lasted only months, until elections for the first all-German Bundestag in December 1990. This position was enough to secure her nomination by the CDU for a seat, not in Brandenburg, but further north in coastal Mecklenburg-Pomerania. Afterward, Kohl stunned this unknown thirty-six year old by offering her a post in his first postunification cabinet, as Minister for Women and Youth Affairs.

During the government's next two terms, Merkel's loyal support of its policies earned her promotions. In 1991, Kohl named her deputy federal chair of the CDU, albeit with little power, and in 1994, she took over Bonn's environment ministry, dealing with issues like climate change and nuclear waste. Kohl's government finally fell in 1998, and his longtime heir apparent, Wolfgang Schäuble became the CDU's new chair, naming Merkel his general-secretary. Just eighteen months later came revelations of Kohl's shady past financial practices. With her party in disarray, Merkel openly urged it to disavow "the old warhorse." When Kohl dragged Schäuble down with him, and others were tainted, she emerged as the shattered CDU's best hope for fresh leadership. Passing over men who had long eyed that post, the party elected her chair in April 2000.

Over the next two years, Merkel did help rejuvenate the party, bringing in fresh blood and encouraging more open discussion, including long-ignored themes like the role of women, yet, her programmatic innovations did not get far. Moreover, Merkel could not control the Union Bundestag caucus, led by another newcomer and rival, Friedrich Merz, as well as Land leaders in the Bundesrat. The opposition chief often found herself outfoxed by the shrewd and charismatic SPD chancellor Gerhard Schröder. For months, she flirted with the idea of becoming the Union chancellor candidate against him in the 2002 election, but her vacillation fed fear among peers that she was not strong enough to exploit Schröder's poor record on the economy. Forestalling a move to block her, Merkel abruptly dropped out, and endorsed the consensus nominee, CSU chief Edmund Stoiber.

After the latter's narrow defeat, things changed. In a deal with Stoiber, Merkel took on a second post: head of the joint Bundestag caucus, strengthening her position as the primary opposition leader. She marshaled Union forces behind her strategy for outdoing Schröder in a contest over who could best reform Germany's welfare state so as to spur growth and job creation. At its December 2003 congress in Leipzig, the CDU endorsed her leadership, and early in 2004 Merkel worked with the Free Democrats (FDP) to elect her surprise choice as federal president, former International Monetary Fund chief Horst Köhler. Meanwhile, her Union was winning a series of Land elections. To be sure, sniping over reform—especially from the CSU—was straining opposition unity by mid-2004. Union approval slumped, as did Merkel's, reviving a leadership debate. Yet, the SPD-Green government's own travails, grim economic news, and two key CDU Land electoral victories in early 2005, revived Union fortunes. When Schröder announced an early federal election in May, her party was again at 45 percent in the polls, and she was quickly confirmed as its chancellor candidate. Nevertheless, her reform platform proved too ambitious for some, and her error-prone campaign failed to rally the Union's base, let alone undecided voters. In September, the CDU/CSU won just 35 percent of the vote and a thin plurality of Bundestag seats, too few for a majority with the free market FDP. Once again, however, Merkel hung in, facilitating Union negotiations with the SPD and emerging as chancellor of a new "grand coalition" in November 2005. Her roller-coaster ride had ended at the top.

Assets and Liabilities: The Biographical Dimension

Throughout Merkel's career, being a newcomer and an outsider often helped her. She admitted that Kohl's initial patronage resulted from him wanting an eastern woman in his cabinet, giving her "an unbelievably good apprenticeship" with more prior ministerial experience than any past CDU chair or chancellor (other than Erhard), or any potential intraparty rival.[10] Schäuble noted that he chose her as general-secretary in part because she represented something "new and refreshing." This reputation was also why the CDU turned to her amid the finance affair.[11]

Specifically, being from the former GDR, she "embodied pan-German history like no one else before," and more than any CDU rival.[12] In theory, that seemed likely to help integrate a party in many ways still divided along east-west lines, and to attract "rootless" swing voters in the new Länder, seen as decisive for strong federal election results. Given her sex, Merkel could also seemingly count on solidarity from women, feeding CDU hopes (and SPD fears) that she would improve its image among female voters.[13] An added benefit of her gender was that male rivals often either underestimated her, or felt compelled to display exaggerated public deference.[14] Being raised in a pastor's household seemed like an asset as well, given that Protestants had risen from 25 percent to about 40 percent of the CDU membership in reunited Germany. Often lost in the focus on other features of Merkel's biography was her youth: even if most rivals were not much older, it was an asset given her party's need for generational change at the top. Being forty-six upon becoming chair gave her a comfort level with pop culture (it was hard to picture her predecessors at a boy band concert, for example) and new technology like text messaging (Kohl had not even used a computer), as well as a bond with youthful colleagues and voters. In 2005, she would become not just Germany's first woman chancellor, but also its youngest. Finally, training as a scientist set her apart from all but a few western politicians, and even the rare exceptions–leftwing rival Oskar Lafontaine, for example, or Britain's Margaret Thatcher–had not made careers of it.[15]

Merkel's unconventional biography had its costs as well. Despite a crash course in "learning by doing," she would long feel disadvantaged by knowing little of western ways or the Federal Republic's history.[16] She had not networked within the Young Union (by 1989 she was already at the party youth group's upper age limit), nor slogged her way up through CDU offices (the so-called *Ochsentour*), nor served as a minister-president–the executive training ground for many previous Union chairs, and every chancellor but Erhard. Indeed, Merkel would long feel like an outsider in her CDU. Early on, as deputy chair, she would still refer to colleagues as "them," and find it hard to say "we" in describing its past record.[17] Being Kohl's protégé also compelled her to compromise her own views at time, and stuck her with the demeaning tag of being his "girl."

While these handicaps could be overcome, a more lasting problem lay in having roots only among minority milieus in her CDU. As an easterner, Merkel came from a part of the party with a "problematic [GDR] legacy," internal divisions and slumping membership.[18] Being an "*Ossi*" subjected her to stereotypes–as a "leftwinger"–and condescension regarding her appearance.[19] Another challenge lay in being the first woman to lead a male-dominated party.[20] Gender bias was implicit even in complimentary monikers like "valiant lady," "*Trümmerfrau*," (referring to the "women of the rubble" who cleared German cities after wartime bombing raids) or "Joan of Arc," but also in snide labels like "Kohl's girl," "Angie baby," or harsher epithets. It was also evident in the attention paid to her appearance, and to one outburst of tears.[21] While citing her own inexperience as a bigger problem, she agreed that male colleagues initially had a tough time taking orders from a woman. Analysts noted that polls understated the reluctance of many men to actually vote for a female candidate.[22] As for her religion, Protestants were still a minority among CDU members, and lacked the cohesion to serve as a power base. Moreover, while confessional differences had long been fading within Union ranks, commentators and even Catholic colleagues saw her faith as more of a negative than they had, for example, with Schäuble (perhaps because it was conflated with her eastern background and economic liberalism).[23]

Worse, Merkel was often doubly handicapped by her biography, for even within each minority milieu her status was ambiguous. While westerners viewed her as an *Ossi*, it was harder for many easterners, especially older ones, to identify her as one of their own. With an apolitical background, she lacked roots in the GDR's power structure or its dissident milieu, had been eager to liquidate a separate East German state, and had assimilated rapidly into the Bonn establishment. She would rarely evince much pride in things eastern, let alone any *"Ostalgia,"* and instead took satisfaction in being, sounding, even appearing "pan-German."[24]

Nor did she fit fully into any familiar category of CDU women. Her religion and personal life—Merkel had left her first husband, lived with her second before marriage, and had no children—did not square with the old conservative "Catholic mother's tradition." Yet while she admired Simone de Beauvoir's independence, saw Marie Curie as a role model, and put up Catherine the Great's portrait in her office, feminism played "no special role" for her. She resisted being categorized as a female politician, observing that, while women in her business did face some unique obstacles, they were otherwise no different from male politicians.[25] At first, she had not even wanted the women's ministry and, aside from some measures on behalf of working mothers, did not pursue a feminist agenda there. Some feminists never forgave her for temporizing on the abortion issue in 1992-93.[26] Merkel even resisted Kohl's proposed quota to make slates of CDU candidates more gender balanced (though she later changed her mind). Later, she did give women's issues somewhat higher profile within her party, but never top billing. Indeed, during the 2005 campaign Merkel long stressed that her sex should not be politically relevant. Only very late did she begin stressing her earlier ministerial experience and appear at some rallies for women voters, thus highlighting her gender, as she put it, "to an unusual degree for me."[27]

Nor did Merkel's Protestantism play a visible role in her personal life (her second marriage was not in the church) or her politics. She admitted being uneasy at first with the opening prayer at CDU congresses, and observers detected her "visible discomfort" with religious themes—one claimed that her Christianity was "evidently limited to being a pastor's daughter."[28] In fact, it was less her Protestantism than her lifestyle that caused comment in a party with church ties (Berlin's Cardinal Meisner chastised her for living in sin), and long led by men prone to praise, if not always practice, traditional family values.[29] While too Protestant for some Catholics, Merkel was thus not religious enough for those of either faith who wanted her party to rally traditional Christians by emphasizing the "C" in its name (though as CDU members and voters were growing more secular with every year, in this respect she represented the future).[30]

Assets and Liabilities: The Stylistic Dimension

Merkel's style was both an asset and a liability as opposition leader. Most assessments began with her intellectual capacity. Since her childhood, associates viewed her as a quick learner (she credited a good short term memory), and as a trained scientist, her ease with numbers and technical data were obvious (aides in both ministries she led noted her ability to master detail).[31] She picked up quickly on the policy process and was comfortable with in-depth briefings–on economic issues, for instance. Interlocutors were struck by her facility in Russian and English. Even Schäuble, a jilted former patron, conceded: "she is one of the most intelligent people that I have come to know in politics."[32] While Merkel could slip up (e.g., confusing net and gross income during the 2005 campaign), she rarely made, let alone repeated, factual errors.

Indeed, her intelligence was less often debated than her intellectual approach. Again partly as a result of scientific training, Merkel often spoke of how "systems functioned," of testing new concepts, and of surprising male colleagues by injecting "rational thought" into discussion. She displayed a high degree of analytical objectivity and disdain for the confines of tradition or dogma, along with an openness to innovation, especially to "new and consistent solutions."[33] At the same time, biographers surmised that "living in two different worlds" while growing up had taught her to bend without breaking by accepting compromise, nuance, shades of grey–in short, to accept that life rarely offered simple, clear choices, especially between moral absolutes of good and evil.[34] She was thus often faulted for being a dry empiricist, mechanistic, overly technocratic–a "wonk," who seemed to lack passion, vision, or even a moral compass.

These observations invariably shaded over into discussion of ambition. From her school days and throughout both careers, Merkel's compulsion to come out on top was evident. She spoke of needing to prove herself, whether as a pastor's daughter under communism, or as a woman in politics. Her taste for power became evident soon after the Wall fell.[35] Kohl's early patronage was like a proseminar on that subject (and, notably, she "studied" under him late in his career, when he had become a wary autocrat). After years of seeking chances to build up her power, as opposition leader "she [could then] create situations" to exploit.[36] "Power as such is nothing bad," Merkel herself stressed, "it is necessary." Noting that in German the noun shared a stem with the verb "to do," she characterized it as a vital and justifiable means, within democratic ground-rules, to achieve a goal. "She likes power," agreed an ally, "and she likes to be underestimated, because that is one of the best ways to fortify [it]."[37] Asked about obstacles facing women leaders, she noted that their smaller stature and high-pitched voices exuded less power. When told that she herself lacked that aura, she reportedly consulted friends, and was advised not to call upon peers, but instead have them come to her, or only to appear in public with an entourage, never alone.[38]

Merkel's sense of power also shaped her interpersonal style. She unsentimentally severed links with allies or patrons in the dying GDR's democracy movement who became liabilities.[39] Upon taking over at the environment ministry, she quickly "sent a sign of strength" by removing its experienced but independent-minded permanent state secretary.[40] In 1999-2000, she not only broke with Kohl, but her letter urging the party to do so also sparked a nasty war between him and Schäuble, from which she emerged as the beneficiary.[41] As one ally put it, it saved the party and advanced her career by "dismantling" both former patrons.[42] As chair, Merkel not only cleared out more staff at party headquarters, but did not balk at firing her own first appointee as general secretary when, after just months, he proved ineffective. Against heavy odds, Merkel pursued the 2002 chancellor candidacy, even having herself nominated to force a showdown. Yet pragmatism tempered her ambition: when headcounts showed her losing, and rumors mounted that CDU colleagues planned to block her, a mortal blow for a chair, she preempted them by conceding the title to Stoiber, campaigning loyally on his behalf, in exchange for his acceptance of her as caucus chair. In taking that post, Merkel dispatched her rival Merz, coolly ignoring his reproaches by arguing that divided leadership would only hurt the Union. In 2004, she did not deny speculation that the opposition would nominate Schäuble as federal president, yet then sprung her personal choice, Köhler, seeing him as more popular with her preferred coalition ally, the FDP. One columnist called it "cynical and unworthy," a "diabolical" Machiavellian game to "secure her political power."[43] By then other monikers were cropping up: "the snake," "ice cold angel," "Lady Merciless," even "man-murdering power woman" (*männermordenden Machtfrau*).[44]

Merkel was also reserved in her interpersonal dealings. This demeanor stemmed from having grown up in a system rife with informants, and in a home where it was vital to keep the concerns of some parishioners quiet. "One of the great advantages of the GDR era was learning how to keep silent," she would later say, "it was a survival strategy ... and still is."[45] She valued discretion, in herself and others (even listing it as her most prized trait on a survey).[46] One observer wrote, she "made use of reticence more than any other politician," and many credited her with an exceptional poker face.[47]

Merkel was also leery of relying on others, another reflection of life in the GDR, and of learning that a close colleague, as well as the DA's first chair, had been police informants. Other suggested sources of her wariness included "having built a political career out of nothing," as well as a "foreignness and distance" that came from never having "completely belonged to any group" in which she moved.[48] While remembering those who had taken her seriously before she was well-known–like Köhler, then a top Bonn bureaucrat, or Thomas de Maizière, later her chancellery minister–she distrusted many westerners who flocked to her only thereafter.[49] Such wariness could only have been heightened by serving under Kohl. She also bitterly recalled how many CDU peers pledged to back her 2002 chancellery candidacy, but then flocked to Stoiber (whereas those who openly backed him and told her so, like Volker Kauder, actually earned her trust). True to her view that "there are no friendships in politics," Merkel largely kept private and public spheres separate, avoiding the informal "du" and preserving a physical distance from most colleagues.[50]

This reserve and mistrust made for a certain autonomy. Merkel was not unduly dependent on any allies or clientele, giving her more latitude and precluding charges of being a tool of any faction.[51] Yet, it also kept her distant: despite a demure charm, unlike many politicians, she could never be a backslapper or hugger. Networking with the attendant danger of dependence did not come naturally to her, and similarly, she was reluctant to consult political peers or opinion leaders on policy, preferring instead to rely more on personal aides or technical experts. That could cut her off from useful input and leave her politically isolated at times. As one colleague noted when her approval slumped in 2004, "Merkel hasn't been able to gather loyal allies around her because many don't know if she would be loyal to them in the worst of cases."[52]

When it came to decisions, Merkel's analytical objectivity, grasp of detail, and wariness of dogma inclined her toward long discussion, not quick, simple answers. Ever attentive to her own power and leery of making herself vulnerable to rivals, she avoided rushing deliberations or imposing her own preferences until adequate information about others' views was available to help determine where a consensus lay. Since Kohl's ouster, when as one critic quipped "the girl" had proven to be her party's "bravest man," few doubted her courage: as she claimed, "I have no fear. Of anything or anyone."[53] Nevertheless, Merkel did not want to risk generating cacophony within her CDU, or the Union as a whole. This penchant for consensus-building could be an asset, making her an effective mediator on complex issues, in defining the lowest common denominator, or in developing detailed formulae in areas like economic policy. More emotion-laden cultural issues could trip her up, like the bitter debate in late 2003 over penalizing a Bundestag deputy (Martin Hohmann) accused of anti-Semitic remarks.[54] Especially early on, her reluctance to commit prematurely often let debate drag on endlessly. She could come across as hesitant, indecisive, tactical, even fickle or opportunistic (a colleague noted in dismay, "one can't lead this way"). For a time, Merkel did appear to lay more effective groundwork on her economic reform proposals, and seemed able to steer her party's decisions in a clear direction. Yet, she soon reverted to "tactical hesitation," reviving doubts about her authority.[55]

As for public style, Merkel exuded "authenticity," if also drabness. Both showed in an initial lack of concern with her appearance, something she traced partly to being a lab scientist. She clung to the casualness of her GDR days–a page-boy haircut, long skirts, and sandals. Determined to preserve her individuality and deterred by an image of the "horrid" dress-suits that eastern career women had to wear, she resisted joining in what struck her as the strange western "competition of self-presentation." Even after Merkel shifted to a more businesslike look, colleagues, journalists and jokesters then took jabs at her dowdy pantsuits, flat bob hairdo and baggy eyes. More perplexed than angry at such frivolous scrutiny, she attributed it mainly to there being more features of a woman's appearance that drew attention, not gender bias.[56] With self-effacing unpretentiousness, she noted that being "mouse grey" also often led foes to underestimate her (in 2001 she even had the CDU seek a new advertising agency by using a comically unflattering photo of herself under the subtitle "make more out of what you've got"). Ultimately Merkel did adopt a more stylish wardrobe, coiffure and makeup, sparking fresh gossip about who was responsible for the changes, and even admitted to taking some pleasure in being more fashionable. But flair would never be one of her political weapons.[57]

Authenticity also described the low-key directness of her rhetorical style, a contrast to the doublespeak or slick sound bites of many rivals. Based partly on experience presenting scholarly research, Merkel rendered complex material in a clear, organized and concise way, but also came across as a dry lecturer, without color or wit. Her most effective speeches, like an October 2003 address on economic reform in Berlin, touched on her GDR past, yet she rarely dwelled on that chapter.[58] In Bundestag debates, she could also deliver points clearly, but when partisan fervor mounted, it raised her tempo and pitch, problems she strived to control, or triggered badly timed gaffes.[59] On the campaign trail, her speeches could come across as painfully detailed and staccato in delivery, with a lack of positive passion, polemical jabs, humor or personal pathos. She worked hard to improve her on-camera talk show manner, and by the 2005 campaign it showed–especially when interacting with women media personalities.[60] In televised encounters with Schröder, she was generally well-prepared and aggressive. But viewers still found her less likeable and less self-confident.[61] In off-camera interviews, her substance came across, but she never fully trusted journalists until she knew them personally.[62] Merkel in turn did not endear herself to reporters, who felt she viewed them warily and seemed distracted, often checking her text messages or stepping away to make calls. Observers detected an uneasiness about being the center of attention.[63] Though she discussed hobbies like hiking and cooking, she kept her private and political lives separate (husband Joachim Sauer rarely appeared with her in public), which made for few human interest stories. Oratory and media-savvy were thus plainly not Merkel's strengths, and certainly not the key to her success. In many respects, she was the "anti-Schröder," and many voters, even Union supporters, found her boring.[64]

In sum, a finely-tuned sense of power and capacity for moderation were for Merkel, like Kohl before her, assets. Weak presentation and tactical caution were weaknesses both shared. What most set her apart, though, was her reserve, bordering on remoteness: it made for an almost apolitical interpersonal style that risked frustrating colleagues and making it hard to muster team spirit.

Assets and Liabilities: The Programmatic Dimension

If Merkel's pragmatism, ambition and caution led critics to accuse her of opportunism—one former GDR colleague grumbled: "In that sense she has become a west German politician"—allies insisted that she "acts out of conviction more than one gives her credit for."[65] In any case, more so than any CDU leader since Adenauer, she did identify herself with a specific program, indeed one largely at odds with traditionally dominant schools of thought in her party. Paradoxically, this effort to rattle the Union's status quo and set it in a new direction bolstered her own power initially, but it also soon threatened to backfire, and she was forced to backtrack.

Merkel voiced broadly liberal views. She placed a premium on individual freedom, due to her experience with and rejection of a Communist dictatorship.[66] In particular, this attitude shaped her outlook on economics. Memories of the GDR's inefficiencies, her ethos as a scientist that merit should be rewarded, and even a "Protestant social ethic" of individual responsibility all fed her wariness of socialism in any form—including more humane versions dreamt of by her father or post-Wall leftwing "utopians."[67] She would instead recall market economics being one of her top three priorities in 1989, alongside a place in parliament and rapid reunification. Attracted by "the CDU commitment to the individual [and] trust in competition from which creative prosperity can arise," in early 1990 she published an article on Erhard's ideas, and endorsed breaking up collective farms and privatizing industry in the newly democratic GDR.[68] Merkel would never share the longing of other easterners, even in her CDU, for a strong state to provide equality and order.[69] She read economic treatises in the 1990s, and as environment minister, grew to favor "liberalizing the social market" system (despite once proposing to add the "leftwing" modifier "ecological").[70] In 2001, she set up a CDU commission to discuss "the new social market," one adapted to changing conditions, but still based on free enterprise and a limited state.[71]

All of this came to a head after 2002. Drawing a lesson from Stoiber's defeat, Merkel argued that her Union could not compete for the center with a charismatic pragmatist like Schröder simply by offering to manage the status quo more competently–especially given the depth of Germany's economic plight, a brewing consensus on the need for reform, and the chancellor's own Agenda 2010, which called for trimming costly social welfare benefits as a way of sparking private sector growth and creating jobs. She insisted that her Union could not allow the chancellor to outflank it by seizing this issue, let alone block his measures. Instead, the opposition needed a more constructive course and a sharper profile of its own. She thus pressed colleagues to help pass Schröder's reform plan in the Bundesrat, albeit by extracting concessions that would take it further and exploit divisions within his own camp. Beyond that, she urged the party to advance its own alternatives as a way of seizing the initiative back, even if that meant tampering with the sacrosanct balance inherent in social market economics. Merkel endorsed proposals by a party commission under former president Roman Herzog for "readjusting the social safety net," by "departing from the ... old Bismarck model" on health care, reversing the CDU's own "mistaken" system of long term care insurance, "reconstructing the intergenerational deal" on pensions, and "reordering the world of work," while also streamlining, simplifying and reducing taxes.[72]

She ardently sold this program. Rather than conceiving of justice in purely horizontal, redistributive terms, Merkel argued, it had to be seen vertically: wage-earners could expect help in turn for their own efforts and contributions to the commonweal. She also defined solidarity in limited terms, as aid for those who could not help themselves, like the handicapped. Merkel even called self-interest functional, and unlike most colleagues, she never referred to the U.S. economy as a bad example, but as a model.[73] She blamed both major parties for too long propagating the "illusion" of redistribution without regard to the economic effects, a way of thinking that had developed into a "very stable political system" by heading off costly social tensions, but that in the end, had also penalized society's most productive elements. "Those who achieve more should not have less than those who achieve less," she insisted.[74] Merkel chided her own CDU for equating equality of opportunity with equality of outcome, and warned that "when distinctions are leveled, society loses vitality and healthy tension," as well as fellow easterners for getting "soft" and echoing the Left's call for state imposed equality.[75] Merkel clashed with her party's Christian social wing—the Catholic traditions and trade union politics that were so formative for an older generation of westerners were alien to her. She was also breaking with the long centrist consensus embodied by Kohl. In her view, as a "classic man of the middle," he had been "especially skeptical" about market forces, but "today the center has shifted more in the direction of political necessities now that we can no longer afford more redistribution ..."[76]

At the same time, despite comparisons, above all in the foreign press, Merkel did not espouse the unabashed free market capitalism of Britain's Margaret Thatcher. For that she was too antidogmatic, too much a product of the German social state tradition, and head of a party that had never questioned the validity of this tradition. In any case, her appeal for market reform also rested partly on claims that it could help make some social security measures more affordable: as she noted pragmatically, her program needed public acceptance in order to work.[77] Even while urging steps to free up the private economy, Merkel still set her program within CDU social market traditions, emphasizing justice and solidarity. She took pains to downplay parallels to Thatcher, even avoiding offers to be photographed with the former British premier.[78]

Of all Union leaders, Merkel thus seemed most well-suited to match Schröder on the reform front. Merz was a more ardent market liberal, but too much so to carry the entire party with him. Hesse's minister-president Roland Koch demanded hardline opposition tactics that struck many as sure to backfire. Stoiber talked of bold reform, but balked at acting on it. Merkel, the economic liberal with consensual instincts and grasp of detail, was equipped to conduct a strategy of constructive opposition, while her own program promised the CDU mainstream a distinct party profile, distancing it from Schröder's SPD. She rode this momentum to the Leipzig congress in late 2003, where delegates embraced her leadership and chancellor candidacy, helping ensconce her in power (even if some later had buyer's remorse about the program and its author).

Merkel's liberalism also came across on cultural issues. She urged respect for individual choice, including on abortion, as well as acceptance of the fact that family structures had grown more varied and women were playing wholly new roles. Cautioning her Union that it could not ignore reality, she urged tolerance of homosexuality, held "good conversations" with an unofficial CDU lesbian and gay group, and welcomed FDP chief Guido Westerwelle's self-outing with his male partner at her 50th birthday—unimaginable for Kohl. Merkel the scientist was also open to stem cell research or embryonic testing.[79] Given negative memories of the GDR's constant pressure "to be frightfully proud" she felt awkward voicing patriotic sentiments, and when she did it struck some as forced: "tears [did] not flow from her eyes at the sight of the German flag."[80]

Thus, Merkel was not comfortable with her party's cultural and national conservatives, and vice versa. She stressed that the Union had always embodied several traditions, and that with a changing electorate could ill-afford to sound reactionary on cultural or national themes. Still, she was careful to redefine conservatism rather than reject it, saying it should be more than a mindset of preservation, but an outlook that favored "progress from a firm foundation."[81] After all, she was by no means on the Left, having long rejected 1960s-style radical progressivism and "naïve" multiculturalism.[82] Moreover, Merkel never put progressive themes at the center of her program or pushed them too far: for example, she did not endorse gay marriage or adoption, and remained ambiguous on stem cell research.[83] Under attack from colleagues for giving away the CDU's "conservative silver," the chair accentuated her wariness of immigration and Turkish accession to the EU, and made family values a theme of her address to the 2004 congress in Düsseldorf.

Merkel explained her views on international politics as an extension of the premium she placed on freedom. Like many eastern

Europeans (albeit fewer in the former GDR) she had long admired America as the mirror opposite of the "sad world of Communism," and also voiced a debt to Washington for reunification.[84] This Atlanticism, as well as a deep disdain for pacifism, underlay her support for U.S. military action against terrorists and more controversially, rogue regimes like Hussein's Iraq. She likewise depicted EU integration as an extension of democracy.

Merkel thus represented a new direction for her CDU. Her indifference to dogma or tradition made it easy for her to talk of updating long-held, time-tested formulae, such as in her proposals for "ecological" or "new" social market economics, and her 2005 reform slogan "we will pursue fundamentally different policies so that everything gets fundamentally better." Especially in the form of her economic reform agenda, she provided strategic orientation exactly when the party longed for it. Yet, her views could also seem out of place in a party wedded to tradition, where change came incrementally, if at all. Her economic liberalism in particular could also come across as "cold [and] technocratic" to those who saw Merkel as "beyond pathos" and wanted her to "risk more emotion"[85] Even allies decried a lack of imagery or inspiration. As a result, she did not convert many followers based on her programmatic assertions. As ambivalence towards parts of her reform agenda grew, she had to backtrack and compromise. Moreover, she failed to connect with, even alienated, the CDU's traditional Christian social and cultural conservatives. Some worried that Merkel's programmatic innovations might not only fail but, worse, could backfire, narrowing her party's voter appeal on both the right and left, locking it permanently into the "30 percent dungeon."

Merkel's Organizational Assets and Liabilities

Leadership of the CDU had long depended on personal connections within the party's structure that could be used to help assess the interests or moods of its various components and generate support for major decisions. Such organizational assets began at the grassroots, but unlike Kohl, Merkel could not count on ordinary CDU members long identifying with her as "one of them." Despite having come on the scene late, however, she did develop a bond. During the grim winter of 2000, CDU leaders had sought to give rank and file a chance to vent over the finance affair, and discuss the party's future, but doing so at the regularly scheduled congresses in all sixteen Länder would have dragged the process out and restricted discussion to delegates. Instead, nine larger conferences were held, open to all Christian Democrats from broader regions. Moreover, the format was less regimented, more talk show style, aimed at fostering open discussion, so that unhappy members felt they were being heard (and so that the media would convey the image of transparency—well-conveyed when, at the very first, one speaker called Kohl an "asshole"). These regional conferences circumvented Land-level officials and drew more participants than at regular congresses—600 to 1500 each, including more younger and female members. The first took place in north Germany, where the old Kohl network was weaker, and anger at the southern men who dominated their party ran deeper.[86] These regional conferences quickly took on their own dynamic. From the first in Wolfenbüttel to the last in Stuttgart, participants greeted their general-secretary with chants of "An-gie, An-gie," and called on her to take over as chair. Despite last minute maneuvers, older, more experienced male rivals could not ignore the mood. As Schäuble noted, "one would have to be fairly deaf not to hear what the rank and file want."[87]

The regional conferences established Merkel's bond with the membership, showing also that she stood for a new, untainted, more open and more diverse CDU. At its congress in Essen, she won 96 percent of the delegate vote as chair, a rapturous acclamation. To be sure, this zeal subsided once the crisis passed. The "old boys" did not go away, and even Merkel showed little enthusiasm for more idealistic organizational reforms to shift power from the party's hierarchy to its membership. Still, the regional conferences did become an autumn ritual. Lacking the packed agendas and orchestration of regular congresses, they would be used to air topical controversies, and thus serve as a useful vehicle for Merkel, whose leadership claim was to be closely linked with substantive policy proposals. She used these fora in the fall of 2001 to discuss immigration, and to promote her candidacy for chancellor. At December's congress in Dresden, her new general-secretary got a huge majority, she again heard chants of "An-gie, An-gie," and reporters clocked applause for her speech at six and a half minutes–just longer than that for Stoiber, a guest speaker. After the 2002 election, 94 percent of the delegates meeting in Hamburg returned her as chair (160 did not take part, which some said was a protest, but others blamed on the fact that most simply had not returned from their refreshment break).

Merkel's support of the United States' invasion of Iraq in 2003 tested her grassroots support, as most members opposed it–several hundred even quit in protest. Yet, with Germany not directly involved, the Union was spared any need for a divisive policy decision. Moreover, in her appearances, Merkel faced little open criticism and was still cheered. As one anti-war colleague put it, she also "accommodated the mood of the populace and in the party" by balancing her own pro-U.S. stance with admonitions to Bush, and openness to dissent. A delegate was even heard admitting "she is not 'the girl' anymore." By proving that she could "swim against the tide" of opinion, this stance even boosted her standing in party ranks.[88] In any case, by mid-2003 all other issues were again dominated by economic reform, and here she played on her grassroots bond most successfully, turning seven regional conferences into rallies for her proposals and her chancellor candidacy. As in 2000, her supporters came out in force–their ranks swelled by Young Union and business activists–to cheer her program, their long applause and chants of "An-gie, An-gie" overwhelming questioners and critics.[89] Harsh attacks on Merkel's "snobbish neo-liberal" proposals by the CDU's old Catholic trade union wing, ironically among her original backers, only further mobilized support for her, as did sharp criticism by Stoiber's CSU, which antagonized many Christian Democrats. Once again, Merkel boosted her own power by appearing as the true servant of her party. At Leipzig in December her reform measures passed all but unanimously, and she received euphoric applause. Even critics conceded "she is at the height of her power."[90]

Developments in 2004, above all her inability to quell debate over economic reform and plans for a petition drive against Turkey's EU accession, tempered Merkel's grassroots support. This time the regional conferences fell flat, and at December's congress in Düsseldorf her vote slipped to 88 percent, her weakest showing. The Union rallied in early 2005, and she was coronated chancellor candidate in mid-summer in Dortmund's cavernous Westfalenhalle. Less conventional congress than orchestrated American-style media spectacle, the brief, three hour event included rock anthems, a daz-zling laser light show, and a multimedia presentation on Merkel. Some 10,000 orange-clad supporters (calling to mind a Dutch soccer crowd) chanted and cheered speeches by all major Union leaders, culminating with the candidate's own address.

Merkel's grassroots backing thus remained strong, but was always based less on confidence than hope that she could deliver, a mood that increasingly required boosting. Support from members was in any case always too inchoate to serve as a permanent instrument of leader-ship. She also recognized the need for a more reliable base, a loyal corps of functionaries from her region and, ideally, like Kohl, beyond it.[91] Since her home was in uninfluential Brandenburg where the CDU was weak and had rebuffed her bid to become its state chair in 1991, it would have to be Mecklenburg-Pomerania, site of her Bundestag seat. She headed the party there from 1993 to 2000, and, despite often being called away by ministerial duties in Bonn, did immerse herself in its management, above all in personnel matters. She mediated effec-tively among factions from the new Land's two halves, from its com-munist-era old guard and reform-minded newcomers, even from its Catholics and Protestants,[92] earning her lasting support. But with just 7,000 members her Land's branch was among the party's smallest and weakest. CDU voter support in Mecklenburg-Pomerania also slumped, except in its far northeastern corner around her constituency. While Merkel could thus count on a warm welcome back in "Meck-Pomm," it was never a powerful political springboard.[93]

There were other pockets of intra-party support for her in the East, but even more in western Germany's Protestant north, namely among CDU associations in Schleswig-Holstein, Hamburg and Bremen.[94] Rap-turous receptions for Merkel at Land-level congresses in populous, Catholic North Rhine-Westphalia had also helped make her chair in 2000, propelled her brief 2002 chancellor candidacy, kicked off the economic reform drive that bolstered her leadership in 2003, and sus-tained her in a later slump.[95] This backing proved a valuable asset, even if it also reflected a backlash against long domination of the CDU by its southern branches (and a desire for unity before pivotal 2005 Land elections). As such, it was not a strong or reliable personal base.

Intraparty associations offered a similarly mixed picture. In 1992-93 Merkel had chaired the CDU's Evangelical Working Circle (EAK). Although its rolls formally listed all of the party's more than 200, 000 Protestants, that was only because they were automatically listed, often without knowing it. The EAK had steadily lost influence since the 1950s: its monthly newsletter's circulation remained low, while its efforts to facilitate dialogue between the party and church leaders on the moral implications of military action or scientific advances had led nowhere. United Germany's electorate and her CDU's membership were nominally more Protestant, but neither was easily mobilized by religious themes (on many issues the party clashed with the clergy anyway). While some prominent Protestants like former president Herzog and Schäuble lent their names to it, the EAK was a "place to shuttle old politicians or young ones not yet important enough for higher office." Thus, its support of Merkel's leadership and policies brought little benefit.[96]

Members of the Women's Union (FU) identified with her and acknowledged Merkel's efforts to modernize the CDU's image on gender issues. She got on well with its chief, Maria Böhmer. This group's zeal for Merkel had always been tempered by her own caution and maverick penchant for going her own way rather than be seen as a female politician—such as in opposing a quota for party candidates. In any case, the FU also enjoyed at best modest intraparty influence, in part because women still comprised only a quarter of the membership.[97] Merkel's support from the larger Young Union (JU) was similarly mixed. She was close to one chair, Hildegard Müller, if not the next, Philipp Missfelder. Before 2003, however, her speeches drew only mild applause at JU rallies: Stoiber, Merz, even Kohl, got more boisterous receptions. Yet, Missfelder's JU did greet her call to ease the social state's financial burden on younger employees, and at the 2003 regional conferences, youth activists gave the chair visible, vocal support, irking older members. Though rivals like Merz also still enjoyed JU backing, and it did not formally endorse her candidacy as early as it had Stoiber's at the last election, the group was largely in her corner.[98]

Moreover, unlike Kohl, Merkel could never benefit from a close, yet balanced relationship with her CDU's influential internal lobbies for labor and business. As an easterner she was at first seen as closer to the trade unionist Christian Democratic Employees Association (CDA), but its old guard attacked her market reform initiatives, and other officials went along only grudgingly. On social policy, Merkel preferred consulting younger, more technocratic specialists in her caucus or at the Land level rather than the heavily Catholic, blue collar CDA, and never had good relations with it until Karl-Josef Laumann took the helm in 2005. On substance, she was closer to CDU groups that spoke for private enterprise—its small-business Middle Class Association (MIT), and a loosely-affiliated advisory group of major firms, the Business Council (WR). Both backed her reform plans, and prodded her to go further. But paradoxically, Merkel rarely networked with their leaders. Mindful of being seen as a corporate shill, she distanced herself from the WR in particular, which grew frustrated that she let her reform plans be diluted. Having alienated or confused both lobbies, Merkel could not completely rely on either one.[99]

In managing her party, the chair would of course have one bureaucratic asset: the staff at party headquarters, Konrad Adenauer House in Berlin's Tiergarten. Unlike Kohl as opposition leader, Merkel never named an ambitious general-secretary who might make CDU headquarters into his own base, even a rival camp, choosing instead low-profile loyalists. Key posts went to Merkel's closest confidantes, whose ties with her went back to the early 1990s. Office manager Beate Baumann controlled access to the chair and was her closest advisor and spokesperson Eva Christiansen steered her media relations. Belying the nickname "girls' camp" given to it by reporters, this inner-circle also included CDU business manager Willi Hausman, another longtime confidante, and other men. Merkel also cleared out most holdovers in mid-level positions, though their role was mainly restricted to logistics, communication and campaigns. Still, her general-secretaries were unable to make headquarters a major asset in managing the opposition. The first, Ruprecht Polenz, lasted just half a year, and the second, Laurenz Meyer, proved too impulsive for his own good or hers. While Merkel's third choice, Volker Kauder, earned more positive reviews, even under him headquarters could never provide much value added in mobilizing the party, and it came under fire for slow reaction time in the fast-moving 2005 campaign.[100] Between the cost of moving to Berlin and

172

paying fines after the finance affair, resources were scarce and staff had to be cut, limiting opportunities for patronage. Merkel drew even less on headquarters after 2002, as key aides moved with her to the Bundestag.

Indeed, the caucus would ultimately make or break her as opposition leader. Merkel could not count on it during her first two years as party chair, thanks to cool relations with Merz. Ousting him in 2002 created some ill-will and saddled her with an executive committee dominated by critics. Even so, she won 92 percent of the vote (214 of 232 deputies) thanks to Stoiber's backing, and her warnings against dividing two key leadership posts. Her elevation to the chair also coincided with a broader generational turnover, given that many older Kohl-era deputies had retired before the 2002 election. One third of the caucus was thus new and, as a result, the average age of its members (including veterans and newcomers) fell. This change increased the size and clout of its Young Group, on which Merkel could often rely (including most CSU members), providing her with a chance to mold this changing caucus after her own fashion. Moreover, unlike Kohl, she did not become chair as a Bundestag novice, having already been a deputy since 1990, and unlike another predecessor, Schäuble, she would not have to mediate between her parliamentary group and an intrusive, autocratic chancellery. Finally, she had allies: the so-called "pasta band," a group of friends who had been bound by mutual oaths of loyalty, first sworn in 1980 at an Italian eatery in Cologne after losing a leadership election in North Rhine-Westphalia's JU. Their leader was Peter Hintze, a former Protestant pastor who won Merkel's trust early on while serving as deputy in her first Bonn ministry, and subtly coaching her on western political norms. Despite a stint as CDU general-secretary that ended with Kohl's disastrous 1998 defeat and subsequent obscurity for him, he had remained a key Merkel caucus ally—as did his colleague Ronald Pofalla, who had served on the committee that dealt with bills from her first ministry in 1990-94. This group later grew to include Laurenz Meyer and Norbert Röttgen, as well as other youngish, low-profile, liberally-minded CDU deputies, like Eckardt von Klaeden, Peter Altmaier, and Volker Kauder. Criticism from older, more conservative, mainly southern Bundestag members bound them together more closely, as did press commentary dismissing them as bland unknowns.[101] Merkel made Kauder caucus manager in 2002, Pofalla his deputy, and Altmaier its legal counsel.

Despite some strains, Union deputies backed her unpopular stance on the Iraq war and her constructive opposition to Schröder's economic reform proposals. In September 2003, she was re-elected with almost 94 percent (209 yeas, 14 nays, and 14 abstentions). Despite annoyance with her indecisiveness, in late 2003, the majority also accepted her decision to banish a deputy charged with anti-Semitic remarks. Merkel mobilized most deputies behind proposals for social insurance, tax and labor law reform. Critics led by the CSU's Horst Seehofer balked at these measures for going too far, while Merz pressed her to take them further. Nevertheless, both lost and quit the group's executive committee in late 2004, opening slots for her supporters. As one observer put it, "for the first time, Merkel has a clear majority of allies in the inner leadership of the caucus."[102] Of her powerful potential foes, only Schäuble remained, but while he could cause problems, she could also circumvent him.[103]

Indeed, if the opposition chief had a solid base, it was the caucus. This helped offset Merkel's organizational deficit at the CDU's top rungs. In opposition, members of the party's top decision-making bodies, its exclusive presidium and the slightly larger executive committee, would have more influence than during Kohl's era as chancellor. Chairs of each Land-party were represented in the former and some in the latter. By 2004, a record eleven of sixteen minister-presidents sat in the presidium, enjoying special clout by virtue of their Bundesrat role (as did even CDU officials who were junior partners in Land governments). Dealing with these regional "barons" would prove tough, especially because Merkel had never been a minister-president, and held no post in the Bundesrat. Worse, her rapid rise had crossed the career ambitions of colleagues like Roland Koch from Hesse, Christian Wulff of Lower Saxony and Peter Müller of the Saarland. All had made the *Ochsentour* and won convincing elections to become minister-president, traditionally a launch pad to the party chair and chancellery. They were, at best, unreliable colleagues, and, at worst, rivals. Moreover, since a 1979 party youth group trip to Latin America, they and several others had pledged never to compete against or even criticize each other. Now as minister-presidents or Bundestag deputies, this band of brothers still honored its "Andean Pact." Merkel received a belated invitation to attend gatherings, but she was not to benefit from its solidarity.[104]

Although Merkel sought to woo them, mutual wariness persisted. Early on, she did not always consult CDU Land leaders closely on key decisions, which helped feed grumbling about her "girls' camp," hurt team spirit and sew public discord. In 2000, she could not stop CDU leaders who were junior partners of the SPD in Berlin and Brandenburg from backing Schröder's tax plan as a way to get federal aid for their indebted Länder and before the 2002 election, a simmering "putsch" by CDU Land leaders killed her chancellery bid. While most went along with her 2003 strategy for constructively opposing Schröder's reforms and advancing alternatives, several still stalemated her. When criticism of her rose in 2004, it was notable how "lonely" she appeared: Wulff and Müller issued ritual pledges of support, but without defending her, and there were even rumors of another planned "putsch."[105] Early in the 2005 campaign, Union minister-presidents undercut her platform by pressing for more revenue for their own budgets, and did not campaign vigorously for her.

At first Merkel could not easily counter these rivals because she lacked allies high up in each CDU Land association, and long had trouble trying to install them.[106] Yet, she did develop a counter-network, including former JU chief Müller and Baden-Württemberg Cultural Affairs Minister Annette Schavan, both presidium members. Hintze brought in other allies from his "pasta band," like Kauder and Röttgen. Merkel cultivated easterners like Thuringia's minister-president Dieter Althaus and education minister Dagmar Schipanski, the CDU's 1999 presidential candidate, as well as westerners like Ole von Beust of Hamburg, Bernd Neumann of Bremen, and Christoph Böhr of Rhineland-Palatinate, along with Land ministers like Lower Saxony's Ursula von der Leyen and Baden Württemberg's Tanja Gönner. These allies were mainly young, low-profile, and not bound to traditionally strong CDU factions, and at least initially, few had strong autonomous bases or broad reach within their party's Land-level associations. Rather than being able to help her, they depended more on association with her success to boost their own careers.[107] That dependence, along with their discretion and pragmatism, bolstered their cohesiveness and Merkel's trust in them.

This group was dubbed the "midnight round" because it often met with her at headquarters very late. She also kept in touch by cell phone (especially text-messaging) from her office, on her travels, or on Sunday afternoons at home in Templin. They supplied intelligence about the party mood (an "early warning system") and on where her peers stood on major issues. That helped her lay the groundwork for key decisions, as even one opponent admitted.[108]

Indeed, her midnight round actually became more cohesive than the Andean Pact, which was strained by clashes of approach, regional interest and personal ambition. Koch, for example, was a hardline conservative, who having been elected minister-president twice by 2003, was already positioned to move up at Merkel's expense. The Lower Saxon chief Wulff, by contrast was an amiable moderate, who having just begun his first term, arguably had a stake in letting Merkel stay on longer until he had proven his bona fides. Pact members viewed themselves as co-equal, which, despite or in fact because of their mutual loyalty, made it hard for any one to take the lead, especially since they could not move up by criticizing a "brother." Finally, a few members, including von Beust and Pflüger, were also Merkel loyalists, and thus potential "moles."

While never able to monopolize power within the party hierarchy, by late 2005 Merkel had accumulated adequate support, arguably as much as Kohl had enjoyed when opposition chief. Her four deputy chairs were Wulff and Rüttgers, along with two close allies, Schavan and Böhr. Of the presidium's seven additional elected members, four were in her camp—Hildegard Müller, Schipanski, von der Leyen and the new CDA chair Laumann (Schäuble, Koch and Brandenburg's Jörg Schönbohm were not supporters). Two of three ex officio members, Kauder and Bundestag president Norbert Lammert, were also Merkel loyalists, as well as several other minister-presidents, advisory participants in presidium sessions. Her outsiders thus gradually surrounded the insiders.[109]

As for Merkel's organizational assets beyond her own party, as a Kohl protégé, she long grasped the importance for her CDU, and for her own aspirations, of unity between the Union sisters, yet in an entirely instrumental fashion. Unlike Kohl, she had no biographical link to Bavaria or intuitive feel for its unique political culture, nor was she at home with its cultural conservatism and populist commitment to a social state. She could never declare "when I say 'my party' I mean CDU and CSU."[110] Her relations with Stoiber were at best coolly correct—they never used the informal "du" for instance. Unlike Kohl, she had not spent two decades building connections among Bavarian politicians to undercut an antagonistic CSU chair, or help against rivals within the CDU. On the contrary, until 2002, Stoiber could rely more on the latter to back him against her. Only by deferring to him as chancellor candidate and campaigning loyally (as Kohl had for Franz Josef Strauss in 1980) did Merkel salvage something from the relationship. He accepted her ambitions to become caucus chair, in which role she would forge a positive working relationship with CSU Bundestag chief Michael Glos and younger, reform-minded Bavarian deputies. Moreover, since Stoiber's 2002 campaign had been a bust in northern Germany, many in the CDU were done with him. Thereafter, his sniping at Merkel's leadership compelled them to rally behind their chair in defiance of the Bavarian boss,[111] as did Stoiber's tolerance of attacks on her reforms by CSU deputy caucus chief Seehofer (even many Bavarian Bundestag deputies, especially younger reformers, resented him as a maverick self-promoter, giving Merkel a chance to play divide and rule). At her nadir, in early 2005, CSU sniping led northerners like longtime Bremen CDU chief Neumann to demand that Christian Democrats back their leader (filling a silence left by others). Still, while able to fend off her sister party's pressure, the CDU chair could not always earn its active support.

By contrast, Merkel's relationship with the FDP under Westerwelle was good. She was more instinctively at ease with the Liberals on cultural and economic issues than with many in her own Union. On one hand, this lent credence to her strategy of restoring a center-Right coalition. More than any leader since Kohl, Merkel came to embody this Christian-Liberal connection. She shaped her economic reform plan and nominated Köhler as president with this alliance in mind. This strategy, however, further complicated her relations with the CSU, and critics charged that Merkel's "Babylonian captivity" by the Liberals made for a narrow appeal, costing her party conservative voters.[112]

She did develop contacts beyond party ranks. Despite some sense that networking was traditionally a male ritual, Merkel spoke of greater connectedness among women. Observers noted that "she knew how to play her woman's bonus" with female journalists, publishers and business leaders, and that she even had a small network of them.[113] She also built ties to other corporate officials, like Siemen's Heinrich von Pierer and tax expert Paul Kirchhof, a former constitutional court judge. Nevertheless, she never formed a large network of powerful allies in business, let alone labor, consulting more regularly with a small circle of about a dozen lower-profile CDU-associated managers or economic specialists. This group did include some business officials, such as Jürgen Kluge, head of the McKinsey consulting firm, which she contracted to help run the data that underlay her major reform proposals in 2003. Yet, this "Group 2020" could not match the array of prominent business barons routinely wined and dined by Schröder. Indeed, Merkel resisted setting up such a group, ostensibly because it would be read as a sign that she lacked expertise. Only late in her sagging 2005 campaign, after a backlash against her surprise choice of Kirchhof as shadow finance minister and his controversial flat tax, did things change. She met quietly with top business leaders after a horseshow in Aachen to persuade some of them to join a campaign advisory board.[114]

Conclusion: From Opposition Leader to the Chancellory

In late 2004, a journalist wrote "Merkel appears to have moved into a strange house ... one in which she has never been at home, that had other owners and heirs."[115] This referred to the chair's unconventional biography, but also to her seemingly almost apolitical style, with its reserve toward others and disregard for tradition; her liberal inclinations on economic policy and cultural affairs; and, above all, her shallow roots in the CDU's historically strongest milieus and networks. While no one could have replicated the Kohl formula anyway, Merkel's leadership in most respects broke his main "rules," except perhaps in his preoccupation with power preservation.

Nevertheless, she had risen to the top and ensconced herself there as securely as had her old mentor when he was opposition leader. How? One tempting explanation is circumstance. Indeed, it has been argued that however daunting the challenges Merkel faced, "fortuna" played a part.[116] She was plucked from obscurity early, promoted by Kohl for his own ends, and became general-secretary at a propitious moment. By her own admission, without the finance affair she might never have become chair.[117] Losing the 2002 Union chancellor candidacy to Stoiber spared her the onus of a costly election setback, opened the path to becoming caucus chief, and undercut the CSU chief's support in the CDU. Schröder's belated embrace of reform, followed by his own travails in getting the SPD to go along, created an opening for her. The simultaneous success of potential rivals in the Länder meant that their aspirations for higher office and challenge to her would in effect offset each other. Even the bizarre epilogue to Schleswig-Holstein's 2005 Landtag campaign, and a fortuitously timed election in North Rhine-Westphalia sustained her at a pivotal point.[118] Finally, the snap election called in May left no rival enough time to mount a serious challenge for the chancellor candidacy.

Such circumstances worked to Merkel's advantage, however, only because she was better able to exploit them. For other potential leaders, the devastating finance affair of 2000 and their party's demoralizing 2002 election defeat might have proven obstacles. Merkel was uniquely able to convert these challenges into opportunities because she embodied something new, lacked compunction about breaking with tradition, proved open to new ideas, and was not too closely linked with or dependent upon any of the CDU's traditional power centers.

But, if Merkel's assets thus outweighed her liabilities as opposition leader, the reverse was true for her as chancellor candidate. In May 2005, her party stood near 45 percent, and had a double digit lead over its SPD rival—electoral victory was already regarded as given. But in the September 2005 Bundestag election, her Union won just 35.2 percent, three points and three million votes fewer than under Stoiber in 2002—the CDU alone garnered a mere 27.8 percent, 1.7 percent less than three years earlier. Schröder was the preferred chancellor of most Germans, including easterners and women. Merkel's CDU won just 25.3 percent in the new Länder, finishing third there, and it won fewer female voters than the SPD, indeed, fewer than it had under Stoiber in 2002.[119] According to pollsters, many conservative male voters, especially in Bavaria, stayed home rather than elect a woman.[120] On balance, Merkel's biography thus helped less than it hurt her party. Tension between her style and program added to its woes. Merkel's quest for consensus within the Union led to her reform program being diluted, and, in the name of fiscal probity, she even proposed tax hikes, confusing voters and leading some coalition supporters to split their tickets by casting ballots for the FDP.[121] At the same time, her flaws as a campaigner and the controversial choice of tax-slasher Kirchhof as shadow finance minister made it hard to fend off SPD charges that Union pledges of "fundamental change" would mean a socially unbalanced, brutally neo-liberal course. Those attacks scared off other swing voters.[1182] Finally, Union leaders made damaging comments or distanced themselves from her campaign, feeding voter fears that she lacked the organizational resources to keep her own team in line. Thus, among the main reasons for the Union's worse than expected showing was a serious "Merkel deficit."[123]

Still, she survived this debacle with circumstances again helping. Schröder's smug insistence on election night that he would form a new government left the Union little alternative but to rally behind its wounded candidate. Merkel was, after all, ensconced as opposition leader, and at the urging of aides, quickly moved to shore up her core support by seeking confirmation as caucus chair. In a secret ballot, 219 of 222 deputies (almost 99 percent) voted to re-elect her. It was also a mandate to try forming a new government and block out Schröder. With her strategy for a reform oriented Union-FDP coalition in tatters, after briefly flirting with some alternatives, Merkel reversed herself and began negotiating with the SPD. The CDU chief's discretion and skill at forging consensus paid off, even if in the process she also dropped major chunks of her economic reform agenda. Despite grumbling, especially from the market liberal wing of her party about sacrificing their profile, Merkel cobbled together a coalition. On 22 November 2005, Union and SPD deputies elected her chancellor.

Merkel had achieved her personal objective, but at the price of a paradox. As opposition leader, her biography, style, program and organizational assets had all represented something different in a CDU that then had reasons for seeking a modicum of reorientation.

By contrast, the Grand Coalition, though of course new, stood for continuity, coming about precisely because most voters were wary of major changes promised (or threatened) by her preferred center-Right alliance. While, as proponents stressed, this bipartisan government (unlike Schröder's) could count on a large majority for bold reforms in both legislative bodies, this would hardly matter if the SPD used its leverage as an equal partner to resist them at an early stage. Merkel would have to rely on the consensus-building skills that had helped her construct this coalition to now make it function, not by fudging policy differences, but by pressing her new partner and CDU/CSU Land leaders to give ground. If she instead advanced only half-measures in the name of harmony, settling for success on style points rather than programmatic consistency, there was a risk that her organizational assets would be insufficient to shield her against resistance from within the Union, especially from among its minister-presidents. In short, difficult though it had been for Merkel to lead the opposition, heading her party as chancellor would create new challenges. But, experience had already shown the risks of betting against her success with even the most daunting tasks.

Notes

1. Gerd Langguth, *Angela Merkel* (Munich, 2005), 328.
2. Frank Bösch and Ina Brandes, "Die Vorsitzenden der CDU: Sozialisation und Führungsstil," in *Die Parteivositzenden in der Bundesrepublik Deutschland, 1949-2005: Göttinger Studien zur Parteienforschung*, ed. Daniela Forkmann and Michael Schlieben, (Wiesbaden, 2005), 23-24.
3. Arnold J. Heidenheimer, *Adenauer and the CDU: The Rise of the Leader and the Integration of the Party* (The Hague, 1960); Geoffrey Pridham, *Christian Democracy in Western Germany: The CDU/CSU in Government and Opposition*, 1945-1976 (New York, 1978); Frank Bösch, *Die Adenauer CDU: Gründung, Aufstieg und Krise einer Erfolgspartei, 1945-1969* (Stuttgart, 2001).
4. Josef Schmid, *Die CDU: Organisationsstrukturen, Politiken und Funktionswesen einer Partei im Föderalismus* (Opladen, 1990), 256-88; Peter Merkl, "The Structure of Interests and Adenauer's Survival as Chancellor," *American Political Science Review* 56, no. 3 (1962): 634-50.

5. Daniele Forkmann and Michael Schlieben, "'Politische Führung und Parteivorsitzende: Eine Einleitung," in *Die Parteivorsitzenden* (see note 2), 19; Anne-Kathrin Oelzen and Daniela Forkmann, "Charismatiker, Kärrner und Hedonisten: Die Parteivorsitzenden der SPD, in *Die Parteivorsitzenden* (see note 2), 64.

6. Clay Clemens, "Party Management as a Leadership Resource," in *The Kohl Chancellorship*, ed. Clay Clemens and William E. Paterson (London, 1998).

7. Frank Bösch, *Macht und Machtverlust: Die Geschichte der CDU* (Stuttgart, 2002).; Ute Schmidt, *Von der Blockpartei zur Volkspartei? Die CDU im Umbruch, 1989-1994* (Opladen, 1997).

8. Evelyn Roll, *Das Mädchen und die Macht* (Berlin, 2001), 17-18. Indeed, Merkel declared that her father's profession meant "more advantages than disadvantages" for her. Angela Merkel, *Mein Weg: Angela Merkel im Gespräch mit Hugo Muller-Vogg* (Hamburg, 2004), 48.

9. Merkel (see note 9), 20, 70-71.

10. "It was clear to me that the constellation was favorable: a woman, from the east and young as well. None of that hurt." Merkel, (see note 9), 86, 136. "Naturally I was advantaged from the beginning, because I came into politics as an outsider from the new Länder," *Stern*, 13 April 2000

11. Wolfgang Schäuble, *Mitten im Leben* (Munich, 2000), 60. As one sign delegate to the April 2000 Essen congress colorfully put it, "[She is one] who does not come from the swamp," *Frankfurter Allgemeine Zeitung*, 15 March 2000. As one study of Merkel's rise suggested, "in extraordinary situations in which male political leaders are tainted by scandal, a 'cleaner,' 'softer' style may suddenly seem appealing. In such situations, traditional attitudes do not block women, but *assist* them politically. Women are seen as best suited to cleanse the soiled political realm. They possess the moral capital necessary to make a clean start." Mark R. Thompson and Ludmilla Lennartz, "The Making of Chancellor Merkel," *German Politics* 13, no. 1 (2006): 106.

12. Langguth, (see note 1), 326.

13. Alice Schwarzer, founder of the woman's magazine *Emma*, was foremost among those who openly backed Merkel. Some surveys also suggested up to a 10 percent increase in voter support for the party nominating a woman candidate who was considered to be as competent as her male rival. Indeed, when the 2005 campaign began, Merkel's lead over Schröder among female voters exceeded that among men. Cited in *Süddeutsche Zeitung*, 30 May 2005. Schröder's wife Doris warned women that Merkel's biography "did not embody that of most women [who] worry about managing a family and a job together"–widely seen as a sign of SPD concern that its Union rival might close the gender gap. *Tages-Anzeiger*, 12 October 2005.

14. SPD spokesman Michael Donnermeyer and former CDU general-secretary Heiner Geissler, cited in Roll (see note 9), 54-55. To be sure that he was not accused of being chauvinistic when tensions between them were high, CSU chief Stoiber once arranged to have the song "She's a Lady" played when she arrived for a guest appearance at a rally in Bavaria.

15. Merkel's background was a bit less uncommon among those who, like her, had lived under Communist rule: before 1989, a scientific career held promise of advancement without deep political involvement. Prominent German examples included the SPD's Matthias Platzeck.

16. Her criticism of the 1960s student movement drew (in her words) reminders that she had no idea of "what was going on in [West] Germany" during those years. Roll (see note 9), 48.

17. Merkel (see note 9), 127.

18. Bösch (see note 8), 138-42.

19. Early on, many in her party simply assumed that any easterner would in effect automatically fall on "the left spectrum of the CDU," including her. Merkel (see note 9), 77, 86.

20. The share of women members had stagnated at 25 percent throughout the post-reunification period. Thanks in part to a quota established under Kohl, their proportion of the federal executive committee had risen from under 20 percent in 1991 to 40 percent by 2004. But only 20 percent of the party's federal policy committee seats were held by women. The share of female CDU deputies had increased between 1990 and 2002, but only to just above 20 percent. And despite some increases, women were under-represented in the party's lower ranks–among legislators and executive committees at the Land-level, and above all among officials at the district and local levels. Frauen Union, *Frauenbericht der CDU Deutschlands 2004*, http://www.frauenunion.de [Lesenswertes], 3-5.

21. Labels cited in *Die Welt*, 26 December 2004; 25 October 2004. Merkel's tearful outburst came during a spring, 1995 cabinet debate, when colleagues blocked her initiative for cutting smog. Langguth (See note 1), 182-84.

22. Merkel (see note 9), 108. "It was socially undesirable to say something against a woman," while harboring reservations, noted pollster Manfred Güllner of Forsa after the 2005 election. Above all in southern Germany, male respondents expressed an intention to vote for the Union but then stayed home. *Tages-Anzeiger*, 12 October 2005.

23. *Der Spiegel*, 5 September 2005, *Die Welt*, 5 October 2005. One went so far as to depict debates over economic reform concepts in the Union as a "a small religious war," between those like Merkel and Herzog, who held to Erhard's more liberal version of social market economics, and Catholics, who had long stressed the social component. Michael Inacker, *Frankfurter Allgemeine Sonntagszeitung*, 19 October 2003.

24. Roll (see note 9), 132-33; Jacqueline Boysen, *Angela Merkel: Eine deutsch-deutsche Biographie* (Munich, 2001), 107, 132. As she recalled, "the economic and political order of the old Federal Republic was incomparably more successful, efficient and reasonable and beyond that more free ... It always outraged me when people who had for years been trying to change [it] now hoped to use the GDR citizens as a sort of critical mass and thereby muster a majority that they would never have had in the old Federal Republic." Merkel (see note 9), 76. Later she dismissed notions that easterners had helped each other more or had placed greater emphasis on things like child care, contending that both had been just temporary ways of making do amid miserable economic conditions. Ibid., 65, 114. As she noted, it was a compliment when people told her that could no longer tell whether she came from east or west. Ibid., 131.

25. Merkel (see note 9), 117-23.

26. She abstained in parliament rather than join a majority of her Union colleagues in endorsing adoption of the western restrictions on abortion in all of Germany or support extending the old GDR's more liberal law, which passed. She would later (wrongly) recall then signing her party's petition to block the latter measure

in court, but also claimed to be satisfied with the final outcome–namely, legalized abortion with counseling about the risks and alternatives. Merkel (see note 9), 88-31; Roll (see note 9), 173.

27. *Spiegel,* 26 September 2005.
28. Merkel (see note 9), 24. Christoph Keese and Christian Reierman, "Die Union muss Kurs halten und um die Mitte kämpfen," *Focus,* 5 December 2004.
29. Without naming her, Meisner told an interviewer from *Bild Zeitung* "Apparently there is also in the current government a female minister of the Christian faith living outside of marriage," *Focus,* 23 August 1993; Merkel (see note 9), 32.
30. Konrad Adenauer Foundation analyst Andreas Püttmann noted that the CDU's membership structure made it "an almost completely Christian party." Even in the East, where only 21 percent of the population classified itself as Protestant and 5 percent as Catholic, 80 percent of party members were practicing Christians–and they were among the most loyal. "Thus the active Christians of both confessions form an essential core membership of the Union with strategic significance for the strength of the party's mobilization," *Frankfurter Allgemeine Sonntagszeitung,* 17 March 2002.
31. Langguth (see note 1), 43-45; Merkel (see note 9), 49; Langguth, 181.
32. *Spiegel,* 4 November 2002.
33. Merkel (see note 9), 132; Langguth (see note 1), 304.
34. Boysen (see note 28), 21; Dominik Geppert, *Maggie Thatchers Rosskur: Ein Rezept fur Deutschland?* (Munich, 2003), 434. Merkel herself conceded later "It is obviously especially hard to understand and make clear today how we lived then. Where were the limits of the compromises that one had to find? ... Everyone had to make compromises, including me. It would be hypocritical not to admit that." Merkel (see note 9), 62, 66; Langguth (see note 1), 99.
35. One ally from the GDR democratic movement observed, "For her it was all a matter of optimizing her political will. She had no trouble picking up the power that we had left lying in the streets." Ehrhart Neubert cited in Roll (see note 9), 131.
36. *Spiegel,* 4 November 2003.
37. Merkel (see note 9), 21; Annette Schavan cited in *Frankfurter Allgemeine Zeitung,* 8 September 2005.
38. Merkel (see note 9), 118; *Spiegel,* 4 November 2003
39. Examples included GDR Prime Minister Lothar de Maizière and Günther Krause. Roll (see note 9), 211-16. Although in later years her apartment in Berlin was only a few floors above de Maser's law office, he reported that she never took up his invitation for coffee. "I have the feeling," he said, "that Angela has a fear of contact with all of the people that once promoted her career ..." *Spiegel,* 4 November 2002.
40. Boysen (see note 28), 167.
41. According to biographer Langguth, Merkel wrote her article without consulting party chair Schäuble, and yet knew what was otherwise still secret–that he too had accepted an unreported donation. She then contacted a newspaper to have it published. Although Schäuble registered irritation at her going behind his back, Kohl was convinced that his two protégés had conspired against him–and in retaliation began leaking information that would trigger an ever more bitter feud. In the end, both men were so badly damaged that the party sought a fully new kind of leader. While Merkel may have acted to help her party, it was also at least possibly a shrewd career move as well. Langguth (see note 1), 200-205.

Merkel herself would insist that she had written the letter in order to free Schäuble from the burden of having to defend their longtime former leader, and had not told him about it in advance since she knew he would have had no choice but to stop her. Merkel (see note 9), 103-04.

42. Lothar de Maizière cited in *Spiegel,* 4 November 2002.
43. Heribert Prantl, "Angela Machiavelli," *Süddeutsche Zeitung,* 5 March 2004.
44. *Die Welt,* 26 December 2004; 25 October 2004.
45. Merkel (see note 9), 33-34, 48; Roll (see note 9), 58.
46. Roll (see note 9), 58. Asked about her most important political virtue, she replied "The ability to keep my mouth closed ... in the sense of remaining silent so as to ensure that things can be discussed behind closed doors without showing up in the newspaper the next day," *Stern,* 13 April 2000.
47. Boysen (see note 28), 179.
48. Klaus Töpfer cited in ibid., 10.
49. Langguth (see note 1), 155.
50. *Frankfurter Rundschau,* 18 October 2005; *Stern,* 7 November 2002.
51. As one close friend, Stralsund mayor Harald Lastovka, put it "There is no web of connections around Angela Merkel, no network, no strings that one can pull. She does not want to expose herself to being dependent on others, but to remain free, without having to take others' interests into account ... Angela Merkel promises no one a career and thus remains sovereign in her decisions," *Rheinischer Merkur,* 15 July 2004.
52. *Die Welt,* 18 October 2004.
53. Hans Herbert von Arnim cited in *Tageszeitung,* 24 December 1999; Merkel cited in *Frankfurter Allgemeine Sonntagszeitung,* 10 November 2002.
54. Martin Hohmann's remarks implicitly drew a parallel between the Holocaust and those killed in the Russian Revolution by Communists of Jewish origin. At first Merkel settled for a mere warning but, as criticism grew—even within Union ranks—she agreed to a vote on expelling him from the caucus. Some critics felt she acted too slowly and mildly, many blamed her for bowing to pressure and not giving him a second chance, while still others faulted the flip flop.
55. Christian Wulff cited in *Frankfurter Rundschau,*18 October 2005; cited in *Spiegel Online,* 22 December 2004.
56. Merkel (see note 9), 131. "After [1989] we got to know this—for us—unusual competition of self-presentation, that we had never known before." She reported being astonished that westerners paid so much attention for so long to her outward appearance. Ibid., 118-19, 128.
57. Ibid., 128-32. The jokes would also never go away. According to one of the most popular, Merkel was, after all, implicated in a party finance scandal because she had charged the CDU for a new hairstyle and no one knew what became of the money.
58. As one reporter noted about her sales pitch for reform in Fall 2003, it was "very substantive, very calm, very analytical"—and thus often still sparked less jubilation from audiences that agreed with her than did the more feisty speeches of leaders who were more out of step with their crowds (such as Stoiber addressing a youth group rally). *Die Welt,* 20 October 2003. She also began holding a political speech on Ash Wednesday back in her home district, but hers were "atypical [and] somewhat dry" compared to the tub-thumbing oratory of CSU leaders that same holiday in Passau. *Spiegel Online,* 26 February 2004.

59. One came at the zenith of her power, during the Summer 2005 debate over Schröder's call for new elections, when she slipped and spoke of her hope to govern with the SPD when she meant SPD, and then described trust as the "lubricant of politics"–a phrase more often used in connection with unreported cash donations, and thus an inadvertent reminder of CDU scandals.

60. Observers credited her with coming across as calm and substantive in a key session with ZDF's Maybrit Ilner at the height of the 2005 campaign. *Die Welt*, 13 August 2005. Some detected a certain sympatico between Merkel and television talk show host Sabine Christiansen. Langguth (see note 1), 326.

61. The survey firm Emnid's poll figures for Schröder and her in those categories were, respectively, 57 percent to 34 percent on competence, 56 percent to 34 percent on personability, and 58 percent to 31 percent on self-confidence. *Manager Magazin*, 5 September 2005.

62. She had long felt that many journalists portrayed an unduly benign image of life in the GDR while harping on the Federal Republic's flaws, and that–even if their coverage later arguably helped her bid to become party chair–focused too much on trivial things like her appearance Merkel (see note 9), 46; Roll (see note 9), 93.

63. From Peter Dausend, "Showdown," *Die Welt*, 14 September 2005; Johannes Leithäuser, "Die Politik als ehrliche Handwerk," *Frankfurter Allgemeine Zeitung*, 14 September 2005.

64. According to Allensbach, as of late 2004, 40 percent of German voters found her "boring"; the comparable figures for CDU colleagues Christian Wulff and Roland Koch were 12 percent and 19 percent, respectively. Elisabeth Noelle, "Sie gilt als kluge Frau," *Fankfurter Allgemeine Zeitung*, 17 November 2004.

65. Lothar de Maizière cited in Roll (see note 9), 148; anonymous colleague cited in *Stern*, 30 October 2003.

66. Once asked what the CDU would have missed without reunification, she answered "me"–by which, she hastily explained, she meant someone who had lived for decades in a system without freedom and thus more fully appreciated its value. Merkel (see note 9), 17.

67. "Those who experienced the GDR's truly feeble-minded economy can have an even sharper view of what is economically necessary today." Ibid., 234. For arguments about the role of religion in her views on economics, see Michael Inacker, "Der christliche Kitt brockelt," *Frankfurter Allgemeine Sonntagszeitung*, 19 October 2003, and Karl Rudolf-Korte, "Neue Sachlichkeit," *Rheinische Post*, 8 February 2006. For her views on other forms of socialism see Merkel (see note 9), 20, 70-71.

68. Roll (see note 9), 119; Boysen (see note 28), 107; Merkel (see note 9), 19.

69. As Thuringia's minister-president Dieter Althaus noted, easterners–even in the CDU–still gave precedence to "equality, consensus, and a strong state that keeps everything in order," *Die Welt*, 24 July 2005.

70. Boysen (see note 28), 192.

71. Their August, 2001 report came with a water color portrait of the pipe-smoking Erhard on its cover and led off with a quote from him: "I want to prove my worth through my own strength; I want to bear the risks of life myself, to be responsible for my own destiny. State, you see to it that I'm in a position to do so." It went on to call, in general terms, for curbing taxes and labor costs by trimming social benefits–albeit not radically enough for some and too much for

others (Blüm dismissed the concept as nonsense). See "Neue Soziale Mark-twirtschaft," CDU, Berlin, 27 August 2001, http://www.neue-soziale-mark-twirtschaft.cdu.de; *Bonner General-Anzeiger*, 28 August 2001.

72. Merkel speech, 1 October 2003, German Historical Museum, Konrad Adenauer Stiftung website, http://www.kas.de, publikationen, Staat und Gesellschaft, Politische Kommunikation/Öffentliche Meinung.

73. Whereas Americans face challenge or change by asking how they can adapt, she argued, such circumstances initially left Germans "depressed" and thinking "perhaps the state is a secure harbor–like a small child who falls while taking his first step and would then rather lie curled up rather than take another risk of getting hurt." She disparaged Europeans for clinging to their "social model" and bemoaning globalization," while Americans seemed eager to master it. Merkel (see note 9), 173-74, 179-82.

74. Ibid., 179-82.

75. Ibid., 232, 243-44.

76. Ibid., 202-03.

77. Ibid., 197.

78. *Die Zeit*, 25 May 2005. When party supporters declared in a public forum "We need a Maggie, and among us she is named Angie," the CDU chair did not look amused, *Die Welt*, 9 October 2004.

79. "Managerin der Macht," *Focus*, 8 December 2003.

80. Given her past experience, Merkel admitted, she had trouble with such "formulations" as "I am proud to be German," and preferred simply saying that she "love[d] her homeland." Merkel (see note 9), 239. Asked what came to mind upon hearing the word "Germany," she once listed things like solid windows, an orderly kitchen, oak trees, and storks. She plainly meant these items as symbols of efficiency and tradition, but as one biographer asked "Would that really touch the soul of many Germans?" Langguth (see note 1), 322.

81. "Merkel is conservative. But is she such a rightwing conservative that the xenophobic and backward-looking slogans of the *Leitkultur* debate are really hers? ... She is for the old family values, but does not want to send women back to the hearth, she is against equal rights for homosexuals but opposed to discriminating against them. The [party's] rightwing clientele will hardly be able to go along with this," *Tages-Anzeiger*, 7 December 2004. For her own views on conservatism, see Merkel (see note 9), 235.

82. "Obviously the damage that was also done [in the 1960s]–the false turns in education, the animosity toward technology, the rejection of elites and many other things–are [downplayed]. In contrast, the alleged achievements of a certain liberalization of society are overemphasized." Merkel (see note 9), 158-59. Just before the 2004 CDU congress in Düsseldorf Merkel declared that multiculturalism had "dramatically failed," and in her speech there she embraced a "free, democratic *Leitkultur*." Associated Press, 20 November 2004; *Spiegel Online*, 7 December 2004.

83. *Focus*, 18 June 2001.

84. Merkel (see note 9), 17; Langguth (see note 1), 316.

85. *Tagesschau*, 3 December 2005; *Die Welt*, 3 December 2005; *Die Welt*, 23 November 2005.

86. *Die Tageszeitung*, 1 March 200; *Frankfurter Allgemeine Zeitung*, 19 March 2000; *Frankfurter Allgemeine Zeitung*, 20 March 2000; *Stern*, 6 April 2000.

87. Some party leaders hastily spoke of selecting the new chair through a first ever member ballot, but there was no reason to think that such a device would have yielded a more representative sampling of the CDU's 630,000 members–or a winner other than Merkel, *Frankfurter Allgemeine Zeitung,* 15 March 2005.

88. Merkel declared that "in an issue of war and peace [she] wanted no streamlined party," that it was "not a question of command and obey, but a matter for each [member] to come to grips with personally." She also admonished Washington against trying to "determine everything on its own," *Tageszeitung,* 7 April 2003. Delegate cited in *Capital,* 30 April 2003.

89. Yet some argued that, in the absence of a real base, she was employing a "Napoleonic" means of "stabilizing" her leadership, encouraging her "mob" of supporters to violate customs of cordiality that upheld traditional party decision-making institutions. Volker Zastrow, "Das Johlen der Eiche," *Frankfurter Allgemeine Sonntagszeitung,* 12 October 2003.

90. Heribert Prantl, "Die Winterkönigin," *Süddeutsche Zeitung,* 2 December 2003.

91. As she noted, "From the beginning, I found it important to have a base in the party alongside my work as a minister. Otherwise you have too little weight ... As [Land-level] party chair one has to learn to think in broader political terms." Merkel (see note 9), 93-94.

92. Boysen (see note 28), 163-65; Roll (see note 9), 222-27.

93. Merkel began the tradition of holding a political address in Mecklenburg-Pomerania on Ash Wednesday, much the way other politicians did, most famously CSU leaders. She could draw up to one thousand of the CDU faithful for beer, sausage, sauerkraut and speechmaking. As one participant noted, "One sees that Angie is still one of us." This relatively low key event, along with her modest oratory, were suited to her region. But in that it also showed how far she had yet to go in her stated aim of making Mecklenburg-Pomerania a "Bavaria of the north," that is a bastion of Union support: CSU chairs could draw eight or ten times that number to their Ash Wednesday event in Passau (more than the CDU had members in her entire Land). *Spiegel Online,* 26 February 2004.

94. Even in late 2004, when Merkel came under strong attack for allegedly weak leadership, Bremen CDU chair Bernd Neumann–among the party's longest-serving north German power brokers–declared that talk of her ouster was "total nonsense," adding that "the grassroots wants [her]," as did every Land-level association in his region, *Frankfurter Allgemeine Sonntagszeitung,* 28 September 2004.

95. When she faced difficulty in 2004, CDU chair Jürgen Rüttgers declared "I support Angela Merkel," and his deputy Oliver Wittke added, "Her support here at the grassroots is stronger than ever. If the Land-level executive committee were to vote, it would be the same result as three years ago: Merkel should be chancellor candidate," *Frankfurter Allgemeine Sonntagszeitung,* 26 September 2004.

96. *Frankfurter Allgemeine Zeitung,* 18 March 2002; *Bonner General-Anzeiger,* 16 March 2002; *Frankfurter Allgemeine Sonntagszeitung,* 17 March 2002.

97. Bösch (see note 8), 240-66; *Süddeutsche Zeitung,* 30 May 2005; *Stuttgarter Zeitung,* 14 November 20005; *Tages-Anzeiger,* 12 October 2005.

98. *Frankfurter Allgemeine Zeitung,* 20 October 2003; *Die Welt,* 20 October 2003; *Frankfurter Allgemeine Zeitung,* 25 October 2004.

99. When the WR greeted her nomination as chancellor candidate in spring, 2005, but set out an even more ambitious set of proposals for reforming the welfare

state, Merkel took note of it, but also underscored that her party was not obligated to follow its prescriptions: "The CDU is the CDU, the Business Council is an association close to it." *Spiegel Online*, 13 June 2005.

100. *Die Welt*, 7 August 2005.

101. Stefan Braun, "Angela Merkel und ihre Mitternachtsrunde," *Stuttgarter Zeitung*, 6 December 2004.

102. *Stuttgarter Zeitung*, 6 December 2004. Though to be sure, she could not always get her way. In 2005, her preference for moving Hintze into the post of caucus business manager ran into resistance from CDU deputies who saw him as still too tied to Kohl, and from the CSU, *Frankfurter Rundschau*, 19 January 2005.

103. Merkel actually offered Schäuble Merz's post as caucus spokesman for economic policy in late 2004, partly in order to get someone high profile into so vital a job, and perhaps as an olive branch—but he spurned the offer publicly. For her part, she often circumvented him as foreign affairs spokesman to deal with his second in command, Friedbert Pflüger, a more trusted ally—although, by the campaign of 2005, their relations were back in good enough standing for Merkel to send Schäuble as her emissary on a high-profile visit to Washington. After the September election he accepted a post in her cabinet, the interior minister—even though it was one he had held before.

104. As one journalist observed, the Andean Pact was "not a bad basis for undertaking, something jointly against Angela Merkel," *Frankfurter Rundschau*, 18 October 2005.

105. Johann Michael Möller, "Fremd im Hause CDU," *Die Welt*, 19 October 2004.

106. In 2001, she struggled to find a mayoral candidate in Berlin, and in 2005, Baden-Württemberg's CDU spurned her preferred choice as minister-president, Annette Schavan.

107. This lack of "continually growing loyalties" made for a "power political deficit" that could leave Merkel isolated. Michael Schlieben, cited in *Stern*, 14 October 2003.

108. *Frankfurter Rundschau*, 18 October 2003. Horst Seehofer, cited in *Frankfurter Allgemeine Zeitung*, 8 September 2005.

109. These allies included two of the three easterners, Althaus (Thuringia) and Wolfgang Böhmer (Saxony-Anhalt), along with von Beust (Hamburg) and Harry Carstensen (Schleswig-Holstein). That left Peter Müller (Saarland), Georg Milbradt (Saxony), and Günther Oettinger (Baden-Württemberg) as independent or hostile.

110. *Frankfurter Allgemeine Zeitung*, 25 October 2004.

111. Whereas Baden-Württemberg's CDU had backed Stoiber's 2002 candidacy, a year later one of its activists noted that he and many colleagues were "sour at the Bavarians," *Stuttgarter Zeitung*, 13 October 2003. All twelve CSU deputies in the caucus's twenty-three-member "Young Group" embraced an ambitious economic reform program that mirrored Merkel's, *Frankfurter Rundschau*, 22 October 2003.

112. As CSU Landtag caucus chief Joachim Herrmann noted of Merkel and Westerwelle, "By background and profile they both do not completely cover the bourgeois spectrum," cited in *Focus*, 13 December 2004.

113. Merkel (see note 9), 116-19. Names mentioned in this respect included above all feminist publisher Alice Schwarzer, founder of the magazine *Emma*, and Ann-Katrin Bauknecht, as well as Frieda Springer of the eponymous media empire, *Spiegel*, 26 September 2005.

114. She reportedly did not seem to know their names, forgot to greet them at key events, checked her test messages under the table while with them and did not stay around for a group photo. In sum, her relations with them had "no spark," *Impulse*, 1 June 2005. Her belatedly-assembled "Council for Innovation and Growth" was chaired by Siemens chief Heinrich von Pierer, *Die Welt*, 30 August 2005; *Agence France Presse*, 11 October 2005.

115. Johann Michael Möller, "Fremd im Hause CDU," *Die Welt*, 19 October 2004.

116. Peter Lösche, "'Politische Führung' und Parteivorsitzende: Einige systematische Überlegungen,"in *Die Parteivositzenden* (see note 2), 360.

117. Merkel (see note 9), 17, 86; Bösch (see note 8), 150.

118. Since the two large parties finished in nearly a dead-heat, incumbent minister-president Heidi Simonis from the SPD had hopes of being re-elected in the Landtag thanks to support from the small Danish minority party. But an unknown deputy from within her own camp kept voting against her, leaving Simonis in tears and no other alternative but a CDU-led grand coalition.

119. Richard Hilmer and Rita Müller-Hilmer, "Die Bundestagswahl vom 18. September 2005: Votum für Wechsel in Kontinuität, *Zeitschrift fur Parlamentsfragen* 37, no. 1 (2006): 212. The CDU share of the woman's vote fell 1.4 percent from 2002 to 2005–under Merkel as chancellor candidate–to 34.8 percent overall and just 24.2 percent of eastern women voted for her party. To that extent, she attracted fewer women to the party than had Stoiber or Kohl.

120. As Allensbach's Renate Köcher observed, "In the polls people boasted of voting for the Union, and then did not." Her colleague Manfred Güllner of Forsa added "perhaps because of a female candidate," *Frankfurter Allgemeine Zeitung, FAZ.NET*, 19 September 2005.

121. Almost half of all the FDP's "second" or list vote came from those who had cast their "first" or constituency vote for a CDU/CSU candidate. On one hand, this may have reflected an effort by Union supporters to aid their preferred ally and thus ostensibly reduce chances of Merkel needing to form a grand coalition with the SPD. But the Liberals were never seen as in danger of falling below the vital 5percent threshold and "loaned" votes could not add to the alliance's overall seat share, but merely shift its internal balance more in favor of the smaller party. Analysts thus concluded that there was also a sense that Westerwelle's more consistent anti-tax message–in contrast to Merkel's mixed signals–exerted a pull factor. The fact that polls continued to show these voters backing the FDP months after the election reinforced the notion that their motives were more substantive than tactical. As one analysis noted, "Those Union supporters who switched to the FDP did it not only on strategic grounds, but on policy grounds: it was a vote for more market economics," Hilmer and Hilmer, (see note 142), 202, 211-212. Certainly Merkel's rival Merz agreed, calling defections to the Liberals an "all too clear response to [the Union's] election program and personnel," *Spiegel Online*, 5 October 2005.

122. Matthias Jung and Andrea Wolf, "Der Wählerwille erzwingt die grosse Koalition," *Aus Politik und Zeitgeschichte* 51-52, 19 December 2005, 6.

123. "Opinion pollsters indicate that Union chancellor candidate Angela Merkel was the one mainly responsible for the Union's surprisingly bad result at the federal election," *Frankfurter Allgemeine Zeitung, FAZ.NET*, 19 September 2005.

Notes on the Contributors

ERIC LANGENBACHER is a Visiting Assistant Professor and Director of Special Programs in the Department of Government, Georgetown University, as well as Managing Editor of *German Politics and Society*. He studied in Canada before starting graduate work in the Government Department and Center for German and European Studies at Georgetown in 1996, completing his Ph.D. with Distinction in 2002. His manuscripts, *Memory Regimes and Political Culture in Contemporary Germany*, and *Collective Memory and Foreign Policy in a post-911 World* (edited with Yossi Shain) are currently under review at several university presses. He has also published articles in *German Politics and Society*, the *International Journal of Politics and Ethics*, the *Forum*, as well as several book chapters, review essays and book reviews. His current project is entitled *Collective Memory and Democracy in Germany, Argentina, Chile and Japan*.

DAVID P. CONRADT is Professor of Political Science at East Carolina University. He has also held joint appointments at universities in Konstanz, Cologne and Dresden. Among his recent publications are Precarious Victory: Schroeder and the German Elections of 2002 (New York and Oxford: Berghahn Books, 2005); The German Polity, Eighth Edition (New York: Longman Books, 2005) and Politics in Western Europe, Fourth Edition (Washington, D.C.: Congressional Quarterly Press, 2006). He has also published a variety of articles and monographs on German political culture, parties and elections. He is currently completing a study of political culture in unified Germany.

HERMANN SCHMITT is a research fellow of the Mannheimer Zentrum für Europäische Sozialforschung (MZES), University of Mannheim and a Privatdozent for Political Science at the Free University of Berlin. He is the coordinator of the European Election Study (EES), a member of the planning committee of the Comparative Study of Electoral Systems (CSES), and a member of the coordination committee of the German Election Study (DWS). He has published widely on public opinion, electoral behavior and political representation with a particular focus on the politics of European integration.

ANDREAS M. WÜST is research associate at the Mannheimer Zentrum für Europäische Sozialforschung (MZES), University of Mannheim. He studied at the University of Heidelberg were he received an MA in political science in 1996 and a doctorate in 2002. His research interests are voting behavior, political parties, migration and survey methodology. His main publications are: *Wie wählen Neubürger?* (Voting Behavior of Naturalized Citizens in Germany, Opladen 2002) and an edited volume on Germany's regular opinion poll "Politbarometer," (Opladen 2003).

LUDGER HELMS is a Heisenberg Fellow and Visiting Professor in the Department of Political Science at the University of Göttingen and Adjunct Professor of Political Science at Humboldt University, Germany. He has published widely on German and comparative European politics. His work has appeared in such journals as *West European Politics, Government and Opposition, Electoral Studies, The Political Quarterly* and *Parliamentary Affairs.* His two most recent books are *Presidents, Prime Ministers and Chancellors: Executive Leadership in Western Democracies* (2005) and *Regierungsorganisation und politische Führung in Deutschland* (2005).

LARS RENSMANN, D.Phil., is head of the research unit on rightwing extremism at the Moses Mendelssohn Center for European-Jewish Studies/University of Potsdam, lecturer at the Department of Political Science at the Ludwig Maximilian University of Munich, and Affiliate Professor at the University of Haifa. He had previous appointments at the Free University of Berlin, Yale

University, the University of Vienna, and the University of California at Berkeley. Recent publications on the subject include *Rechtsextremismus in Deutschland* (Berlin, 2005, with Hajo Funke), *Populisten an der Macht: Populistische Regierungsparteien in Ost- und Westeuropa* (Wien, 2005, ed. with Susanne Frölich-Steffen), *Demokratie und Judenbild* (Wiesbaden, 2004).

MYRA MARX FERREE is Sewell Bascom Professor of Sociology and Director of the Center for German and European Studies at the University of Wisconsin-Madison. In 2005 she was a fellow at the American Academy in Berlin. Her most recent books include *Shaping Abortion Discourse: Democracy and the Public Sphere in Germany and the United States* (2002) and *Global Feminism: Organizations, Activism and Human Rights* (2006).

DOROTHEE HEISENBERG is the Richard S. Hirsch Professor in European Studies at the School of Advanced International Studies, Johns Hopkins University. Her most recent book is *Negotiating Privacy: The European Union, the United States, and Personal Data Protection* (2005) and she has written several articles and book chapters on Germany in the European Union.

JACKSON JANES is the Executive Director of the American Institute for Contemporary German Studies at the Johns Hopkins University in Washington, D.C. He has been engaged in German-American and European affairs for more than three decades, joining AICGS in 1989. Dr. Janes has lectured throughout Germany and the United States and has published articles and op-ed pieces on topics dealing with Germany, German-American relations and transatlantic affairs. Dr. Janes was selected for inclusion in Who's Who in America and Who's Who in Education. He is a member of the Council on Foreign Relations. He received his Ph.D. in International Relations from The Claremont Graduate School (1981), his Masters Degree from the University of Chicago (1971) and his Bachelors degree from Colgate University (1969).

JEFFREY KOPSTEIN is Professor of Political Science and Director of the Centre for European, Russian, and Eurasian Studies at the

University of Toronto. He is the author of *The Politics of Economic Decline in East Germany, 1945-1989* (Chapel Hill, 1997). Recent articles have appeared in *Comparative Politics, Theory and Society, and The Washington Quarterly.*

DANIEL ZIBLATT (PhD, 2002, University of California at Berkeley) is Assistant Professor of Government and Social Studies at Harvard University where he is a Faculty Associate at the Minda de Gunzburg Center for European Studies. He is the author most recently of *Structuring the State: The Formation of Italy and Germany and the Puzzle of Federalism* (Princeton, 2006). He is currently a Research Fellow at the Max Planck Institute for the Study of Societies in Cologne, Germany

CLAY CLEMENS teaches Government at the College of William and Mary. His work has appeared in German Politics and Society, German Politics, West European Politics and International Affairs. His analysis of the 2005 CDU/CSU election campaign will appear in a forthcoming volume from Berghahn. His authored or edited books include The Kohl Chancellorship (Frank Cass/1998) and Reluctant Realists: The CDU/CSU and West German Ostpolitik (Duke/1989).

Index

Deconsolidation:

post materialist issues → Greens (federal structure)

vote splitting (→ FDP, Greens benefit at expense
                    of catch all parties)

unification (→ PDS,) Greens!

breakdown of core support (church goes, other
cohesive holes, *)   unionized

decline in psychological identification with
parties (60% in best, 20% in 62)

*   just now 30% (1950: now 50%)
*   unionized blue collar support 50 (73: now 70%)
#   decline in union membership

Consequences of the erosion of social / demographic
bonds of the parties :
  → millions of undecided voters
  → candidate personality votes
media-driven
  → campaign event votes

                              Consequences for party
                              system / political style
Problems : P. 23
            P. 24   • coalition formation

Prediction : p. 26